Political Science
in America

Political Science in America

Oral Histories of a Discipline

MICHAEL A. BAER
MALCOLM E. JEWELL
LEE SIGELMAN, Editors

THE UNIVERSITY PRESS OF KENTUCKY

Scholarly publisher for the Commonwealth,
serving Bellarmine College, Berea College, Centre
College of Kentucky, Eastern Kentucky University,
The Filson Club, Georgetown College, Kentucky
Historical Society, Kentucky State University,
Morehead State University, Murray State University,
Northern Kentucky University, Transylvania University,
University of Kentucky, University of Louisville,
and Western Kentucky University.

Editorial and Sales Offices: Lexington, Kentucky 40508-4008

Library of Congress Cataloging-in-Publication Data

Political science in America : oral histories of a discipline /
    Michael A. Baer, Malcolm E. Jewell, Lee Sigelman, editors.
        p.   cm.
    Includes index.
    ISBN 0–8131–1758–5 (alk. paper).—ISBN 0-8131-0805-5 (pbk.)
    1.   Political scientists—United States—Interviews.   2.   Political
science—United States—History—20th century.   I.   Baer, Michael
A., 1943–   .   II.   Jewell, Malcolm Edwin, 1928–   .   III.   Sigelman,
Lee.
JA92.P63   1991
320'.092'273—dc20   91–9064

CONTENTS

INTRODUCTION

This book is an effort to enable political scientists to find their intellectual roots through the study of interviews with prominent political scientists. Unlike some of the other social sciences, political science, has done relatively little to convey a sense of disciplinary heritage to those who are just entering the field. The history of psychology is recognized as a respectable subfield of that discipline, and the *American Economic Review* regularly publishes photographs of past presidents of the American Economics Association, but political scientists seem relatively unconscious of their discipline's past. The most recent history of the discipline is *The Development of American Political Science: From Burgess to Behavioralism*, which has appeared in two editions (Albert Somit and Joseph Tanenhaus, 1967 and 1982).

The Political Science Oral History Program began in the late 1970s as an effort to preserve the experiences and perspectives of major figures in the profession so that future political scientists will be able to hear and read what they had to say about their lives, their careers, and their involvement in the discipline. The American Political Science Association (APSA) operated the program for several years with financial assistance from Pi Sigma Alpha, the political science honorary. APSA's attempt to attract external funding for the project proved to no avail, and, in 1982, Pi Sigma Alpha accepted responsibility for the program and continued to provide some financial support. In the period from 1981 through 1986, about ten more interviews were completed, and most of them were transcribed and corrected, but the pace of interviewing slowed.

In 1987, Pi Sigma Alpha and the American Political Science Association decided to transfer the program to the University of Kentucky and to provide financial support beyond that offered by the university. The change gave the project a stronger professional base and increased the rate of interviews. Since the program was transferred to Kentucky, fifteen more interviews have been completed and transcribed, and several others have been scheduled.

Malcolm E. Jewell of the University of Kentucky political science department directs the program and is responsible for planning and scheduling interviews. He is advised by a five-member committee from the American Political Science Association and Pi Sigma Alpha, chaired by Karl Cerney. Their plan is to complete and transcribe about ten interviews per year. The experienced oral history staff of the University of Kentucky's M.I. King Library, directed by Terry Birdwhistell, has assumed responsibility for compiling transcriptions and maintaining materials.

These interviews trace the intellectual and institutional growth of political science by recording the very words and ideas of individuals who have played important roles in its development. When the program was initiated, it was already too late to interview those who might be described as the early giants of the profession: A. Lawrence Lowell, Charles Merriam, Edward Corwin, Arthur Holcombe, Leonard White, and Frederic Ogg. Sadly, we also missed the opportunity to record the views of many leaders of the second generation, including Harold Lasswell, V.O. Key, E.E. Schattschneider, Carl Friedrich, and Ralph Bunche.

In its early years, the program did interview a number of the men and a few of the women who played major roles in the development of political science. Typically, these people received their graduate training in the 1920s and 1930s. Many of them served in Washington during the war years, and their teaching and research careers spanned the period from the end of World War II into the 1970s. Charles Hyneman was the first subject, interviewed initially by Elinor Ostrom and later by both Austin Ranney and Evron Kirkpatrick. About a dozen political scientists were interviewed between 1978 and 1980, chosen as a result of a survey of leading political scientists conducted by the American Political Science Association.

In the last few years, we have filled some gaps by interviewing more people from that early generation, and we have begun to interview members of the second generation, typically those who either retired or achieved senior status during the 1980s. Because the number of political scientists in that generation who made important contributions is so large and their activities and interests are so diverse, it was challenging to select a small group of "great men and women" for interviews.

For recent interviews, and those that will be done in the next few years, we have followed a strategy of diversity. The subjects are interviewed, in most cases, by professional colleagues who have known them for many years and therefore are able to ask detailed, informed questions about their careers, research, and viewpoints. We interviewed people who played significant roles in the major intellectual developments in the discipline and who participated in major research projects in recent decades. Several of the individuals are political scientists who have held major university administrative positions. We are particularly interested in interviewing those who have been deeply involved in major institutional developments in the profession, such as the American Political Science Association and its *Review*, the Social Science Research Council and its major committees, the Inter-University Consortium for Political and Social Research, and the National Election Studies. We also intend to interview more persons who have played leading roles in regional political science associations and journals.

We are currently giving priority to interviews that trace the role of black and women political scientists. Interviews have already been conducted with a few of the senior blacks and women in the profession. Funding has been obtained to expand the number of interviews with black political scientists, and a similar effort is under way for women. In both cases, we will try to interview some members of the earlier generation and some of the leading political scientists who are still active in the profession.

Just as the selection of political scientists to be interviewed must be limited by the funds and time available, the material selected for this volume has been restricted to a small portion of the recorded interviews. Several guiding criteria determined what materials would be included. First, we wished to provide a description of the development of the discipline from the viewpoint of scholars involved in several subdisciplinary areas: public administration, international relations, comparative politics, political behavior, political theory, and so on. Second, we wanted to present a perspective on the influence of the major institutions involved in the training of political scientists in the early days of the discipline, the ways these institutions and their faculty and graduates interacted, and how they influenced the development of the discipline in other institutions. The University of Chicago and Harvard trained large numbers of early political scientists, with Yale, Columbia, and the University of Illinois developing a bit later. Of course, while these schools had the largest doctoral programs, there were others that provided an academic home to the serious study of political science, some located in major metropolitan areas and some in what were then considered the boondocks.

Third, we wanted to convey the flavor of the professional lives of political scientists presented in this book—to show how they became interested in political science, who influenced them as undergraduates and as graduate students, whom they interacted with while they were students, and where they began their careers. We were interested in the development of their careers, their teaching and research interests, whom they interacted with as colleagues, and who their students were. The interviewees who had government or administrative experience were encouraged to describe how this affected their professional development. Of course, most of those interviewed have been active in professional associations, and our selections from the interviews often touch on such participation.

This volume includes a sampling of both the earlier and the more recently completed interviews, which cover a spectrum of the material available in the oral histories that have been collected. Faced with a great volume of primary materials and the problem of deciding what to include in this book, we also considered how the interviews could best be presented. Oral history can be presented in many formats. Often material is organized by topic, with excerpts from several interviews speaking to each topic. On occasion, oral histories are edited into first-person essays, as if written by the person interviewed. Because we wished to maintain the individuality of each interview but to cover a similar set of topics for the interviewees, we have chosen the interview format. But we also have taken the liberty of editing interviews freely, often rearranging the order of questions and answers. Generally, subheadings within an interview indicate a major break in theme or subject. To make the interviews more readable, we have often shortened the questions and the answers, and we have added or changed words, while always trying to maintain the meaning and the context. A few words have been added or changed to allow greater readability and to maintain the flow of the text. In all instances, we have maintained the original thrust of the remarks by the interviewer and the interviewee. For those readers to whom the original phrasings are a vital concern, we invite inspection of the transcripts from which we prepared our extracts.

As we touch on the various topics in this volume we hope we spark the interest of our colleagues and thus encourage others to take advantage of the materials currently available in the Pi Sigma Alpha Oral History Collection. Many of the interviews number over one hundred pages (and some over three hundred). As we explored the histories, we noted a great deal of material on the politics of the American Political Science Association; on the development of the Inter-University Consortium for Political and Social Research and of the National Elections Studies; on the unique role of women and minorities in the earlier days of the discipline; on the involvement of political scientists in the development of many government policies; and on the role of political scientists as administrators in the development of several universities. Each of these topics, as well as many others, could be explored using material available in the interviews. We hope that many of our colleagues will utilize the materials to shed light on the intellectual and institutional development of the political science profession. Teachers and graduate students should gain insights from learning how the craft of political science has been practiced by some of its leaders. One of the major purposes of this volume is to alert political scientists to the existence of this professional resource, which is waiting to be tapped.

The Pi Sigma Alpha Oral History Collection is located in the M.I. King Library of the University of Kentucky. The completed transcripts are kept on file there, with copies in the Pi Sigma Alpha archive at Georgetown University in Washington, D.C. All transcripts have been checked for accuracy by the participants, and the earlier ones have been transferred to computer disks using optical scanning techniques. A list of transcripts that are available for loan to scholars appears in the appendix.

We are grateful to those who have consented to be interviewed and to the interviewers, who have devoted substantial time as well, for their participation in this project. Their work will allow us to maintain an ongoing archive of the history of political science. We especially appreciate the willingness of the interviewees to permit us to excerpt their interviews in this volume.

The efficient work of the oral history staff of the University of Kentucky library has made it possible to get the more recent interviews transcribed promptly. The financial support and the continuing commitment of Pi Sigma Alpha and the American Political Science Association have been indispensable to the development and ongoing success of the oral history program. We are particularly indebted to Cathy Rudder, executive director of the American Political Science Association, for her encouragement and support for the publication of this volume.

Charles Hyneman

Charles Hyneman was born on May 5, 1900, in Gibson County, Indiana. He received his B.A. and his M.A. from Indiana University and his Ph.D. from the University of Illinois in 1929. In 1930, after teaching a year at Syracuse University, he moved to the University of Illinois, where he taught for seven years. He also taught at Louisiana State University (1937–42) and at Northwestern University (1947–56), serving as department chairman at both institutions. In 1956 he returned to his alma mater, Indiana University, where he taught until his retirement in 1971. He died in 1985.

His intellectual curiosity led him to explore a wide range of issues, reflected in such publications as Bureaucracy in a Democracy *(1950),* The Study of Politics *(1959),* The Supreme Court on Trial *(1963),* Voting in Indiana *(1979), and* The Founding: A Prelude to a More Perfect Union *(published posthumously).*

He was active professionally, serving as vice president and later president (1961–62) of the American Political Science Association. During World War II he served in several agencies in Washington, including the Bureau of the Budget and the Federal Communications Commission.

He was also a gadfly in the profession, challenging both conventional wisdom and traditional methods for teaching and studying political science.

Hyneman is perhaps best remembered as a teacher. According to his memorial in PS, "he left no disciples, only students," and most who knew him said he was the most gifted and dedicated teacher they have ever known.

Charles Hyneman was interviewed by three people. Austin Ranney, whose interview took place November 6, 1979, has taught at the universities of Illinois, Wisconsin-Madison, and California-Berkeley and has written extensively about political parties and elections. Evron Kirkpatrick interviewed Hyneman on November 15, 1979; he served from 1954 to 1981 as executive director of the American Political Science Association and also taught for many years at Georgetown University. Elinor Ostrom, who helped to inaugurate the oral history program and has taught since 1965 at Indiana University, interviewed Hyneman about 1976.

Early Interest and Training in Political Science

KIRKPATRICK: How did you come to be interested in political science when you were in college?

HYNEMAN: Well, I'm afraid it doesn't bestow much credit on me. I went to Indiana University without any doubt in my mind that I would major in English. My elective in my freshman year was English and American literature. I didn't like the prof because I thought he was a sissy and it was impressed upon me that most of the males who were taking that course were a bunch of sissies also. So I was not going to take any more English.

Then a roommate said he was majoring in political science. I asked what that was, and it turned out that the thing that attracted me most was that there were only seven majors in political science. I thought a lonely existence was the thing for me. Probably, for no reason other than that there were very few people traveling that path, Hyneman the Loner decided he would travel the path of political science.

If I had had, in my freshman or sophomore year, the course in physical geography that I took in the last semester of my senior year I probably would have been a geologist breaking rocks somewhere today. That course attracted me as no course in political science ever did. I never did fall head over heels for political science. I never did in my subsequent career read as much in the field of politics as I should have.

KIRKPATRICK: Something, though, about that college experience must have led you into graduate work in political science, because you could have picked some other field.

HYNEMAN: Well, I knew that I was going to teach in high school for a little while after getting my A.B. degree. By the time I'm a senior, I've decided I want to do graduate work and make my career teaching in a college rather than in a high school. I taught one year, but by then my father and my mother both were dead and I had a very small amount of money—less than two thousand dollars—that I could draw on. So I decided that I was going to graduate school and earn my living as best I could.

KIRKPATRICK: Why, then, did you decide on political science when you went back to graduate school?

HYNEMAN: I had some earning power if I went on in political science. It's trite to say that a man picks up a second father, but, if that is an allowable remark, it applied to my relationship with Professor Frank G. Bates. He took me to raise. He asked me what I thought he ought to say in his class, told me what he had decided to say; I listened to what he said in the classroom, and later he told me what he wished he had said. When I went on from Indiana to the University of Pennsylvania for further graduate work I noticed that no one I encountered in a course at Penn knew more than one-half of the accepted subject matter of political science as I did. That was not because I was bright; that was because I had been spoon-fed by Frank G. Bates with his hand on my throat to make me swallow it.

I applied for fellowships and got a half fellowship at Brookings and a full fellowship—the Harrison fellowship—at Penn, which was a good one. My main concern was to get east. I had never seen a mountain, even as big as what I saw going across West Virginia on the C&O railroad. So I went to Penn. I had a year there; it was a good year for me. I had an extraordinary course in constitutional law. I had an excellent course in economic theory, which I offered as my minor.

KIRKPATRICK: And then you went to Illinois from there. How did you decide to leave Pennsylvania, and how did you decide on Illinois?

HYNEMAN: I was not going to stay at Penn even if my fellowship had been renewed. I never asked about it. I saw the Penn political science department as having no interest in what I thought was political science. I had met Professor James W. Garner at a conference the year I started my graduate work at Indiana. Bates took me up to Chicago to a conference on the politics of science. I went up there and met several University of Chicago graduate students—Harold Lasswell, Amry Vandenbosch, Walter Laves, maybe Fred Schuman. I chose a section that James W. Garner, down at the University of Illinois, chaired, and I made a big hit with him at that time. And during my first year of graduate work, I went from Bloomington to Urbana to talk about making a career, and he was very reassuring. Sure, go on east and have your year there. If you want to come back to Illinois, we'll undoubtedly have an assistantship for you. So I decided to go from Penn to Illinois.

Teaching and Research Career

KIRKPATRICK: Charles, how did it happen that, given the fact that you went out to Illinois and got a degree in international law and wrote a thesis in that field, you then went off to Syracuse, but not to teach international law?

HYNEMAN: I quickly got disillusioned with the state of international law. It wasn't definite; it wasn't positive enough; it was a bunch of uncertainties. In my second year at Syracuse I got a course in American constitutional law and I believe in both years a seminar to do whatever I chose to do with it. I chose to make it an examination of the authority of administrative officials. In those days we were making great use of the term discretion—the range of choice administrative officials had in interpreting and extending public policy and establishing levels of compliance with public policy. I could see so much still to do that I sunk myself in that.

OSTROM: You go ahead and review for us just a bit of your own sense of the intellectual course of Charles Hyneman and political science.

HYNEMAN: My old professor, Frank Bates, used to say that a political scientist was a cross between a poor lawyer and a poor historian, and he might have added "a not-too-busy journalist." We described institutional arrangements, common practices, interesting deviations from the expected, and we criticized institutions and practices on the basis of judgments which were not firmly based on thorough investigation of actual experience. Now, I'd say I carried on in that style through my first two years of teaching at Syracuse University.

When I went to the faculty at the University of Illinois in the fall of 1930, there were five full-time faculty members already on the job and two were added that year—Charles M. Kneier, and me. This makes a department of seven. At that time I think, without question, the Illinois department would have been rated among the top ten of the country and conceivably among the top five or six. As a matter of fact, within ten years, two members of that department—James W. Garner and John A. Fairlie—became presidents of the American Political Science Association.

The study of political science, as I knew to be the case at Illinois and as I understood to be the case around the country at that time, was essentially a descriptive job—the description of political institutions, organizations, processes, and so on. That's not to say that there was no critical examination and evaluation of these institutions. I'm certain a great deal of very, very good thought came into the classroom and into the books and articles about "What are your expectations of a political system which would enable you to say this is good or this is not good?" But it did seem to me then that there was also a very cheap passing of judgment on institutions and processes. By cheap, I mean that sure knowledge of what actually was the case was just simply lacking. Judgments rested entirely too much on a traditional view of things. There was no venturing outside of what had long been established as the aspects or sectors of political society that should be examined.

I understood at the time, and I guess had strong reasons to believe, that I was regarded by some people as a sort of troublemaker at that period, and I think that was in fact an unwarranted conclusion. If they had said a dissatisfied person, this would have been the case. For it did seem to me that we were shortchanging a student by taking him on descriptive tours where he didn't really need much help. He could read; if you insisted that he read, he would read.

I thought that the task of the teacher of American Constitutional Law (in a political science department, not in the law school) was to help the kid come to see how authority expresses itself, how decisions which are authoritative in the political system get formulated and become law. What's the process, the steps, by which they get to the decisional point? And what can we say about the persons who make these decisions and what rules them? And in addition to this, one has to examine the alternatives to the decisions which they did make, in order to get some sense of who's winning and who's losing. I remember making the statement that the Supreme Court is where authority is most clearly defined and lodged so that you can get at it and see what it is. My office mate's reply was: "Well, I guess about all I have to say to you is you'd better not let the other members of the department know what you're up to. This is not what the course is for. The purpose of the course is to tell the students what the Court has said, what the Constitution requires, permits, and forbids."

There was not anything I would call pressure for publication at the University of Illinois in the 1930s when I was there. There was a high regard for it, and Professor Garner especially made a great thing of saying how important it is to do research and publish. But I never doubted that if you were a fairly good teacher you would be honored for that and thought valuable to the institution, and you'd go right up the promotional ladder, and possibly just as fast with no publication record.

But I had a kind of curiosity that attracted me to neglected problems and important experiences that had been overlooked. And I have an idea that, in large part, I was kind of a show-off. I thought it would be nice for other people to discover that I had found some things to talk and write about that they'd had under their noses all along and never noticed.

If you cited out of all my publications the items you'd most likely say were worthy of notice, there are several things that date from those early days at the University of Illinois.

One was cumulative voting. Cumulative voting is that system for electing the members of the Illinois state House of Representatives which divides the state into three-member districts; all districts for the House of Representatives in Illinois send three members to the lower house. Each voter has three votes, all of which he can give to any one candidate, spread out one vote to each of three candidates, or divide between any two candidates. If you gave all three votes to one candidate, that was called plumping. By plumping for an agreed-upon candidate, the minority party could get a member into the House of Representatives in almost any district in the state; I would guess there never was a time that, out of the fifty-one districts, there were fifteen that sent to Springfield three members of the same party.

Except in one or two printed pieces, the cumulative voting system was condemned as an anachronism. I went to work and, with a graduate student to help me, we put out an essay that did relate this cumulative voting to strength of minority positions on various kinds of legislation, the distribution of the party vote over the state, and the stability of legislative membership.

I got intrigued by some nonsense I encountered in the two years I taught a course called State Administration, a course I inherited when I went to Illinois. That two years convinced me that we had going all over the country a holy crusade, favoring the reorganization of state government. It was supported by a package of dogma that totally ignored what I thought were the broader requirements for testing administrative organization against objectives, goals, and a variety of interests. So immediately after I left Illinois for LSU, I wrote an article for the first issue of the *Journal of Politics* which gained me a considerable notoriety if not fame for having torpedoed the entire line of goods of the leading specialists in public administration.

I have no doubt that if you ask anybody else about Hyneman in those days, he'd say: "Well, all I know about him was tenure and turnover in state legislatures." I fell into that by accident. There was a body of data that anyone not totally blind could collect and anyone who could cut out paper dolls could put on IBM cards, so I created an assembly line, and we put out a number of articles on tenure and turnover in state legislatures. I never felt good about this until Harold Lasswell said once: "This is very important. Whenever the political scientists wake up enough to study elites, why, then they'll find some valuable work already done for them."

I regard the brief period at LSU as the most formative of my adult years so far as determining my character is concerned. I must say, however, that I do not think that my conception of the job of a political scientist—my job as a student teacher of politics—was notably enlarged while I was at LSU. What I picked up there was learning about people and how to deal with people and proving to myself that I could function in some role outside the classroom. The subsequent five years in Washington was essentially an extension of the LSU experience. The World War II experience, of course, greatly enlarged my knowledge of government in operation. It reinforced my determination to explicate and justify democratic ways in my writing. And five years in Washington also convinced me that I wanted a career as college teacher or a career in an outfit like Brookings. I'd learned I did not want to be an administrator in government or on a university campus.

Three things seem to me to loom up in my ten years at Northwestern, which began at the close of the war and terminated when I moved to Indiana in 1956. First, it was there that, just short of fifty years of age, I made my first entry into serious writing that went beyond the reporting of research results. That first piece was the book *Bureaucracy in a Democracy*. Whatever esteem that book enjoyed arose out of the fact that it induced a lot of people to consider the placement of bureaucracy in the political structure of a country that is committed to certain tests of democratic character. Second, Northwestern gave me my first experience as advisor of graduate students and supervisor of their dissertation research and writing. Third, at Northwestern I became interested in and started my learning about the nature of knowledge, nature of inquiry, the uses of and bounds to scientific inquiry. It also had an effect on my later writing running far beyond the fact that it made possible the little book on *The Study of Politics*. My awareness of some problems of the nature of supposition, belief, and something you want to call knowledge—how this is acquired, and the slippery character of all of that—I expect that's reflected in nearly everything I've written since the Northwestern decade.

In any event, by the time I left Northwestern and descended upon Indiana University I had gone an enormous distance from where I had been in 1937, when I left Illinois for LSU. Back at Urbana in 1930 to 1937, Hyneman was problem oriented. In those days and perhaps ever since, I saw puzzles as something that needed to be worked. It seemed to me in those days to be an awful waste of human energy for someone to make a crossword puzzle and no one worked it.

Roland Young, on the other hand, had something you can call guiding principles which directed him to what he decided to study. I think I took on a measure of that kind of direction over the years, but still at my present age I'm attracted to puzzles.

Coming down to Indiana University from Northwestern at the age of fifty-six, I would now say in retrospect that I had probably been created by the time I got here. I see my fifteen years at Indiana as a period of continuous learning but not as a time when my thought or investigation turned in new directions. What did happen to me here, and these were very important to me personally, related to my teaching rather than to my study and writing. First, the importance of putting information in the student's head receded, and the importance of developing ability to analyze overwhelmed me. At the age of sixty, I wrote the dean that heretofore I had been engaged in developing a subject matter in my courses, but that henceforth I proposed to commit myself to the development of the young people that came to me. I did not want to be strapped in any way by a feeling of obligation to get through a particular subject matter; therefore I did not want to teach any courses that anybody thought essential to the education of a major in political science. I got approval for such free wheeling, and, while I did announce a subject matter, it never was with intent to explicate that subject.

This became my whole concern in the last ten years of my teaching, and I do believe if there were any way of itemizing and putting measures on the gifts I made in the classroom (lecture course or seminar) it would be found that I did more good in my last ten years than I did in all my previous years of teaching. That's the way I feel about it but there's no way of knowing.

A second thing that happened at Indiana was: my personal study and writing turned to what I called pre-theory analysis. What I wrote was intended to do for a reading audience essentially what we were doing in the classroom. Then, third, at Indiana University I became impressed by the old man/young man relationship. I tried to connect myself, especially to a very few graduate students, in a joint thinking/ joint research relationship. Byrum Carter told me once, and I recognized that he was right, that it was a matter of instituting and cultivating apprenticeship. I've often mentioned my puzzlement by a statement in one of the biographies of Pasteur—Pasteur saying that education is the cult of the great man. At the time I read that I had to say: I just don't know what the Sam Hill the man means. But I concluded later that he sure could well have meant that a young person really learns at his maximum rate when he is connected with a person he accepts as a model and comes to view as a great man. Wanting to shine in the presence of the model, he gets the incentive, the drive, the motivation and all of that, as well as the observational knowledge that enables himself to move faster and further than he otherwise would have.

Now, lastly, looking over the whole span of years, I would say that my principal commitment as an explainer of American government and politics and as a bestower of approval, which I did do in the classroom and in writing, has been to the democratic ideal and to the American effort to achieve democratic way in government. I have grown in my conviction that it is the right way of life for the American people and in my confidence that in America responsive government is firmly based. But concurrent with that persisting faith there has been a sharpening of conviction that we are confronted by need for repair and reconstruction on a broad front.

Comments on Evron Kirkpatrick

HYNEMAN: I went to the Illinois faculty in the fall of 1930. I think Kirk [Evron Kirkpatrick] was a senior that year. I don't know whether Kirk moved into my orbit while a senior or in the fall when he was back to do a year of graduate work, but we got very, very well acquainted. I want to put a note in here as to why I think it's very important to know all we can know about Kirkpatrick. Now, we've got luminaries in this profession in the sense of what I'll call productive scholarship—scholarship that got into print. We've also had a number of very great scholars who did not put much into print. Kirkpatrick, I think, is a man of extraordinary learning as a political scientist, extraordinary learning running far beyond the social sciences. Kirk's one of a half a dozen.

RANNEY: Yes. That's a very important point, and I can only confirm that. I have, in my time, commissioned him to do two articles. There was the review of the Parties Committee report published in the *APSR*. And then, more recently, a paper for our AEI volume on the 1960 presidential debates. And in both of those cases, he did a truly learned piece.

And I think that you're absolutely right to emphasize this side of Kirk that most people don't know. But I see a great deal of him since I moved to Washington, and I know what his pleasure reading is, and more than anything else he reads philosophy, technical philosophy, epistemology and aesthetics and political philosophy, too. He reads enormously, retains everything.

HYNEMAN: One time I talked to Kirk about what kind of reading he had been doing. He came out with a statement like this: "Well, I have not only read whatever Wittgenstein put into English,

but I own all of Wittgenstein's books and I've reread most of them."
And I said: "Well, what about Heidegger?" "Well, that's another mat-
ter. Actually, I don't take to Heidegger. I've read enough of
Heidegger to find that he's not my dish."

He was sitting in my office one day, and I said to him: "How in
the hell can you find so much time to sit here and talk? Aren't you
taking any courses?" "Oh yes, all they'll allow me to take." "Well," I
said, "How many's that?" "Well, this semester, actually, only twenty-
two hours. Fifteen hours is standard load." "Well, how do you do this
and still have time to talk?" "Oh," he says, "no problem to handle a
course. The first thing I do is I read the textbook, and within the first
two weeks I read it all the way through, and if I'm going to mark it
up, I mark it up. The first two weeks I read the textbooks in all my
courses and I know what's in them. Then, the second thing—I don't
intend to miss any meetings of the class. I don't care how much com-
plaining there is, if you listen carefully you get something out of it. So
I listen carefully in class, and I take notes. Now, that only takes so
many hours a day, going to class to take notes. I've already read his
stuff, and I know what's in that, so I don't have anything to do until
final exam." "Oh, no," I said, "you've got some term papers." "Well,
any term paper can be written in two weekends. I work like a dog at
exam time getting ready for the exam, so then it's all over with, and
you don't need much time for all of this, and that's why I've got time
to sit in your office and talk."

Well, he and I became great friends.

American Political Science Association

HYNEMAN: There was a famous remark about a character in
Macbeth that nothing became his life so much as his leaving it. I
think you might say nothing became my career in the APSA so much
as the manner of my entry into it. When I was a youngster, of course,
it seemed to me very important to be noticed by the profession, and
to have been appointed to a committee or in any other way given
recognition by the Association would have seemed very important
to me. But I got that almost totally out of my system during World
War II.

Well, I went to the Association meeting at Christmas time, 1949,
and nearly conked out. I didn't think I was sick, but I did become
aware that I was all but totally exhausted. I did not have a room in the
hotel where we were meeting, but I went up to a friend's room and
lay out up there for quite a while. Something was in fact working on
me because in February I had a coronary occlusion. Well, at that

time I just made a resolve: This is it between me and the American Political Science Association; I'll go to meetings when they are here in Chicago and nowhere else.

Having severed myself from APSA in my own mind it came to me as a total surprise when I got a phone call in the early spring of 1960: Would I accept the nomination for president-elect if I was nominated? I still remember my response. My first remark was: "For Christ's sake!" And my second one was: "You can do better." The phone call was from Johnny Masland, the chairman of the Nominating Committee and then at Dartmouth. I recall that of the members of the committee, there was only one person I could think of as a friend. This reassured me a great deal; if a committee like this would nominate me for the place, they must have done it on some evaluation of my position in political science and not simply on a friendship basis.

So I did accept the nomination. And probably not solely for the considerations just mentioned or because it was fine for my ego. My wife probably would never have quit talking if I had turned it down. I guess it is appropriate to say I had a platform. One avowed goal you may view as personal: I was not going to appoint anyone to an important committee who was on the shady side of forty. This promise to myself I was pretty successful in keeping.

There were some appointments of importance to be made: to the Nominating Committee that would select the next year's officers, the Program Committee, some committees that judged dissertations and made awards. Well, I was determined that I was going to give these assignments to younger persons who had not been noticed as much as I thought they should have been and who, I had reason to believe, were persons of first class quality. To that I must add a further resolve to be brashly discriminatory; I was not going into the Ivy League with any of my appointments. Their faculty members were well enough known; they had hogged the patronage for years.

I happen to know that in many cases, the selection of persons for committees and other posts in APSA had been most casual. There may not have been a deliberate effort to favor an in-group. There was just the flopping around of a man who didn't know anybody. I've often told, but won't put on tape, the story of one of my friends who was president of the Association. It turned out he could name only two people on the West Coast when he was told that there must be somebody from the West Coast on the Nominating Committee because there hadn't been anyone from out there for a year or two. He knew two persons, each of whom had been his former student.

I had one matter of a different type that I wanted to do something about. That was about teaching political science in the black colleges. Over the past few years I had attended a few of the seminars for teachers in small colleges, which APSA sponsored and Howard Penniman managed. One that I had attended in Atlanta was an exception to the rule. There were at least a few black persons attending that seminar and I became very much impressed by the liveliness of their interest.

I learned that life in some of the colleges for Negroes—colleges not represented by anybody who got to the Atlanta seminar—was to me hardly conceivable. About that time, Howard Penniman made a survey of conditions in the black colleges and he found such things as: only four books in the whole field of political science had been added to the library in the last year or the last two or three years. One man teaching political science, and he also teaches part of the history curriculum. Except maybe for a beginning course, a rarity for a man ever to be able to repeat a course in three years because they want to offer something they call a major in political science.

Well, I did some inquiring and a good deal of thinking about this, beginning well before the St. Louis meeting where I was named president-elect. I remember a seminar down at Berea. I remember sitting out on a bench during an afternoon session that didn't interest me much and thought the whole thing through and worked out an idea for foundation money for the American Political Science Association to give teachers in black colleges a full summer of instruction by the best men the country could produce.

Well, I had the problem pretty well solved in my own mind, so, when I came into the meeting of the Council in September, I just cleared the decks. I did get complimented for getting business done. We shut up the talk; we got the voting done, and we had the entire afternoon session to talk about this Negro problem. Well, I don't remember too much about what was said but I definitely do remember one impression I had. I said to myself: am I the only man here that ever gave this matter a passing thought? It seemed to me that hardly anybody there had given the slightest bit of thought to the condition of black colleges, let alone how to improve them. This was the fall of 1962. That's eight years after the segregation decisions.

Possibly it wasn't altogether a matter of not having given any thought to the black colleges. Possibly some or even most of the members of the Council believed that the less done for the small black colleges the better for everybody. I still have a pretty distinct memory of a meeting I convened at St. Louis two years before—September 1960. I asked Sam Cook and Lucius Barker to corral up to a half-dozen of the few blacks who were attending the convention to meet with Howard Penniman and me and talk about what needed to be done for teachers in those little colleges scattered about the South. I think five or six black teachers sat with us that afternoon.

They would all have been teaching in white institutions or upper status black colleges, of course, since people teaching at Stillman College or Tougaloo weren't spending a month's salary to attend a political science meeting in St. Louis. I was totally unprepared for the reception I got that afternoon for my proposal to rescue these people that I figured to present a first priority need. The black teachers in that little meeting were totally uninterested in doing anything for these down-at-the-heel places; indeed, I think it may be proper to say that some of them were adamantly opposed to it. They viewed those colleges as illegitimate and their faculties as unfit for offering college education. I knew Sam Cook, then at Atlanta University, to be a man of remarkable charity; I had only a slight acquaintance with Lucius Barker at that time. So I put the reaction down to the snobbery I had been told was rampant in black educational circles. I had to make an exception for Sam Cook and I have to make an exception now for Lucius Barker.

But the story I got out of the group, consistently, was: You can't bring the quality of instruction in those institutions up to the minimum level that should be tolerated; sink your investment in something that promises some payoff. Possibly none of the blacks in that sitting looked with favor on the survival of schools that advertised themselves as refuges for black people; they may have been thinking: Wipe these submarginal run-down places out and give these black kids a chance to get a decent education in an institution that white people think good enough for their own kids. If that was in their minds, very little of it got said out loud in St. Louis that afternoon. Well, back to the Council meeting in 1962. Kirkpatrick thought we ought to be able to get some foundation money. Later I was told that Kenneth Thompson, who was a member of the Council and a well-up official in the Rockefeller Foundation—I was told that he said to Kirkpatrick: "Why don't we just fix an amount of money right here and now to get this thing started." Kirkpatrick understood that Thompson was sure he could get a commitment to twenty-five thousand dollars out of Rockefeller without filing a formal application. I don't know whether he changed his mind, or whether he asked for the money and got turned down. The foundation said: "No, we just do not see ourselves doing anything in the way of an educational improvement program for colleges that select one class of schools. We'll not do this for black schools—God knows they are lousy—unless we do it for lousy white schools, too." And there never was an American Political Science Association program of the proportions that I had in mind either for blacks only or for all races.

At least in a small way this gets to your question: What was the Council like? Well, the Council was really viewed as a rubber-stamp-ing organization. It met only once a year, at the time of the annual meeting. They were sent a notice of items on the agenda, reports of committees, reports of the executive director and of other officers. All Council members had a file in advance, and, as far as I know, they may have very religiously studied that file. But most of the actions they took were simply confirmations of things already accomplished or affirmations of recommendations made by the Executive Committee. I carry memories of a lot of very interesting conferences that I have attended, but I don't call up a memory right now of any thing ever happening in a Council meeting that I thought was an intellectual discussion.

Southern Political Science and the Journal of Politics

HYNEMAN: When I was beginning my teaching, you had to look awfully closely to find anybody in the South that was known by political scientists in the North to be a good man, meaning by that, a man of sincere commitment to the study of political science, a good mind hard at work and, hopefully, some publications. On the whole, the southerners did not have the publications.

But the big thing that occurred in the South, as I saw it, was the move of Roscoe Martin from the University of Texas to Alabama. We went into the South at the same time; maybe he beat me by a semester. Roscoe had got himself a Bureau of Government Research which was well funded; I inherited a Bureau of Government Research at LSU which was meagerly funded—little more than enough to employ three or four graduate students for a few hours per month. Roscoe, having been several years in Texas, had a feel for the South that I did not have. I saw myself as a guest who had no right to be giving advice until I had been around a while; Roscoe saw the South as his empire—rather, as terrain on which he's going to build an empire. "And, Hyneman, you're going to be very important to this New Reconstruction Era." So he offers a high price for my services. Well, I didn't cotton up to all of this, but, as I look back on it, Roscoe Martin really did something for political science in the South, both in setting models for the kind of thing all good departments ought to be doing but also in organizing things and taking them over.

RANNEY: Well, it's said that he was the prime force in getting V.O. Key to do *Southern Politics*.

HYNEMAN: Oh, hell, he was not the prime source, he was it. He birthed the idea and he raised the money. Jasper Shannon told me that Roscoe first offered it to him and Jasper said: "If it had been anybody other than Roscoe I would have done it, would have loved to do it. But I was not going to put myself under Roscoe's thumb."

Well now, Roscoe gave you the *Journal of Politics,* and get this on the record—Hyneman voted against it. Roscoe moved the creation of a committee to consider creation of a journal in the annual meeting of the Southern Association and the motion carried. Roscoe was made chairman of the committee, and I was made a member, no doubt at Roscoe's suggestion. I am equally free of doubt that Roscoe had selected all members of the committee and nailed down chairmanship before he introduced the motion.

Roscoe made his case for a journal, which we did decide to create and name the *Journal of Politics.* Hyneman voted against it, but I do believe he made a positive contribution. Hyneman gave them the name. "Don't give it a regional name," I said, "because the sons of bitches up North will never look at it. But if you give it a name that does not denote that it's a southern journal, well, they won't know if it's any good until they do look at it."

RANNEY: I don't know if that's the reason, but that certainly is one of the great successes of political science, I'm sure.

HYNEMAN: Now the reason I opposed it was because the terms in which we were talking were that this would, indeed, be a journal of the Southern Political Science Association. All these southerners who have had no place to put their stuff can put it here. And Hyneman said: "If what they're going to put here is not of any higher quality than what they are not able to put somewhere else, it is not worth putting where people can see it." "Yes it is," says Roscoe. I remember some of his illustrations. Now take the case of the Louisiana legislature which has just passed some interesting legislation. We ought to report here all of the innovations in legislation around over the South. But we'd also have articles, and we'd have the kind of articles, the way Roscoe was presenting it, that we get as presentations to Southern Political Science Association meetings.

Well now, believe you me, Hyneman, having so far attended two of those meetings, is not thinking that that needs to be preserved for posterity in a journal. Well, it comes out that the University of Florida, says Manning Dauer, would put up the money so we can make a go of this. Roscoe says: "Hyneman, you must be the editor." Well, that may have given me a nice thought for five minutes, but I would think more likely five seconds.

But I saw a chance of getting a little glory for my department, so I said: "Well, since no one's suggesting anybody else, what would be wrong with Bob Harris as editor?" "Well," says Roscoe, "if you ride herd on him and see that he's well managed and all of that, why that would be all right." So I go back and ask Bob Harris would he be editor? He would. And he opened the first issue up with a piece by Corwin. I think Coker had the lead article in the second issue.

Before long there had been an article by Ben Lippincott, J.A.C. Grant, Peter Odegard, and I don't remember who all.

RANNEY: Well, it's a national journal.

HYNEMAN: From the first issue, it became a national journal. So there was Hyneman's contribution; I didn't foresee that that could be. Maybe you can credit me with something for saying: "Sure, Bob Harris will do this." Bob turned it away from Roscoe's whole intent. Oh, Roscoe wanted one thing. He wanted to be the book review editor, which would give him such patronage as there is in being able to give out books for review. So Roscoe's book review editor. Bob Harris becomes editor, and he launches a national journal.

E. Pendleton Herring

Pendleton Herring was born in Baltimore, Maryland, on October 27, 1903. His baccalaureate degree in English was awarded in 1925 and his doctorate in Political Science in 1928, both by the Johns Hopkins University. He began his career as a political scientist at Harvard University in 1928, where he taught until he joined the Carnegie Corporation of New York in 1946. As an executive associate he oversaw programs in public administration and international relations. In 1948, he was named president of the Social Science Research Council, a position he held for more than twenty years.

In 1941, Herring was asked to consult with the Bureau of the Budget as an advisor on the Records of War Administration. This began his long-term contributions on advisory committees for the army, the navy, and the air force.

His research on American government included the publication of six books. The first, Group Representation in Congress *(1929), was a pioneering effort based on interviews with representatives of such groups as labor unions, farmers, and business leaders. His next three books dealt with aspects of public administration including client interactions with the government, the impact of administrators' backgrounds on their actions, and presidential leadership. His most significant work was* The Politics of Democracy: American Parties in Action *(1940), which argued the case for decentralized parties in American government rather than parties of greater discipline and purity. His* Impact of War: Our American Democracy under Arms *(1941) was an innovative study in national security and public policy.*

As president of the Social Science Research Council, Herring appointed several committees that played major roles in the behavioral revolution in political science, including the Committee on Political Behavior (1949–63). He was an organizing editor of the Public Opinion Quarterly, *served as editor-in-chief of* Public Administration Review, *and was a member of the editorial board of the* American Political Science Review. *Herring served as a member, and as chair, of the National Science Foundation Social Science Advisory Committee for over ten years. He served as president of the American Political Science Association in 1953, and, since 1962, he has been president of the Woodrow Wilson Foundation.*

Pendleton Herring was interviewed in Princeton, New Jersey, in July of 1978 by Fred Greenstein, who taught at Wesleyan and Yale before joining the Princeton University faculty in 1973. His research includes work on the presidency and on political behavior, particularly among young people.

Graduate Study at Johns Hopkins

HERRING: I enrolled as a graduate student in the Department of Political Science at Johns Hopkins in the fall of 1926. I found as my classmates Marshall Dimock and Ted Dunn, and two or three other students. This suggests a contrast in terms of numbers with the situation in many graduate departments today. There was an atmosphere of congeniality and informality. One entered into something of a collegial relationship, even with senior members of the faculty. Surely there was nothing that could be accurately described as training. There were seminars and lecture courses and much assigned reading, but especially there was the experience of close association—of learning by example.

We had seminars and participated in lectures with graduate students in history and economics. In political science, one was confronted with a formidable reading list and urged to work one's way through it. The most memorable teaching/learning experience was with Frank Goodnow, who was president of the university, but who had time to conduct a class in constitutional law. I was rather awed by the thought of the president of the university presiding over this class, but he was a most sympathetic and kindly gentleman and it remains a memorable experience.

W.W. Willoughby was to be found in his study, the door ajar, and if you ventured in he would look up from his writing and greet you. No prolonged discourse was involved, but it was impressive to see a scholar at work. The attitude of the faculty and the nature of the instruction were probably closer to a condition of 1876. That fifty-year period had not witnessed any great change in the nature of

instruction. I recall from the papers of Woodrow Wilson that he became rather irked at what he regarded as somewhat pedantic requirements in historical research and begged leave to pursue his own
studies without following the prescribed course. This was granted. I
didn't have the precedent in mind when I went to my mentors with a
proposal for a dissertation topic that seemed perhaps somewhat unconventional. I wanted to study the activities of lobbying organizations in Washington. This meant a conference with W.W. Willoughby
and his twin brother, W.F. (The only way you could tell them apart
really was W.F.'s nose had a slight northeast slant. Otherwise they
were almost identical.) One of the problems that had to be confronted
was whether interviewing was an acceptable method of inquiry, could
be trusted, and came within the rubric of scholarly research.

Field Research in the Early Days

HERRING: I was aware of no other graduate students engaged in
research on governmental affairs in Washington in the summer of
1927. I went to the Library of Congress to find a place to carry on my
studies, and was greeted in a friendly fashion by the director of the
Legislative Reference Bureau, who carried forward his work in a single desk in the Library of Congress. He suggested that I might focus
my research by selecting one organization, and he took me deep into
the stacks to confront me with the proceedings of the Wool Growers
Association extending over a good many decades. I can still see those
dismal, serried ranks of reports. Woolgathering and wool growing
were too closely associated for my taste. I escaped that hazard and
launched out onto a rather unfamiliar theme, but there was no problem of access. I made appointments readily. I don't recall any difficulty in seeing any of the leading lobbyists. For example, the
"patriotic organizations" were exceedingly ready to help and, indeed,
called a meeting of all the representatives of the various associations
in the DAR Building for an afternoon discourse.

GREENSTEIN: This was for your purposes? They were that cooperative?

HERRING: Yes. They sat around in a circle and answered my
questions, which I dare say were not too penetrating.

On the Hill, I simply wandered around the congressional corridors, as though I were the white rabbit in *Alice in Wonderland.* The
corridors were deserted. I remember distinctly knocking on a very
large door that was opened by a little man with a florid countenance.
He invited me in, and it was only after we had been talking for some
time and he had likened lobbyists to coyotes that I realized he was
John Nance Garner. I don't remember what Senator Borah said, but I

do remember his long underwear poking out from under his shirtsleeves. There was no protocol involved. The congressional staffs were very modest, indeed, and the whole atmosphere was very placid.

Early Political Science Experiences

HERRING: In the fall of 1928, I turned up at Harvard. For the first time, the Department of Government had decided to give up the practice of inviting law school students to serve as "section men" in the introductory course, and, to that end, young instructors were appointed to assist in Government I. My other duties involved participation in the tutorial system, which was in its early stages at Harvard. Like all new academic developments, it attracted a good deal of enthusiasm, and full professors were ready to act as tutors, along with instructors. The expectations of the tutorial system were unrealistic, but that's another story.

Life on $522 a year, while not sumptuous, was very pleasant. I discovered that, by careful planning, I could get three meals at a dollar a day around Harvard Square. The Boston Symphony came for a season at Sanders Theatre. Some of us became acquainted with members of the orchestra and discovered that we shared an interest not only in music, but also in finding some restaurants where wine might be served, even though in very thick porcelain coffee cups. Does it sound too dated if I suggest that another of our amusements was playing charades?

My salary left sufficient surplus to go off to Europe for the summer of 1929 and visit England, Germany, France, and Czechoslovakia and gather material for articles that were later published on aspects of economic and functional representation of those countries. It was toward the end of the summer that I received a letter from Louis Brownlow, inviting me to organize a round table for the American Political Science Association meeting to be held in New Orleans. With this very formidable responsibility looming, I returned home somewhat sooner than I had planned and wondered how one went about preparing a round table.

The Association had never met in New Orleans before, and, since it was far away, it was a long train journey, so there were not many more than a hundred people in attendance. My round table was very sparsely attended, but that was hardly surprising in view of the total attendance and in view of the subject matter. Brownie had suggested that I organize a round table on group representation in public administration, an uncultivated field. There was no literature on the thing and I couldn't find anybody who was interested in the subject.

At any rate, I didn't know how to go about it. Brownlow was present and perhaps half a dozen others. That didn't deter me from having a memorable time, though I must say I remember more vividly getting acquainted with Harold Lasswell, Jim Pollock and others than I do remember about the papers that were delivered.

GREENSTEIN: Could that have been your first awareness of what was happening in Chicago during those years? Harold Lasswell's propaganda book must have come out during that year. Where did Merriam, Gosnell, and the whole spate of University of Chicago publishing fit in your view of things in those years?

HERRING: During 1929, I prepared my manuscript for publication. Soon thereafter, I was invited by the Social Science Research Council to serve on a committee on Pressure Groups and Propaganda. Lasswell was chairman. That led to my first contact with the Council. Harold was in fine fettle, and the committee was apparently generously supported. We met at the Hotel Roosevelt in New York for several days. In New York, we met with leaders of the most prestigious advertising agencies. There would be a morning session and then a new group would come in at lunch, and then they would be succeeded by another group in the afternoon. In other words, we were in constant session and one group of guests would be relieved by another group. It was a most arduous experience.

GREENSTEIN: These were, in effect, collective interviews that you and they were having?

HERRING: With Harold doing most of the interviewing.

GREENSTEIN: At that stage, was Harold speaking a rather jargon-free English that communicated itself to the general public?

HERRING: It was very difficult to understand what he was talking about. And the other thing that puzzled me was the vision he entertained. It seemed to involve a highly organized arrangement whereby monitors would study the state of public opinion across the country. It seemed to me a very fantastic scheme. These meetings were exciting, and I thought if this is field research, this is a heady diet.

I gathered from this experience the impression that somewhere there was money for research. I didn't know where, and I didn't know how one went about it, but it seemed to me that there must be some key to the store. So, in the early 1930s, I journeyed to Chicago to get acquainted with Charles Merriam and his colleagues.

From that time on I was in touch with Charles Merriam, who was consistently friendly and supportive in his characteristic way. He had an avuncular personality. One felt rather close to him personally. You felt his interest in you as an individual. And there was Harold in his office: there was a couch, and the walls were lined with waxed cylinders, and I had never quite experienced a study that was furnished that way.

The Eagles at Harvard

HERRING: I felt rather close to W.Y. Elliot since he invited me to his home, and socially we had an agreeable relationship at the outset. I came to know Carl Friedrich quite well. I remember babysitting once—the only experience I ever had in babysitting—for one of the children—it must have been Otto. I think I changed his diaper. I didn't think I would ever do that for an editor of the *Saturday Evening Post*. It was a very happy time because there was this warm friendship in the department. But the relationship between Elliot and Friedrich grew more tense, and it was some years later that the rivalry grew between the "eagles," as a junior colleague called them.

It's not uncharitable to say that both of those men had egos of rather massive portions. If your ego is as large and well-developed as that you have a hell of a lot to live up to. Friedrich was rather in the tradition of a European professor—you have a chair, and you have your little entourage. And Friedrich liked to win the friendship and loyalty of younger colleagues through various collaborative arrangements. He invited me to collaborate in a seminar. He was awfully good and had a powerful conceptual mind.

GREENSTEIN: Was Elliot less disposed to form a circle?

HERRING: No. Each man had his little following of more or less congeniality. And if either one took a junior under his wing, a very protective covering was provided.

The Depression Strikes Harvard

HERRING: The depression even reached Harvard University. There was a certain amount of attrition, and there was talk of a salary cut. The senior members of the department felt they should take the cut and not have it fall upon the shoulders of those who were getting along on a couple of thousand dollars a year. So the state of the world was grim, and very able associates were there briefly and off they went. You never knew whether there would be a reappointment or not. One is reminded of the part that good fortune as much as anything else played in it. The "publish or perish" atmosphere was something of a motivating element, but I don't think that people can be driven to write and publish if they don't have something they want to say; they certainly are not likely to do it happily or effectively.

An even more bothersome problem was the realization on the part of the topside that they were overcommitted, that the university would be in serious trouble if they didn't go about the whole problem of promotion in a more orderly fashion. That's when Dean Ferguson undertook an analysis of what had to be done about promotions. That resulted in my being classified in a "semifrozen" category—semifrozen in that no promotion could be made until an opening appeared on the ladder. This finally worked through, and I was granted tenure. At Harvard when you are granted tenure and do not have a Harvard degree, you're given an honorary master's degree and become what they call a "child of the house." It is a meaningful and heartwarming gesture.

Training for the Public Service

HERRING: In 1936, Lucius N. Littauer arranged for a gift to Harvard University to set up a school to train for the public service. Well, how do you train for the public service? Can you train for the public service? And wasn't Harvard already training for the public service? A chemist who had not long been president of Harvard didn't really know quite what to make of all this and was as skeptical as only a chemist could be, confronted by such a situation.

The faculty decided that they would play for time and started a series of conferences. For five days every week officials from Washington were invited to come to Cambridge and talk about training for the public service. I was designated to serve as secretary of the school, which made me the first person on the payroll. Thinking that one way to keep track of all this flow of discourse would be to use the latest technical devices, I got a system which consisted of wires that were strung around the faculty room so that all the wisdom could be recorded on waxed cylinders. The secretary was supposed to produce the minutes of that discourse by the next morning. You can't listen all night to what's been said all day, so I went back to my notes and dictated the minutes and had them mimeographed and ready. Well, I don't think that really the faculty got much enlightenment from it, but it did get word around that Harvard wanted to do something about public administration, and it did persuade the faculty that a good deal of help could be had from getting officials to participate.

With the title of secretary, I was in the position of, in effect, "associate dean" for nearly ten years. During the war years, I commuted back and forth every week from Cambridge to Washington and, in the school, had the excitement and experience of participating in an interdisciplinary seminar on fiscal policy.

There was this skepticism about public administration. The dean had no interest whatsoever in public administration. Indeed, the faculty in general looked with scorn upon what was being attempted at Syracuse as mere management. It fell to me to serve as a link with the non-Harvard world of public administration.

Unifying the Armed Services

HERRING: My bibliography dealing with mobilization apparently came to the attention of Ferdinand Eberstadt, who was very active in the War Production Board and a close friend and associate of Forrestal. When Forrestal was confronted with the problem of how to respond to Truman's interest in unification of the armed services, he turned to Eberstadt and asked him to head up a task force to formulate a defensible position. The Navy was by no means enthusiastic about the unification of the armed services.

In response to a call from Eberstadt, I went to Washington. He said he wanted me to help him by applying "the lessons of history." That was rather a stopper, since I'd never quite thought of history in that fashion. I talked with some of my historian colleagues to see if they agreed with me that that was hardly a feasible assignment. I convinced Eberstadt, apparently, that while there were no neat lessons of history, maybe there was something that I could do by way of assistance that wasn't quite so pat. He forgot about his "lessons of history" approach, and we worked very closely together during the summer of 1945.

Eberstadt was an enormously intelligent, driving, quick-witted man—a highly effective "Wall Streeter" of a rapierlike intelligence. We were in that miserable relic of World War I on Constitution Avenue across from the Federal Reserve Board, a great firetrap of a temporary building. The summer was very, very hot, and Eberstadt called upon a succession of outstanding individuals to come and talk. Our task was essentially to construct some administrative organization that would relate the armed services to the White House and to the State Department. Each of the armed services departments feared losing its identity, losing the degree of autonomy and of responsibility that it felt was essential. Well, I kept at that task during the summer of 1945, and I seemed to be useful to Eberstadt. I can't precisely tell you why, but he seemed to feel that I performed a useful service, and I think my contribution was in helping to give some form to the data.

Leaving Harvard

HERRING: After I came back to Harvard in '45, Charles Dollard asked whether I would be interested in joining the staff of the Carn-

egie Corporation. I expressed an interest and went to New York for
an interview with Devereaux Josephs, president of the Carnegie Corporation. I was very much taken with his personality, his keenness,
his intelligence. He had just taken over as president, and they were
getting off to a new start now that the war was over. They had great
plans. Their plans were certainly not very realistic, but I think the
attraction of a different setting, of venturing on a new course, was
more important than the precise nature of what it was all about.

GREENSTEIN: In your writing, had you reached a phase where
you may have had no more to say? Perhaps the time had come to
move from primarily focusing on research and the written word?

HERRING: I think that's a very perceptive point. In Washington,
I had had a very good experience and had tremendously enjoyed the
arranging and organizing and dealing with people and trying to get
things done and seeing them happen. At the university I had enjoyed
my work as secretary of the school. My office door was open, and if
you try to write, act as a consultant, have administrative responsibilities, and serve on faculty committees, you are a busy person. I had
reached the point where I wondered about such proliferation! I was
wondering about priorities. I think I had about written what I wanted
to write.

I agreed that I would join the Carnegie Corporation. Josephs
didn't want me to take a leave of absence from Harvard because, if
you're a foundation officer but on leave of absence from a university,
where are you? So I talked to Paul Buck, who was dean of the faculty,
to tell him that I was planning to resign. He said, "But I'm just about
to put up your name for appointment to a full professorship, but I
can't do that if you don't promise to come back." "Well," I said, "that's
very nice, but I'm not planning to come back, and I don't think I
should promise to come back if I'm not planning to. I want to try
something else." It would have been nice if my promotion could have
been realized—it would have been so much more symmetrical!

Public Opinion Quarterly

HERRING: Harwood Childs, a friend from the late 1920s, developed an interest in public opinion and decided to start a quarterly.
He invited me to serve as one of four editors. To start a journal is an
awfully quick way to spend money, and the *POQ* was started with
quite limited resources. How Childs ultimately supported it I'm not
certain. But he divided up the responsibilities of these four associate
editors and also asked us to see if we could raise money. I remember
calling upon the head of the Chamber of Commerce of the United
States. He confronted me with a cold and unarguable response by

saying that he never subscribed to magazines that he didn't read, and he had no intention of reading still another magazine.

One thing that came of this association with *POQ*, on my part, was a heightened interest in public opinion polling. My first and only foray into that resulted in an article published in the *POQ* called "How Does the Voter Make Up His Mind?" It was a rather naive, exploratory, and certainly not very significant venture. The only thing to be said in its favor was that there weren't any precedents that I knew of at the time. I got the cooperation of the League of Women Voters to circulate a form with a good many questions, and the underlying purpose was to see what correlations I could find between the expressed political attitudes of the respondents and personal information about themselves. I recall consulting with Wassily Leontieff's statistical staff to see if I could learn anything about random sampling, but to little avail.

The main significance of all this was that here was an effort initiated by a group of political scientists under the leadership of Harwood Childs. We had no methodological skills. Certainly what made for the *POQ*'s continuity was the fact that other social scientists developed methods, and they have carried on over the years. There was for me a profound realization that it isn't enough to have an interest in the field, you have to have some tools that are appropriate for developing it.

Modernizing the American Political Science Association

HERRING: Kenneth Colegrove had given devoted service to the Association for a long period. He ran the Association with what time and energy he had left from his teaching duties at Northwestern. We're talking about the period just after the war, and in that context many of us felt that the Association needed a fresh start. When the discontent with Colegrove had reached a peak, I was attending the annual meeting of the APSA. George Graham called upon me in my hotel room one morning to say that they had to have a candidate to run against Kenneth and I should be the man.

I explained that, while I agreed with all that, I was not going to be the stalking-horse in this political venture. Happily they turned to an elder statesman, Henry Spencer at Ohio State. Soon after he took over, he wrote me a letter. It starts out, "My dear Herring, as I try to perform the functions of President of the APSA just thrust upon me, there comes from various quarters on various topics the suggestion, 'See Pen Herring about this' " etc., etc.

I was able to get a grant from the Carnegie discretionary officers' funds that enabled the Association to activate a committee dealing with the reorganization, and later a grant was made that enabled the Association to undertake the study that eventuated in Goals for Political Science. A third grant helped to underwrite the Washington office of the Association for the first year. Ed Litchfield, who'd been active in military government in Germany and very effective in his work with Lucius Clay in Berlin, and I worked very closely in planning for a Washington office. After the first few years of Ed's concern with the Association, it became necessary to find a successor. He was succeeded briefly by John Gange, but Gange didn't want to hold on to the job. The question of finding someone for the post of executive director came along just at the end of my presidency and at the beginning of Ralph Bunche's, and I think Luther Gulick and Ralph Bunche and I were the three involved. I recall canvassing the membership. I believe in one canvass there were ninety-one different people mentioned as possible candidates.

Dealing with Association "Activists"

HERRING: A difficult question that persists is how to deal with the activists. Let me hasten to say that it's not activity that creates the problem. It's the nature of the aspirations and the projected actions. When you look back over a span of a good many years concerning some of the proposals that were hard pressed, you're very much relieved that these objectives were never realized. For example, W.Y. Elliott was convinced that we needed to rewrite the Constitution of the United States. Arthur Macmahon, during his presidency of the Association, was confronted with a long, rambling memo from Elliott about the great desirability of setting up a constitutional convention at each meeting of the Association in order to give continuing concern to constitutional revision. Our own APSA constitution we had enough difficulty with, but now he was interested in the Constitution of the United States! Another committee that seemed to me even more bothersome was the Committee on Political Parties.

GREENSTEIN: The Schattschneider Committee report was very commonly used for the teaching of political parties, but doesn't seem to have moved the wheels of the political system.

HERRING: Fine: a stimulus to internal debate. But there's very little to be said for provocative proposals as an indication of the wisdom and skills of political scientists for dealing with immediate and practical political issues. The responsible officers of the Association have this task of dealing with matters of that delicate sort.

Truman and Eisenhower

GREENSTEIN: There was a phase when public figures were brought into Association meetings. I remember the year of Lasswell's presidency, Harry Truman giving an extremely amusing banquet speech.

HERRING: The Association meeting was at the Mayflower, and I was told to go to Truman's suite and escort him down to the speaker's platform in the ballroom. When I reached his suite, I found a smoke-filled room. Apparently his Secret Service men were having a very convivial time with him, had coats off and collars loosened and so on. I escorted him, in the elevator, down to the assembled crowd. He was most pleasant, characteristically cheerful and friendly, and when he was introduced, he said, "Now I understand you're all concerned with government and politics. If you want to know anything about politics, you just ask me, and I'll tell you all you need to know."

Litchfield was convinced that it was a good idea for us to involve public figures. So when he was executive director, we would start off planning the annual meeting by being turned down by the president.

Ed arranged a nine o'clock appointment with Eisenhower at the White House; Ralph Bunche and I and Ed were greeted most affably by Eisenhower. He seemed to be in very good humor that early in the day, and we sat around his desk and chatted. He was very interested to hear that there was a Political Science Association and that we were teaching people that they should take an interest in government. He thought civics was a very good thing, that it was very wise to get people to consider their duties of citizenship. He said, "You know, my doctor tells me I shouldn't smoke these things, but I do. But that doesn't mean that he isn't right." He was very glad to see Bunche, although he was a little vague as to Bunche's present connection with the UN. He seemed to feel that Bunche was still in the State Department.

When we explained the purpose of our call, namely to invite him to speak to the Association, he said he would like to, but it came just at the time of year when he felt he had to take his vacation, and were he to speak, with all of the video preparation, he didn't feel that he could do it. But he was most appreciative of the invitation. And then he went on to say, "You know, if I want to do this or if I want to do that, somebody comes in and tells me, 'That's not good politics; this is not good politics.' You know," he said very confidentially, leaning forward, "this job will drive you nuts. It's enough to drive you nuts. It really is."

Well, by that time a worried aide was standing before us, and we realized we'd been there quite long enough, but the president accompanied us to the door of the Oval Office as we shook hands and left. As we filed out, I can see the grim face of John Foster Dulles and members of the Joint Chiefs out there, feeling they'd been standing waiting quite long enough.

The SSRC Committee on Political Behavior

HERRING: The Committee on Political Behavior that served so actively over a number of years in the Social Science Research Council was set up in 1949, with V.O. Key as chairman. Key had recently moved to Johns Hopkins, and we had become good friends, worked together during the years in Washington, and I prevailed upon him to undertake the chairmanship of this new committee. The first event of any importance that I recall in the committee was a conference at the University of Michigan. Key, Truman, and Angus Campbell all played a very active part. This conference helped to establish a certain esprit, and Oliver Garceau was commissioned to prepare a memorandum that would help to lay the basis for committee discussion. That memo later appeared in the *American Political Science Review*, entitled "Research and the Political Process."

Looking back, I'm impressed with the planned and deliberate way in which that committee proceeded. The committee meetings could most accurately be described as faculty seminars. The discussion was substantive in character and dealt with basic questions. We spent many hours beforehand planning and arranging for these meetings. The committee deliberations transcended administrative tasks. The excitement was about ideas.

Fortunately, John Russell of the Markle Foundation offered $100,000 or so if we would propose some worthy way of using it, and that prompted me to invent the summer seminar as a device. These occasions took advantage of the summer recess for bringing together scholars from different universities. The seminars were planned to encompass what could be achieved within that relatively brief span of time and also what one could expect for $25–30,000 worth of effort. So they were used in quite a variety of situations and by a number of committees, but they fit in very well with the needs of the Political Behavior Committee.

The program wasn't simply the exchange of ideas at committee meetings. It provided training opportunities; an excellent illustration was that V.O. Key spent at least one summer with Angus Campbell at the University of Michigan. His *Primer of Statistics for Political Scientists* probably was prompted by his experience there.

It's unfortunate that this minor debate over just how important the committee may have been ever occurred. I would say that the activity of this group was a part of the broader spectrum of changing attitudes, and this particular group had an opportunity to articulate ideas that were developing, and it had the means to encourage and reward people who chose to work along lines that the committee was concerned with. Perhaps its chief accomplishment was to find a way of operating in an efficient and meaningful fashion. We took proposals that came before the committee and, in one or two instances, saw that the independent interests of several individuals appeared to converge. This was the case with Buchanan, Ferguson, Wahlke, and Eulau. And it was at that stage that we brought these individuals together and invited them to share one another's thoughts if they cared to proceed as collaborators.

It was the policy of the Council that once programs were safely launched, they were then carried on under other auspices that we regarded as appropriate. The policy of the Council was to keep us free from operating duties and thereby leave us free to initiate and facilitate and pick up something else rather than to hang on to things that we had started. The Council was thought of as a facilitating agency and never a rival. If a university could perform a given function, the SSRC lent support but did not attempt anything that could be regarded as competition. For example, in the studies of the presidential elections, the grants went directly to Michigan.

The SSRC Committee on Comparative Politics

HERRING: We held a meeting in order to forgather with a number of younger political scientists who had been appointed to fellowships and were on their way to carry forward their research in various foreign countries. I said, "Could we think of the questions that these fellows should have in mind as they set forth on their field work that would enable them to compare notes when they return home? What sort of curiosities, what sort of questions, what points of inquiry would you suggest to them, so that they might have a better chance of developing comparable data?" One of the members of the committee some years later recalled that as being a question that played some part in our quest for finding a conceptual scheme for comparative analysis. My role in this committee, and, indeed, in any committee where I had any substantive reason—or any reason at all—for being present, was to listen patiently to seemingly interminable talk for some lead or idea that could be related to the resources or devices that we had in the Council. That was the reward. If there was something that had enough shape to it or enough potential so that it could be identified and developed in some fashion, I'd have a private sense of satisfaction that I'd accomplished something. But there were intervals of what is best described as "exquisite tedium."

Establishing the Woodrow Wilson Center

HERRING: I want to review what seems to me a rather neat study of bringing something to a successful termination by being in the right place at the right time, knowing the right people, and having the right idea to begin with. This is the story of the steps leading to the establishment of the Woodrow Wilson International Center for Scholars. It starts toward the end of 1965, when I was attending the Advisory Committee for the Social Sciences at Johns Hopkins. There was a discussion of the problem of research in Washington and of the need for arrangements that would be more efficient and satisfactory. I brought up the idea of a center—such an idea had come up in various connections in the past—and I agreed to write to various people at different universities to see what their reaction would be.

Dean Sayre, Woodrow Wilson's grandson, was chairman of the Woodrow Wilson Memorial Commission. They'd become mired down, and Sayre was discouraged and wanted to resign. It occurred to me that if the idea we were trying to advance could be joined with the responsibility Dean Sayre had, to find some sort of memorial for Woodrow Wilson, those two ideas might coalesce and strengthen one another. So I incorporated this in a revision of my original memo and circulated it to a number of people. My very close friend Charles Frankel, who was then assistant secretary for educational and cultural affairs in the Department of State, responded favorably and agreed to see what reactions he could get within the government.

We organized a meeting in Washington, bringing people together who had an institutional interest—the Pennsylvania Avenue Planning Commission, the Smithsonian, and the Library of Congress. Out of this session we then arranged to bring it to the attention of the White House. Douglass Cater picked up the ball, and, through his interest, it was brought to Johnson's attention. He turned to John Gardner, who was in HEW, and John turned to the vice president of the Carnegie Corporation, whom earlier I had brought on my staff from the SSRC, Lloyd Morrisett, to make a staff study.

All this eventuated in a paragraph supporting the idea in the District of Columbia presidential message. So then the attention shifted to what we should do on the congressional side. One of the first things Johnson's interest did was to reactivate the Woodrow Wilson Memorial Commission. Dean Sayre was a bit weary of being the grandson of Woodrow Wilson, but it happened that the vice chairman was Harrison Williams, senator from New Jersey, who took an active interest. Pat Moynihan and I decided that we needed a sales document for Congress, so I got the Princeton University Press to design a very handsome presentation. We saw that every member of Congress got copies of it. Ultimately the bill was passed.

Testifying before Congressional Committees

HERRING: The Cox Committee and the Reese Committee were congressional committees attempting to savage the social science research endeavor. The Cox committee came first. There was to be an investigation of foundations. The established foundations must have experienced a sense of shock that they were up for investigation. Their whole mystique is based on philanthropy in the most exalted sense of the word. They're conscientious, try hard and hope to do good.

The SSRC was to be included in this, and the social sciences were under suspicion. Congressman Cox got hold of a lawyer who asked me, someone from the ACLS and two or three other organizations to come to Washington to meet with him. What I remember most clearly from that meeting is his saying, "I want your cooperation." I'm nothing if not ready to cooperate. But he went on to add that "I'm from Chicago, and I've dealt with alley fighters," saying, "We want you to cooperate." That was the first time I'd ever confronted quite that attitude, so I came back and consulted with my pals about the best way to handle the situation. We concluded that since the investigators were so nervous about the radical nature of whatever it was they were worried about, we would try to get a reassuring witness to address the committee. And we agreed that the man to do it was William Myers of Cornell, a member of the Federal Reserve Board, an agricultural economist, and a solid citizen. The whole notion of an agricultural economist from a state agricultural institution seemed to me to be a very good choice. So we got him down to my office and put it up to him, you know, for the good of the cause. And we gave him some coaching as to what it was all about. He went down to Washington and testified, and it went smoothly.

The possibilities were not pursued by the Cox committee, but about a year later, Congressman Carroll Reese of Tennessee appeared on the scene. This was to be a *real* investigation. One day a man from the staff of the committee came to see me. He wanted to hear all about the way in which the SSRC was organized. I tried to explain it. Well, this man happened to be a refugee from Vienna. He'd gotten this job, I guess, because he needed the job. As I tried to explain how we went about our organization, I remember his saying, "Oh yes, I see, just like the college of cardinals!" The whole thing had an air of the bizarre about it. To be more specific, their charges were bizarre. The Council, they asserted, was the apex of a pyramid of power. And this power was maintained through interlocking contacts that brought together the overweening influence of private philanthropy and the scholarly world, and all this impinged upon government and public policy, and the whole thing was, in effect, a conspiracy to take over the control of public affairs.

How do you deal with anything as bizarre as that? They expressed their horror at all this by calling attention to "empirical inquiry" as being very dangerous. So that's what led me to give a little thought to how to explain to somebody who doesn't know what he's talking about what empirical inquiry means. And it was to that kind of an audience that I addressed my comments. The hearings had been under way for quite some weeks, and there had been a parade of crackpots.

In preparation for testifying, it seemed clear that I needed legal counsel. Timothy Pfeiffer was accustomed to trial work. He would come to the office and ask me questions I might be asked on the stand or encourage me to think of answers to the kind of charges they were making. So I approached that hearing with a certain amount of élan. I had had no experience with this kind of thing, but I thought it would be exciting to see what happened. I found myself responding rather vigorously to some of the committee's questions. It got very extensive press coverage. The foundations were criticized for supporting social science research. That research was staunchly defended, and it was clear that the committee had no ground to stand upon. After my testimony, the hearing ceased.

It wasn't very long thereafter that the heyday of the behavioral science division of the Ford Foundation came to an end. They got into trouble over the study of juries, for one thing. At any rate, the foundation decided they'd have no more to do with the behavioral sciences. It was very shortly thereafter that the Rockefeller Foundation's program changed. They had been supporting the social sciences for decades, but their program changed, and the Carnegie Corporation also developed a strong interest in education and took less interest in the social sciences.

GREENSTEIN: This seems to suggest that the same kind of attack you were able to fend off in that meeting nevertheless represented a viewpoint that was in the air and that independent foundations were sensitive to. So many of them seemed to pull in their horns on behavioral science.

HERRING: It's a complicated set of currents. But from the standpoint of public relations, foundation officers have to be mindful of the predilections of the members of their boards and what's generally going on in the society around them.

Establishing the NSF Political Science Program

HERRING: The status of the social sciences within the National Science Foundation and within the larger science community was so uncertain. NSF officials felt so defensive and just couldn't face the thought of congressional criticism. Of course, there was congressional criticism, so that the officers in the NSF, at the beginning, didn't want their appropriations threatened by the social sciences. When there was a social science division, they didn't want their little beachhead threatened by something called political science. What brought about a change in that, other than a more maturing attitude and greater sophistication? I give credit to Evron Kirkpatrick particularly, and to the American Political Science Association, in getting congressional interest—in getting people like Hubert Humphrey to ask, "Why aren't you doing something for political science?" That was the way this flank attack made it expedient for these officials to do something, whereas, in my opinion, if an advisory committee had attempted to jolt officials, that would have been ineffective. That would have been the wrong pressure, because they look upon advisory committees as support groups. Building support in Congress made it possible—in fact, made it desirable—for NSF officials to decide that political science was "admissible."

Belle Zeller

Belle Zeller was born in New York City on April 8, 1903. She received her baccalaureate degree from Hunter College in 1924 and her master's degree (1926) and Ph.D. (1937) from Columbia University. She began her teaching career in 1926. In 1930, she was among the first instructors at the new Brooklyn College, where she spent the remainder of her career, until retirement in 1973.

Her research specialties were the legislative process and, in particular, lobbying. She is best known for her book Pressure Politics in New York, *the first comprehensive study of lobbying at the state level. She also was co-author and editor of* American State Legislatures, *which was the first comparative study of state legislatures encompassing all fifty states. This volume provided considerable information that was used by promoters of state legislative reform.*

She was chairperson and legislative representative of the Legislative Conference, which began as a faculty lobbying organization and became a union in 1969, and then the faculty bargaining unit for the City University system. Putting into practice her scholarly expertise in legislative lobbying, she was instrumental in leading the negotiations for collective bargaining agreements in New York that have become models in higher education for their due process protections and innovative professional provisions.

She served as a research consultant to the U.S. House Select Committee on Lobbying Activities. She was appointed to the New York State Commission to Study the Government and Structure of New York and to the New York Task Force on Higher Education.

She served on the Executive Council of the American Political Science Association from 1947 to 1949.

Belle Zeller was interviewed in New York City on July 2, 1985, by Benjamin Rivlin, who was a colleague for many years at Brooklyn College and who has taught since 1970 at the City University of New York. He is a comparativist with particular interests in Africa and the Middle East.

Early Interest in Politics and Political Science

RIVLIN: Can you tell us where and when you were born and a bit about your family background?

ZELLER: I was born in the city of New York, the lower end of the island of Manhattan, on April 8, 1903. I was a member of a large family. My parents were immigrants who came here with little education but hoped for more for their children. I had two older sisters, five older brothers, and two younger sisters. My father was a laborer who worked in the early years in a shoe factory.

RIVLIN: Where did you go to school?

ZELLER: I went to the public schools of New York City.

RIVLIN: When did you first become aware of politics?

ZELLER: I became aware of it—really consciously aware of it— during the election of 1916, when Woodrow Wilson ran for reelection. And prior to that time, there was always a great deal of discussion around our dinner table. You see, I had parents who were interested in politics, and I also had older brothers and sisters.

RIVLIN: Were any of them involved actively in politics?

ZELLER: No.

RIVLIN: Now, you became aware of politics around 1916. When did this interest in politics transform itself into political science?

ZELLER: I was very active at Hunter College. I entered Hunter College in February 1921. I specialized in history and the social sciences and was, as I said, very active in the Social Science Club and other activities on the campus.

RIVLIN: Was political science a course at Hunter College at the time?

ZELLER: It was part of the Department of History and Social Science, and, as I recall, only the introductory course was taught at that time. It was history in general, and that carried over when I went to Columbia for my graduate work.

RIVLIN: Hunter College at that time was exclusively a women's school, right?

ZELLER: That's right, exclusively women.

RIVLIN: Were no other students there whom you recall—classmates who shared your interest?

ZELLER: Yes. Ruth Weintraub, for example, was at the college at that particular time. She became a member of the Hunter College faculty. There was Margaret Gustaferro, who became a member of the Department of Political Science, and Elsa deHaas, who became a colleague of mine at Hunter and at Brooklyn College.

RIVLIN: So there were a group of women interested in politics. Did you women feel like you were pioneers in this field?

ZELLER: Well, political science and politics were a man's field.

RIVLIN: Which political figure at that time impressed you most?

ZELLER: I had what you would call a crush on Woodrow Wilson. I loved to read his speeches aloud. In fact, after he left the White House in 1921, the following year I sent a volume of his speeches to his home on S Street in Washington and asked for his autograph. I brought that book in this morning to show you the signature of Woodrow Wilson dated 1922.

RIVLIN: I read from a little note addressed to Professor Zeller, Miss Belle Zeller, by Woodrow Wilson's secretary, dated 29 September 1922: "Dear Madam, It has given Mr. Wilson pleasure to autograph the book sent to him with your letter of September 24. I am returning the book in this mail and hope that it will reach you safely."

Were you aware at the time that Woodrow Wilson was an eminent political scientist as well as a politician?

ZELLER: Yes. I knew he had been a professor and president of Princeton.

Graduate Study and Early Years as a Faculty Member

RIVLIN: You entered Columbia University, the graduate school, as a graduate student in history, or was it then called the faculty of—

ZELLER: Public law. So I was in history during the period when I was getting my master's degree. I was appointed as a tutor at Hunter College and taught, I believe, a course in English history. But the following semester I was given a course in political science, and that's when I switched at Columbia from history to political science and fulfilled my requirements for the Ph.D.

RIVLIN: Who were the professors at Columbia at the time in political science?

ZELLER: The ones that stand out and I did most of my work with: Arthur Macmahon, whom I consider the most outstanding teacher. He didn't publish as much as some of the others, but he was an inspirational teacher. Raymond Moley, Lindsay Rogers, Schuyler Wallace. I was the first Ph.D. student to do my dissertation under Schuyler Wallace. Luther Gulick was there at the time.

RIVLIN: You taught at Hunter College. As a tutor, did you have a full schedule?

ZELLER: Yes. Tutors in those days had full fifteen-hour teaching schedules with only one or two courses that you repeated in small sections.

RIVLIN: How long were you a tutor?

ZELLER: I was a tutor from 1926 to 1930, when I became an instructor. I started at a salary of $1,600 a year, full time. Note, I said a year, not a month. I taught as a tutor at Hunter College in Manhattan, and then I taught as part of Hunter College in Brooklyn from 1927 until it became Brooklyn College in 1930.

RIVLIN: What department were you in at this time?

ZELLER: At Brooklyn in 1930, after it became Brooklyn College, it was called the Department of Government and Sociology. I was appointed chairman by Dean Fradenburgh, who was in charge of all the social sciences.

RIVLIN: And how did you divide up the discipline among yourselves?

ZELLER: We had our specialties in political science—a B.A. curriculum in political science that was one of the best in the country. We searched every college catalog in the country to see what was being offered there so that we could present to our students a rich curriculum. And I think we succeeded. We expanded rather rapidly.

RIVLIN: Many people are interested in the question of women political scientists. What was the experience of the Brooklyn department, and your own experience, with regard to women?

ZELLER: First of all, what was very unusual when Brooklyn College was established in 1930, Hunter College sent to Brooklyn a contingent of four women and one man. So that we began with a fine base of women representation in the field of political science. I wish I could say that was true of the other colleges in the City University system. As I said, political science is considered a man's profession.

RIVLIN: Oh, I don't know about that.

ZELLER: Well, listen. I'll tell you one thing. You know, we have had eighty presidents of the American Political Science Association. But not one woman. It's time we had one.

Research on Interest Groups and Lobbying

RIVLIN: All this time while you were teaching and introducing the new curriculum, you were doing your research for your doctoral dissertation. Who was your mentor at Columbia for your doctoral?

ZELLER: I actually did the dissertation under Schuyler Wallace, as I told you. I think I was the first one to complete a doctoral dissertation under him. But there were others very much interested in what I was doing: Lindsay Rogers, even though it was not his field.

RIVLIN: Well, tell us about your dissertation.

ZELLER: And Arthur Macmahon. My dissertation dealt with lobbying in New York State.

RIVLIN: Were there any earlier studies on lobbying that you were aware of?

ZELLER: Not as comprehensive, no. Mine was the first, as I've been told, and I think it's so—the first comprehensive lobbying study at a state level in the United States.

RIVLIN: How did you go about doing it?

ZELLER: Well, as part of my extra curricular activities, I became interested in what was then called the Legislative Conference of the City Colleges. In the four city colleges, there were committees on legislation. You understand, we were public institutions, and our funds came at that time chiefly from the city of New York and from Albany. So my interest in lobbying, from a practical point of view, grew out of my academic interests and the extracurricular activities. I studied the lobbies that were active, in particular, in New York State, and an examination of my doctor's dissertation will show an introductory chapter describing sociological and political conditions in New York State, and then there are chapters on industry, labor, farmers, professional groups, etc. And lobbying regulation constituted a separate chapter in the study.

So I had this wonderful opportunity, combining my academic work with the so-called practical work of actually going to Albany and lobbying at the same time that I was gathering material for my doctor's dissertation.

RIVLIN: How often did you go to Albany at the time?

ZELLER: At the beginning I would go up maybe once every two weeks. I would leave my classes—I had permission from the administration to do that—and a substitute would take my class, and I would go up to Albany and then come back and teach my course. I had courses in American politics and a course in the legislative process. So I was able to tell my students in the legislative process course and the American politics course what I did up in Albany as a lobbyist.

RIVLIN: And when did you complete your dissertation?

ZELLER: It was actually completed by the end of '36 and published early in '37 by Prentice-Hall.

RIVLIN: Well, your work on lobbies is considered to be pioneering work in the field of political science. I think you know the story that when I went up to graduate school after World War II at Harvard and I walked in to see Arthur Holcombe. And he asked me where I went as an undergraduate, and I mentioned Brooklyn College, and he asked me who did I study with. I mentioned the name of one of the male professors. He didn't know who I was talking about, and he said, "Didn't you study with Belle Zeller?"

ZELLER: I always considered that very flattering because I had tremendous respect for Arthur Holcombe. One of the advantages of being a member of the American Political Science Association, of having served on its Council from 1947 to '49, was meeting not only the professors under whom I studied at Columbia but the outstanding political scientists across the country, like Arthur Holcombe, like Charles Merriam.

Morgenthau and Almond at Brooklyn College

RIVLIN: Well, what about the New Deal? How did that affect people?

ZELLER: Roosevelt received warm support from the overwhelming number of faculty and students. Remember, we were looking for a campus and finally got one out in Flatbush, and a number of the buildings were built with aid from the federal government at that time. The Public Works Administration was under the able leadership of Harold Ickes, and I recall Roosevelt coming at that particular time to dedicate our gym building, which we named Roosevelt Hall.

RIVLIN: Were there any refugees from Nazi Germany who came to teach at Brooklyn College?

ZELLER: We were able to welcome, among others, Hans Morgenthau, and, believe it or not, we had only an opening for him in our evening session. It's hard to believe that we were able to bring Hans Morgenthau from Spain at that particular time and have him teach in the political science department at $3.50 an hour. Unfortunately, we could not find an opening for him in our regular day session at that time, so he left. I think he went out to Missouri.

RIVLIN: University of Kansas City. You were chairman during the war, and, at the end of the war, you were working to recruit somebody, and who was the first person you brought in?

ZELLER: Gabriel Almond. Gabriel Almond, at that time, was a young man in his twenties who was working with Charles Merriam at the University of Chicago; he was his research assistant. And we had an opening in the department as tutor, and I had been writing around the country asking for candidates for this opening. At that particular time, I was eager to get someone from outside New York. We had a department, as has been described, whose members had been doing most of their work at Columbia University. And Merriam recommended Gabriel Almond and released him from his contract as research associate or assistant so that he could come in February 1939.

RIVLIN: How long did he stay at Brooklyn College?

ZELLER: He stayed at Brooklyn College for several years, and then we entered the war. He was a very active member of the department and had all sorts of excellent new ideas for teaching, particularly our introductory course. We lost him to the war effort.

Interest in State Government and Activity in the American Political Science Association and the Council of State Governments

RIVLIN: I want to deal a little bit with your intellectual history, your intellectual interests. I notice that you wrote an article in 1938 called "Lobbies and Pressure Groups: A Political Scientist's Point of View." It's a long time ago.

ZELLER: You bet it's a long time ago. I think what I was trying to do in that was to show the constructive and positive side of lobbying, that it was an excellent source of information, biased as it might be at times; a great aid for legislators, provided they knew what the source was. Lobbying played an important part in the process of government, in the legislative process. That's what I was attempting to show.

RIVLIN: I gather that, from your work on this—your dissertation—you became interested in state government, and you became interested in state government beyond that of New York State, and you eventually did some very important work in the field of state government. Would you tell us a little bit about that?

ZELLER: Yes. The American Political Science Association had a committee on the reform of the Congress. That was headed by George Galloway, who was a political scientist and then went to the Legislative Reference Service of the Library of Congress. They were also interested in a model congressional lobbying law. And we worked on that and played an important part in the passage of the lobbying act in 1946. And then the American Political Science Association decided to widen the scope of this committee and extend it to the state legislatures, and I was appointed to that committee.

My analysis of the first year of operation of this general congressional lobbying law was published in the *American Political Science Review* of April 1948—and reproduced *in full* in the *Congressional Record* of March 8, 1950. It was a long article with many, many footnotes. What a cost to the taxpayers!

I believe I was the first woman appointed to the chairmanship of a committee of the American Political Science Association. And that committee undertook a study of state legislatures in this country. Most of the state legislatures were sadly in need of reform if they were to be effective policy bodies of their respective states. And out of that committee grew the study which was published by Thomas Crowell in 1954 entitled *The American State Legislatures*. I was co-author and editor of that volume. It dealt not merely with one state, it dealt with the problems of all the states. And that volume really became the bible for state reform of their state legislatures.

RIVLIN: You were chairman of the committee?

ZELLER: I was chairman of the state legislature committee—the first woman. Remember, before that I was a member of the Executive Council of the American Political Science Association.

RIVLIN: You were first woman on the Council?

ZELLER: I don't think so. I know Louise Overacker was and there may have been others.

RIVLIN: As I recall—I remember that period when you were working on state legislatures. You would disappear every once in awhile. You were called in as a consultant on state legislatures.

ZELLER: We used to meet annually and hold conferences in different parts of the country, and I made a number of very good friends as a result of my contacts. Then also there was the Council of State Governments with headquarters in Chicago at 1313 East 60 Street, just off the campus of the University of Chicago. I was very active in this group and wrote on state legislatures for its magazine *State Government* and regularly for its *Book of the States* for almost twenty-five years.

RIVLIN: You mentioned that you had been in contact with Charles Merriam with regard to Gabriel Almond's appointment. Did you have any contact with Charles Merriam in regard to this work in state government and state legislatures?

ZELLER: And pressure politics in New York. Yes, I did. You may recall that Charles Merriam in 1922 published his *American Party System*, and he used the pressure group approach to the study of political parties. In fact, I think he was really the first one. And during these years—it took several years in the '30s to complete my dissertation, because I was teaching full time—I sent Dr. Merriam chapters of my dissertation, and he would make valuable suggestions.

RIVLIN: Were you active in 1313?

ZELLER: Yes. I used to attend meetings there, I used to go there to gather material for my research and stay at the International House on the University of Chicago campus. Yes, I was quite active in the Council of State Governments.

Politics and Civic Activity

RIVLIN: Could you tell me, Belle, were you active in any civic groups in New York City at this time?

ZELLER: Oh, yes. I was very active in the Citizens Union of the City of New York. This is an organization in existence for over a hundred years, whose members are concerned with the welfare of the city of New York and the state, particularly with respect to their civic activities. I served on several committees of the C.U. On one, we reviewed the records of state legislative candidates and published the results as guides for voters. I was an active member of the C.U. Constitutional Revision Committee, too. I was also a member of the Board of Editors of the New York Legislative Service, a nonprofit organization that informed its clients what interest group was in favor or opposed to pending state legislation. In fact, I collaborated with the editor of this service—Elisabeth Scott—in a study under a grant from the Social Science Research Council, "State Agencies and Lawmaking," which was published in the summer 1942 issue of the *Public Administration Review.*

RIVLIN: Were you active in the League of Women Voters?

ZELLER: Yes, I've been a member and used to do some speaking for them. In addition, I have held some public positions, such as: I was a research consultant to the Constitutional Convention of New York State in 1967. I prepared some papers for that commission. And, in 1953 and '54, I served on a commission to study the government of New York City, by appointment of the then governor Thomas Dewey. Oh, and prior to that time, I served as lobby consultant to a Congressional House Committee on Lobbying—the Buchanan Committee. Now, these are just a few of the positions I held as a so-called public servant.

Politics and Change in New York
and in the City University

RIVLIN: In your career as a political scientist, I think you would have seen a number of political reforms introduced, and one particular one that I was wondering if you would comment about is the charter revision in New York City that Mayor La Guardia was instrumental in bringing about.

ZELLER: In the old days before LaGuardia, we had a Board of Aldermen made up of some sixty-five aldermanic districts, small districts. Among the sixty-five, there might be one or two Republicans. In fact, the Republican representative frequently couldn't get a second to his motions; the board was completely dominated by the local bosses.

This board was done away with under charter revision. A smaller council was established under proportional representation, which gave representation, for the most part, on the basis of the voting strength of the different parties. The council lasted under proportional representation for some twelve years. Unfortunately, at that particular time—or fortunately, depending upon how you look at it— they succeeded in electing a communist member, one or two, as I recall—I think it was just one. But that was enough to arouse those who could easily be aroused against proportional representation in general, so proportional representation went out the window.

I, along with Hugh Bone, then at Queens College, examined New York City's experience with P.R.—this article was published in the *American Political Science Review* of December 1948.

RIVLIN: As a public institution, the City University and its component colleges have been often subjected to political pressures. Has that been common or rare?

ZELLER: Well, as a public institution, political pressures are to be expected. The City University has grown rapidly. As you know, the City Colleges of New York, since 1847 and until 1976, had a policy of free tuition.

Former Students

RIVLIN: Can you tell me a little bit about some of your most memorable students whom you've had, who either have made their mark as political scientists or in the field of politics?

ZELLER: Yes, I certainly can. I can remember some of my colleagues who are teaching, like Martin Landau, who is now at the University of California at Berkeley; Marilyn Gittell, who is with us here at the City University; Sam Konefsky, a former student and distinguished member of the faculty for many years until his untimely death. Furthermore, they're not only colleagues in the field of teaching but many of them are in the state legislature. For example, at the present time, the Speaker of the State Assembly in New York State is a former student of mine.

What would some of these people be doing today if it weren't for free tuition? That's why we are so concerned about adequate financial backing, about aid and loans to our students, about low tuition.

RIVLIN: Well, you mentioned the City University. When did the municipal colleges become the City University?

ZELLER: As early as '60?

RIVLIN: That's when the legislation was passed.

ZELLER: Yes, but I think the implementation came later. Yes, it became a university. And it also established a separate graduate cen-

ter. And that caused quite a controversy, as you know, especially outside of the City Colleges. Problems arose with Columbia, with
Fordham, with New York University, and with other private universities and colleges offering master's and doctorates. Why do you need a
City University? they asked. So that was a struggle.

RIVLIN: Well, why should we establish the graduate school?

ZELLER: Many of our people couldn't afford to go to a place like
Columbia or New York University. Our rates were lower and our university as a *public institution* took into consideration the special needs
of the people of the City of New York.

But we didn't do it overnight. We didn't do it overnight. As I
recall—and here great credit goes to Mina Rees, who was the first
president of the university. She started very slowly. It's remarkable
that, in a period of twenty years, we have built a City University that is
now receiving national and international attention. We didn't come
smack from an undergraduate institution right into a Ph.D. program.
Many of our colleges had outstanding courses and faculty that granted
the master's degree, so we moved into the Ph.D. quite gradually and
naturally. It gave our better faculty an opportunity to teach at this
higher level and to retain them so they didn't go elsewhere.

Funded Research and a Perspective of Entire Career

RIVLIN: What kind of grants did you have from the SSRC?

ZELLER: I had two grants—one in '45-46, and another one '47-
48—and spent most of my time in Washington—on legislative clear-
ance by the administration of bills before Congress. I think that
second grant was later than '47–48. It was '49–50. And I had access to
the Bureau of the Budget; I had a desk there, and access to their files
in Washington. It was a very interesting study of the administration's
position on bills in the legislature. The Interior Department might
have one view and another department might have a different view
on the same bill. And it was the Bureau of the Budget that had the
responsibility of clearing up differences so that the administration
spoke to a Congress through one voice. As I said, it was a fascinating
study.

RIVLIN: If I were to characterize your career, it seems to me that
you certainly feel that—you've demonstrated that—you're not interested exclusively in the ivory tower and that you think that the ivory
tower has to come down into the practical arena.

ZELLER: And it can. I haven't any doubt that it can and it
should, but, at the same time, we know that even in the practical
arena you need a strong theoretical background. That is why I am

concerned that we're moving a little too fast into the vocational studies area and not stressing enough of the richer liberal arts curriculum.

RIVLIN: As you look back on your career—although your career is in the City University of New York, you have been all over, you have had wide contacts with all groups. What would you say the highlights of your career are?

ZELLER: I think we've hit the high spots. I'm eighty-two years; I've lived a long, happy, full life. I'm sure there are other things we could add, but, I think, Ben, you've done a masterful job in questioning me and in refreshing my memory at many points, and I'm very grateful to you.

RIVLIN: Thank you very much.

Emmette
S. Redford

Emmette Redford was born on September 23, 1904, in San Antonio, Texas. He grew up in Johnson City, where his lifelong friendship with Lyndon Johnson began. He entered the University of Texas in 1922 and, after a brief career as a public school teacher, received a B.A. in 1927 and his M.A. in 1928. He received a Ph.D. degree from Harvard University in 1933. Almost his entire teaching career was centered at the University of Texas, where he joined the faculty in 1933. During the war years, he served in several federal agencies, an experience that enhanced his interest in public administration, one of his major fields of specialization in research and teaching, along with the regulatory process and public policy. His first major publication was Administration of National Economic Control *(1952), a study of the administrative system of government regulation that emphasized the role of interest groups. In 1969, he published his major study,* Democracy in the Administrative State, *as well as* The Regulatory Process, *an in-depth study of the regulation of civil aeronautics.*

For many years, Redford has been associated with the Lyndon B. Johnson School of Public Affairs. In the late 1970s, he undertook the direction of a large-scale project to prepare a multivolume administrative history of the Johnson administration, to be written by a number of authors. In 1986, he authored one volume in that series, White House Operations: The Johnson Presidency.

Redford was president of the American Political Science Association (1960–61), following his terms as vice president and as program chairman and the three years he served as book review editor of the American Political Science Review. *He was also president of the Southwestern Political Science Association (1966–67).*

Emmette Redford was interviewed in Austin, Texas, in July of 1980 by William Livingston, a colleague who has taught at the University of Texas since 1949 and who became vice president and dean of Graduate Studies in 1979. Livingston is a specialist in British Commonwealth studies.

Hill Country Roots

REDFORD: My father died when I was five years old, and two years later my mother became postmaster of Johnson City, Texas, in 1912. When we went to Johnson City we took the train from San Antonio to San Marcos, spent the night there, took a mail hack to Blanco, spent the night there, and then my uncle took us on to Johnson City the next morning, fifteen miles further. This was two and a half days to cover a distance that I have since covered in less than an hour. It was a farming and ranching community. The people were of north European stock and there was uniformity of opinion about most matters.

LIVINGSTON: Did that mean there was no politics in Johnson City?

REDFORD: There was politics but, with two exceptions, everybody in the community was Democrat, and, except for one ex-Union soldier, everybody was of southern origin. Modern descriptions of American society, which have us becoming more and more homogeneous, don't ring true to me, because I recall the conditions of rural Protestant America.

LIVINGSTON: You and Lyndon Johnson were boyhood friends. Can you tell us something about the relationship between the two of you back in Johnson City?

REDFORD: Lyndon was four years younger. He was really closer to my two younger brothers, between the two of them in age and with them in high school. The Johnson family lived two blocks from us, and I suppose Lyndon spent more of his hours when he was awake at our house than at his own because there were other boys at our house. Lyndon had the run of the town; he needed to be home only at mealtime and bedtime, and hence he arrived at our house after breakfast and came back during the day if something was going on that interested him. So I knew him well and I knew the family well.

If you go to a high school that has no science equipment and no real science program and happens to have teachers who are good in history and government, your interests are turned that way. As a boy, I saw no books in our school library except books on history, and my first memory of pulling a book out of the library was reading the life

of Woodrow Wilson. The circumstances were such that if you had intellectual interests, they turned toward the area of history and government.

One time in Washington when I was at the White House waiting
for lunch with Lyndon, a lady of the press asked me how it could
occur that, from a small place like Johnson City, two people with an
interest in government would arise. I said there wasn't anything to be
interested in in the town except the churches and the court house.

LIVINGSTON: Did your relations with Johnson continue to be
fairly close over the years?

REDFORD: I saw him only occasionally because an academic
career and a political career are different. But we were friendly, and
I helped what little I could in campaigns. We shared political ideals. I
think there was a populist element in Lyndon's background, and
I know there was in mine. Another thing that Lyndon and I shared:
neither of us had any racial prejudice.

Lyndon's political attitudes were affected deeply by a couple of
things. One was that a person growing up in humble circumstances
tended to think in terms of the interest of people who were in humble circumstances. That led him to think about the needs for education, equality of opportunity, and so on. The other was that he
believed in the ability and the obligation of government to contribute
to the personal or individual well-being of the citizen. When he went
into Congress and spent so much time as a congressman trying to do
things for people, it was in line with his idea that government should
do things for people individually. I think he derived that attitude from
his father.

If there are any influences on my intellectual development from
youth, they come from the circumstances of humble beginnings and
the sympathy for those in similar circumstances that goes with it. I
remember one time my mother saying in some wrath to one of my
brothers: "I don't see how a person who grew up in the circumstances
you did can think of voting Republican!" The other circumstance was
that we grew up in Johnson City under the influence of the churches
and, in my case, under the influence of a very religious family. So I
believe that my interest in studying the ethical aspects of public administration derives in part from the influences on my youth. The
influence of the Bible and religious teachings produced an interest in
ethical issues that stayed with me all my life.

Discovering Political Science

REDFORD: The schooling in Johnson City was all in one building: three teachers for the elementary grades and two for high school.

The high school had no accreditation, so that anybody who went to school there had a problem getting into college. We had no laboratories, and, consequently, science training was not very good. Those of us who took language usually took it under somebody whose knowledge was pretty limited. On the other hand, my education in English, social science, history, and civics was very good. Going to college from Johnson City was not a common event, but, as far back as I can remember, my mother had taught her children that they were going to rescue themselves by getting a college education.

After one term at Southwest Texas State Teachers College in San Marcos, I decided that I ought to go to as good a place as I could, so I decided to see if I could get into the University of Texas. I entered the University of Texas in 1922, having overcome the formal deficiencies of my earlier education, even if not the substantive deficiencies. For the two years from 1923 to 1925, I became a public school teacher, with the exalted title of superintendent of schools, in a two-teacher school in Hunt, Texas—even more isolated from the world than Johnson City. I taught twenty-two subjects a day to students from the sixth to the tenth grades. Included were social sciences and also some subjects I had never studied, such as physical geography.

After two years, I returned to the University of Texas, still not knowing what my major would be. It was not until September of my senior year that I decided that I wanted a career in law; so in my senior year I had to build a major. I thought I ought to major in something related to law. I registered for three courses in government to give me a major and had practically the same amount of course work in economics.

In May of my senior year, I was offered a "tutorship" in government. A tutorship was a full-time appointment involving complete responsibility for four sections of the introductory course. The professors in the department, at the end of each year, picked one person to be a new teacher in the department, gave him a tutorship the first year and, if he did all right, promoted him to an instructorship the second year. The rules of the university allowed you to take one course, which I did. I served one year as a tutor and one year as an instructor and decided that I liked political science enough to make a career of it.

LIVINGSTON: What was the department like in those days?

REDFORD: It was primarily an undergraduate department. It gave a few M.A.s, but the energies of the staff were devoted to the undergraduate students and their instruction. And that task it performed very well. Quite a chain of people who achieved distinction in political science who went through the Department of Government in the '20s, including Ben Wright in '21, Irving Stewart in '22, Luther

Evans and Francis Wilson in '23, Charles Zimm about 1923, Roscoe Martin in '24, Taylor Cole in '25, Alton Burdine in '26, Emmette Redford and Jimmy McCamy in '27, V.O. Key in '29. No doubt there were others. Among the graduates of the University of Texas between '24 and '29, three became presidents of the American Political Science Association and one became president of the American Society for Public Administration. Our interests were stimulated by the teachers in the department. We might have had an interest in the field earlier, but certainly we had stimulating instruction; and we got a good background for graduate study in the subject.

LIVINGSTON: Did you find when you got to graduate school that your undergraduate education fitted you adequately for graduate study in a place like Harvard?

REDFORD: Yes, and not only I but the others who went from Texas. Alton Burdine, Taylor Cole, and I all went to Harvard at the same time, and we all did well. I had had two years of full-time teaching of government—Alton had had three years, and Taylor four—at the time we went to Harvard, so we had an advantage.

LIVINGSTON: Looking back at your early days in the department, you speak of it as committed to teaching. Was it also a research department?

REDFORD: Not to the extent it is today, though there was research going on. The conditions for research were not as favorable then as they are today. The teaching load was heavier—people taught nine or twelve semester hours—and subsidization for social science research was meager.

Graduate Studies at Harvard

REDFORD: My greatest experience at Harvard was in the full-year course in ancient and medieval political philosophy given by Charles Howard McIlwain. Political theory was required for all Ph.D.s in government at Harvard, and no one dared to offer the field without the basic course given by McIlwain. I don't know whether I've ever been in the presence of anybody who impressed me so fully with the depth of his scholarship and an equal enthusiasm for his subject. It is an inspiration that stayed with me all my life, to think of the profound knowledge that man had of his field and of his ability to communicate it to us. None of us in that course would have dared anytime in the nine months to ask a question. We would have known that we were robbing ourselves of something that it was our privilege to get. He sat down and began to talk, crisscrossed his material, apparently without any clear plan to where he was going, but as he worked his way backward and forward over the material, you realized you were getting a profound understanding of the subject in a way that you'd never experienced before. I also got from McIlwain a great deal of substantive knowledge to buttress my knowledge of constitutionalism and its evolution in the modern world. All through my life what I learned from McIlwain about the history of constitutional government in England, and the West in general, has helped me tremendously.

I also have been inspired by McIlwain's great integrity as a scholar. We had a course thesis to prepare in political philosophy, which we turned in about two weeks before the end of the course. I wrote mine on the political ideas of Philip Hunton. On the next to the last period of the class, McIlwain explained his own interpretation of Hunton's major work. It was in opposition to my interpretation. He already had my paper, so I went up to his desk afterward, thinking that I had busted that course, and told him that I had interpreted Hunton differently. He said, "Well, Redford, you read it again, and I'll read it again, and let's see where we stand." The following meeting of the class, he spent the first half of the hour saying that my paper had changed his interpretation. That has stood for something I had not seen in the same way in scholarship before. Here was a man who could admit error, perhaps because he was such a scholar, but whose intellectual integrity was such that he would admit from one class to another that he had not read something carefully enough. I said to my wife on occasions afterwards that I spent a lot of money at Harvard University, but all the money I spent the first year was worth it to have had the opportunity to study under a scholar with the integrity and depth of knowledge Charles H. McIlwain had.

I wrote my doctoral dissertation on the constitutional problems in American economic planning, a choice I reached reluctantly. I decided I could not major in political philosophy because my language ability was deficient and McIlwain did not think one should major in political philosophy unless he knew French, German, Latin, and probably Greek. So I set out to write a dissertation with (Carl) Friedrich, but, when I took my general examinations, Friedrich was in Europe. I was anxious to get through, so I went to Arthur Holcombe, and he gave me a topic. I don't remember that I ever discussed my dissertation with anybody until I had it done.

LIVINGSTON: Not even Arthur Holcombe, your dissertation advisor?

REDFORD: No. I saw Holcombe several times while I was working on it, but I don't recall any discussion of the dissertation. I just wrote it and turned it in. That's what he said to do.

LIVINGSTON: What kind of fellow was he?

REDFORD: Holcombe was a great fellow. Like the other professors at Harvard, he had a great interest in students, and students enjoyed him. They could see him any time. He was chairman of the department, in charge of the introductory course and all of the teaching fellows. He taught his own courses, but his door was always open, and you could walk up, tap on the door, and he'd say, "Come in," turn around from his typewriter and talk to you, and before you got down the hall when you were leaving, you would hear the typewriter clicking again. Very well-organized man, gave a very well organized course—if anything, too well organized because he stayed completely within his organization. Holcombe always took an interest in any problem of any graduate student, considered it with a kind of father-like attitude.

One thing that impressed me about Harvard was the feeling that the faculty were interested in students and didn't mind whatever amount of time was necessary to give to students. Most of them entertained students in their home. I can remember teas in Friedrich's home to which he invited some of his students. I think he had them every Thursday afternoon, a different group of students perhaps each time. I met A. Lawrence Lowell at Thanksgiving dinner at Professor Yeomans' house. Yeomans had his wife's three nieces and President Lowell and me for Thanksgiving dinner.

All the courses I had at Harvard, except the seminar in constitutional law and the one I had with (W.Y.) Elliott, were pure lecture courses. We felt free to interrupt Elliott, and he liked it, so we had some discussion in Elliott's course. The lecture method was characteristic. They gave you what they knew in the lecture, and you gave them what you knew in your course theses, as they were called, and your examination.

Except for sleeping and eating, we practically lived in the library. Except for Saturday evenings and the *New York Times* on Sunday mornings, we worked constantly. We were at the library by the time it opened in the morning, we were there between classes, and we stayed until dinner time in the evening. Maybe we went back at night or maybe we studied in our rooms.

The Prodigal Son Returns

LIVINGSTON: You finished your degree in '33 and came back to Texas promptly. Was that your intention all along?

REDFORD: No. I had an instructorship for the following year at Harvard and had been offered a summer teaching place at the University of Texas that would pay the expenses for my wife and me to get back home and live during the summer. When I arrived at the University of Texas, I was offered an assistant professorship in government. I spent about six weeks debating whether to go back to my instructorship at Harvard or take the assistant professorship at the University of Texas. I had confidence that I could make a success in a career at the University of Texas. But how your career shapes up, if you go back to an instructorship at Harvard, is problematic. I ultimately stayed at the University of Texas. You often wonder about what your life would have been like if you had taken another route.

One of my problems in accepting the job at the University of Texas was carving out some kind of teaching field that would be acceptable to the established people in the department. I couldn't teach constitutional law, theory, or comparative government because those fields were taken. So I put in a full-year course in government and the American economy, which was a very exciting subject in 1933. A little later, the European comparative government field opened up, so I taught an upper division course in European democracy and one in European dictatorships.

I had the two most interesting subjects to be taught in the '30s in the Department of Government. The New Deal having come, government and the economy was an attractive course, and, with the events occurring in Europe, my European dictatorship course was very popular. So I had large classes and good students. From a teaching viewpoint, it was a very satisfactory period in my life and exciting for me. But it allowed no time for the development of any research or writing. So six years of my life I spent practically in just a teaching career, chasing the facts that I had to know in order to teach my courses.

That period ended in '39. One factor was that I became convinced that I had to make some change in my program. The other factor was the evolution of my interest in government regulation of the economy. When I started teaching it, a very big segment of the course dealt with constitutional issues. After 1937, those issues were being resolved quickly. The two things I knew best when I left Harvard were the American constitution and the Weimar constitution in Germany. Hitler did away with the significance of my knowledge in one of those areas, and the Supreme Court did away with the other, indicating that learning facts alone is no way to endure in a profession. I became more and more interested in the regulatory agencies and decided to move into the field of administration, even though there had been no courses in public administration in the curriculum at Harvard. From then until I left the Department of Government at seventy years of age, I did my work in government and the economy and in public administration.

Public Administration and Public Policy

REDFORD: My four years' experience during the war in administrative positions deepened my interest and knowledge in public administration, so I stayed with it. Like most other people of my generation—a bit too old for military service but still young enough to move around—I worked for the national government during the war. I started in a regional office of the Office of Price Administration in Dallas, three weeks after Pearl Harbor. Personnel of the national government were at the American Political Science Association convention in December after Pearl Harbor, searching for staff. I was asked to stop in Washington on December 31, and I went to work before the end of the day. In the fall of '44, I moved to Washington, into a job that was, in effect, the assistant head of the rationing department.

Before World War II, I was a purely academic student of administration. I came out of World War II understanding, by experience, the various aspects of administrative operations, and, from that time on, I was able to illustrate almost any aspect of administration by something I'd been introduced to by experience. So it added a kind of behavioral aspect to my teaching of administration.

LIVINGSTON: It didn't change your ideas necessarily?

REDFORD: I don't think so. My position in the contending set of ideas about teaching administration was probably not changed by it. At the end of the war, a group of about twenty scholars put together a new text in administration called *Elements of Public Administration*. It is almost the call of the roll of the forty- to forty-five-year-old scholars in the area—Harvey Mansfield, Wallace Sayre, Jim Fesler, and so on. The book was very rich on the behavior of administrative organizations and the people within them, and it indicated how the teaching of public administration was enriched by this wartime experience.

More significant was the Inter-University Case Program. The cases were not intended to enlarge our knowledge of administration. They were developed for teaching purposes, and they did enrich our teaching of the subject. I was on the Inter-University Case Board for almost twenty years and came to give one-third or one-half of my attention in classes to case studies, as did many of the other teachers of my time. This, too, provided an inside view of administrative behavior for the teachers of the field.

LIVINGSTON: One of your great contributions was the examination of the role of interest groups in the administrative process.

REDFORD: Yes, that was an interest of mine, reflecting the interconnections of administration with the political order. It was a continuation of the Wilson-Gulick tradition of administration as a separate area of study. Of course, people in the field of administration varied in the extent to which they accepted that doctrine, but there was a deep division in the field. I remember going to a meeting in the middle '50s at which Luther Gulick was chairman of a committee that had been constituted by the American Society for Public Administration to study education for the public service. We held only one meeting because, on one side of the table, people were arguing that public administration and business administration were alike and should be taught together. I remember Wallace Sayre saying, "Public administration and business administration are alike in all respects except the important ones." We never had a second meeting because we couldn't get agreement as to what kind of organization it was appropriate to locate this subject in.

Another channel of influence in the study of administration was the impetus toward the scientific study of the subject. Of course, the subject had started with the idea that it could be made a science. After World War II, there was a new beginning of efforts toward a science of administration, coming out of operations research, sociology, and psychology. Whereas some people were interested in the political aspects of administration, others were interested in trying to build a science of administrative management. But, following both of these currents, at the end of the '60s there began to develop an interest in policy, and it has tended, in recent years, to engulf public administration.

It was easy for public administration to fit into this new, broader study of public policy. The public administration people have always had an interest in public policy, if for no other reason than that they were interested in the making of public policy within administration and interested in the effective administration of policy. And, as the scope of policy making in administration expanded, it was easier for the scholar in administration to fit into a policy school.

Field Research in Washington

REDFORD: In the spring of 1958, I got a wire from Pen Herring, president of the Social Science Research Council, just out of the blue, offering me a $20,000 fellowship. That was sufficient money to finance me for fourteen months in Washington. They didn't ask for a topic, and I was so busy that I left Austin without having had a chance to give a single hour of thought to what I was going to work on during those fourteen months. I decided to do an in-depth study of one area of regulation and chose civil aeronautics, which was ultimately published as *The Regulatory Process: Illustrations from Commercial Aviation*. It was a good book, but it didn't get a great deal of attention.

LIVINGSTON: You spent more than a year on this study in Washington. How did you go about doing this?

REDFORD: I had a niche to study in at the Brookings Institution, but I did most of my work in the CAB [Civil Aeronautics Board] library and certain other libraries, did some interviewing and fell into some rather helpful aids for my research. And I went over to the Air Transport Association and got acquainted with them, and they opened up everything they had to my research associate, Orion White. I was writing about the passage of the Federal Aviation Act of 1958 and, by chance, in the library, I made the acquaintance of the man who was operating in the White House on that bill. He took me to see Tom Finney, who was operating in Senator Monroney's office—Monroney was the author of the act. So I did that study largely out of those two men's files. Tom Finney had a file two feet high that he brought out to my house one night, and it was the first of three or four evenings that we spent together talking about it. If you show some initiative in Washington, you can sometimes find people who will make research easy for you.

Speaking Truth to Power

LIVINGSTON: You've been a student of public administration all your professional life. To what extent has your career involved you in the actual administration of public affairs?

REDFORD: My only significant experience in public administration was during the four years of World War II. Other things I've done have been usually on a consultant basis or for brief periods of service, usually carrying the title of consultant. I faced the decision at the end of the war as to whether I would take some job in Washington or return to the university, and I decided that I preferred the academic life. But I've had enough connection with government to diversify my interests and give me more joy than I would have had if I were just doing one thing. I've been happy to have had the academic career, but with the diversified opportunities that come to people in the academic world today to do things on a consultant basis, or otherwise, for government.

REDFORD: In 1960, I was asked to do a study for the President's Advisory Committee on Government Organization, a committee set up by President Eisenhower to advise him on government organization. I was asked to do a study on the president and the regulatory commissions. I remember the conversation with the executive director of that committee. I said to him, "Well, you know that I am a Democrat." He said, "Yes, we knew that, and that doesn't matter. We've been told that party affiliation won't have anything to do with the kind of study you make." Well, I said it certainly wouldn't. "But," I said, "I would like for you to know that if I'm working up here on this project in the summer, that I will probably be working at night over in the Lyndon Johnson headquarters." And he said, "That's all right, too."

I got the report written by November. I narrowly missed getting some fame out of this study because of a Democratic victory. I was told by President Eisenhower's press secretary that my study would be released at 10:30 the next morning. It was not released, and I was told it was because the president's brother, Milton Eisenhower, who was a member of the committee, had objected that it would not be in good taste to release my study—President-Elect Kennedy having just appointed James Landis to make a similar study.

That study has had some influence. I incorporated into it a recommendation I had made in my 1952 book that the president should be allowed to give policy directives, not inconsistent with law, to regulatory agencies. That became one of the recommendations in this report. I think the committee was pleased, but the proposal was not well-regarded in legal circles, and a noted court of appeals judge, Henry J. Friendly, in the Holmes Lectures at Harvard, referred to my proposal and said, "Quite simply, I find it hard to think of anything worse." Despite this statement, my proposal is now in respectable consideration.

Several years ago the American Bar Association set up a committee on law and economic policy. They held a meeting at which they discussed a proposal whose details were different, though the idea was the same. One of the attendees told them that this was not a new proposal, for it had been made by Emmette Redford in 1952 and in 1960; it was reported to me that Judge Friendly said he had misunderstood the proposal and now was for it. Recently I received a copy of the report of this committee to the American Bar Association setting forth proposals for reform regulation. And proposal number three is, with different wording, the proposal that I made in this 1960 study. I get appropriate recognition in the Bar Association report. Sometimes something in one of these studies opens up the possibility for some fruit later on.

REDFORD: About 1966, I conducted a study on the administration of selective service for the President's Commission on Selective Service. Burke Marshall, the executive director, asked me to give them a study with this guideline: If we were starting over in the administration of selective service, how should we administer it? I prepared a report that outlined a very different method of administration from the one that had been employed.

I condemned what I regarded as the departure from the rule of law in the administration of selective service, that is, the amount of discretion that had been left to separate boards. It seemed to me it would be better to have national rules and a uniform system of administration. I visited a number of local boards. There were nine local boards in San Antonio. You could be on one side of a street and you could be deferred—if the board didn't need you to make its quota—for any kind of graduate work. You could cross that street and move into the jurisdiction of another board with a different kind of clientele and you could get an exemption only for the study of medicine or science. You could cross another street into a different part of the community and not get deferred for any kind of graduate study. It seemed to me that this program ought to be based strictly on the principle of the rule of law. Also, I thought that most initial decisions on classification could well be made by paid help with an appeal process, because that was what was really occurring anyway. Another thing was that record keeping was woefully out of date. It was an old pen and pencil operation, and, after some consultation with computer experts in Washington, I determined that the whole thing could be computerized with a great deal of saving and more uniformity.

The Commission on Selective Service accepted my report in toto, and it was contained in recommendations to the president. President Johnson didn't push it. He referred it to an internal task force dominated by the military. They didn't see anything wrong with the existing system of administration. It would have been difficult for President Johnson to have done anything about selective service. He was caught with the man who had been administering it all through its history, a highly revered man—somewhat the same situation he was in with regard to the FBI.

Service to the Profession

REDFORD: I was book review editor for the *American Political Science Review* for three and a half years—January '53 through sometime in '56. Being a book review editor is a re-education in general political science. We looked at books and determined which ones deserved full-length reviews, which ones deserved short reviews, and which ones deserved notation. In order to see that you didn't prevent a full review being given to a first class book, you had to give some attention to all of those books. The two times when I've known most about political science were when I got my doctor's degree and when I completed my three and a half years as book review editor.

I enjoyed being president of the American Political Science Association. I learned how to manage administrative chores early in life, so it was no burden, and the Washington office did all the things a Washington office could be expected to do to help a president.

LIVINGSTON: Were there any particular crises or controversies during your presidency?

REDFORD: I think not. Fortunately, I was president before the onslaught of divisions within the Association.

LIVINGSTON: B.C.—before controversy.

Illustrious Political Scientists

REDFORD: Roscoe Martin and I were closely associated for over fifty years. We were fellow students in a history class the first semester I was in the University of Texas in 1922. We became friends then and remained friends always afterwards. Roscoe and I were simpatico as to our professional interests and as to the slant by which we looked at things. Roscoe went to Alabama about 1937, and he became the focus for the blooming of political science in the South. He not only established his own research bureau, he used his influence to get research bureaus established in other universities in the area. He fostered some first-rate studies, including V.O. Key's *Southern Politics*. He was among those who started the Southern Political Science Association. Along with Manning Dauer, Taylor Cole, and a few others, Roscoe Martin was a great stimulus to the development of political science in the South. Beyond all that, he was loved by several generations of students.

Harvey Mansfield has been as close a friend as I've had in the profession. I have gone back to Harvey for advice and help repeatedly. He has consented to read my books when I asked him. He has always improved my copy, for he is as good an editor as we've ever had in this profession, and he's been generous with his time. I marvel at the man, at the breadth of his knowledge, at the memory he has of detail from the *New York Times*—five, ten, thirty, forty years ago. As a teacher, Harvey is continually drawing on this storehouse of detailed information from newspapers and from the anecdotes he's accumulated over the years. His scholarly work is tops. The books that he has written are always the best on the subject. He has been a great contributor to political science. Among other things, as editor of the *American Political Science Review* for ten years, he helped make the transition from the old political science to the more diversified political science that we have today.

I was fortunate to develop a strong friendship with Paul Appleby. When you talked with Paul Appleby, you wished you had a note pad there. I sat on several occasions for two hours or longer and never opened my mouth. Paul just talked. And that's not true of me only; it's true of other people. This was a man you wanted to listen to.

LIVINGSTON: Was it technical talk?

REDFORD: No, it was perceptive generalizations drawn from experience. Here was a man who started in the newspaper world, became a public official and then later became a dean in a university. All his life he was trying to think about what was the meaning of all this, how it all tied together. His influence was tremendous, both by the continual emphasis he gave to the interrelations of politics and administration and by the personal friendships that he had with people. I have known no one who was more thoroughly a democrat than Paul Appleby. Paul Appleby believed that the infusion of the influence of the people into all the processes of government was good.

R. Taylor Cole

Robert Taylor Cole was born on September 3, 1905, in Bald Prairie, Texas. He received his B.A. in 1925 and M.A. in 1927 from the University of Texas, where he studied at the same time as several others who also were to become eminent political scientists. After serving as a member of the faculty at Louisiana State University for three years, he attended graduate school at Harvard University while also serving as an instructor. With stints on the faculty at LSU and Harvard from 1926 to 1935, he was awarded his Ph.D. from Harvard in 1936. In 1935, he became an assistant professor at Duke University, where he rose through the ranks to become a James B. Duke Professor in 1953. He served as provost from 1960 to 1969, during a period of rapid change in southern higher education, and was instrumental in the racial integration of the student body at Duke.

He was a student of comparative politics, with particular interest in the bureaucracies of Canada, Europe, and Africa. His books Responsible Bureaucracy and European Political Systems were standards in the field for many years. His major interest was in the Commonwealth nations, and in 1955, he served as a leader and the chair of the committee that established the Commonwealth Center at Duke University. He was active in special wartime service in Washington and Sweden during World War II and was a consultant to General Lucius Clay in Germany following the war. He held both Guggenheim and Fulbright fellowships during his research career and also served on the council of Ahmadu Bello University in Nigeria.

He served the discipline of political science as editor of the Journal of Politics (1945–49) and of the American Political Science Review (1950–53). He was elected president of the Southern Political Science

Association for the 1951–52 term and of the American Political Science Association for 1958–59.

Taylor Cole was interviewed in Durham, North Carolina, on May 20, 1980, by James David Barber, a colleague at Duke University, who has written extensively on American politics and is best known for his work on the character of American presidents.

Early Education and Developing Interest in Political Science

BARBER: Taylor, how was it that a ranch boy in Texas got interested in intellectual life and scholarship? That seems a little contradictory.

COLE: Dave, I'm not sure that there is any special explanation. There were several factors that influenced me. I think the most important one was my mother, who had a deep intellectual interest in our hometown, where she was a bit of a leader in academic and educational affairs. But, perhaps as important, there was a rather highly competitive atmosphere in this small town of Franklin, Texas. She expected one to do well in school. She also made available different types of literature, some of which interested me and a great deal of which didn't at that time. She tried to get me to study music, which didn't take. The point is that she made available in our home all kinds of literature and books, such as the Harvard Classics. Originally, it was thought that I would go into law. That was my own decision. My parents never tried to influence us in these decisions except to facilitate our own plans.

It was an expectation that came really from outside family influences. It came from individuals in town; it came from the local state legislator in the community. My interest in politics really stems from the same factors, I think, that led me originally to plan to study law. My father was the business partner for a number of years of Dr. N.D. Buie, who was the political mentor and financier of Senator Tom Connally.

BARBER: Did you think you might go into politics at that time?

COLE: No, not necessarily. Politics interested me, but then politics interested the whole family. We spent a lot of time in political talk in our family. My father always took the position that each person should say his piece and stand on his own, but he was the one who frequently initiated the political discussions, sometimes from a rather provocative, and even semiridiculous, position.

BARBER: Then I suppose it was in college where your interest began to jell more around political science.

COLE: I got into political science by accident. But, in my sopho-more year at Texas, although I had a full schedule, I was permitted to take an extra course because of my academic record. And, just as I was in the registration line, I decided to add "government," and this is how I took my first course in government.

BARBER: Almost impulsively; standing in line.

COLE: Standing in line, impulsively. I actually was doing more work in history at that time. But, with my background and with the vague anticipation of studying law, I was attracted by the course in government because it had the legal emphasis that one found in those days in the early editions of textbooks by Ogg and Ray and W.B. Mu-nro.

BARBER: Did you do an undergraduate major in political sci-ence?

COLE: I graduated with a double major in 1925. The term "gov-ernment" was used, then and today, at the University of Texas and at Harvard, interestingly enough.

The Influence of Harvard

BARBER: Was there any one teacher of politics or related sub-jects in college who stands out in your memory as having affected your thinking?

COLE: Yes, I think there was. At the University of Texas, I en-tered at the age of fifteen. One of the teachers I had my junior year was B.F. Wright, Jr. Ben Wright was working on his doctorate at Har-vard at that time. I took a course in political theory under him just after he, Ben Wright, had had a history of theory course under Charles H. McIlwain. I got McIlwain via Ben Wright and found it a very stimulating experience. On the history side, I graded papers in my senior year for one semester for Charles W. Hackett, who was quite a distinguished professor of history of the Southwest. The expe-rience in grading papers for him was a factor in making me think about teaching as a career rather than law. A second thing that I re-member, which influenced me very much, was the experience of one of my roommates at Harvard, Emmette Redford. Emmette later re-ceived special recognition in the course from McIlwain. Of course, theory was very basic at Harvard in those days. Harvard and Chicago, you know, were the two schools that were considered to have dif-ferent approaches—Merriam versus, let's say, the Harvard theory emphasis.

BARBER: Could you just characterize that difference?

COLE: Well, Chicago was viewed then, in our untutored way, as the Merriam school, as the institution which was training people to engage in practical politics and to learn about pressure groups and political parties, or about public administration with Leonard D. White. Lasswell then had not really appeared on the Harvard scene. I remember Arthur Holcombe showing us a copy of Lasswell's *Psychopathology and Politics* when I was a graduate student at Harvard. He was shocked by it as coming from a so-called teacher of government.

In contrast, the individuals who came out of Harvard had the conviction that somehow or other you had to have your roots in political theory, especially the history of political theory, in order to maintain a perspective on the more temporary and current events of the day. Merriam's own work in the history of political theory was not very highly regarded at Harvard.

BARBER: Could we get into your Harvard experience in the early 1930s a bit, especially with some of the individuals in government to whom you were especially attuned?

COLE: Well, the one who had the greatest impact was Carl Friedrich, but I did continue to do work with Ben Wright. I was Ben's assistant during my first year at Harvard in a course in American constitutional theory. Ben Wright was the chairman of the American Political Science Association committee, in later years, that asked me to serve as editor of the *American Political Science Review.* Carl Friedrich interested me because I had gone to Harvard originally to study international law under George Grafton Wilson. Almost en route, I had an opportunity to switch my fields. That is to say, I was given a Harvard fellowship that I could substitute for the Carnegie International Law fellowship that I had originally accepted. I took the more generous Harvard fellowship, the one with greater flexibility, and wound up with a continuing interest in the international field. Friedrich had recently arrived at Harvard from Europe. I think there was just something a little intriguing to Texas boys in seeing all this foreign influence. But as time went on, the European scene became more and more genuine and interesting and significant. In a way, Friedrich always represented a kind of bridge between the American scene, in which he attempted all of his life to incorporate himself, and the European scene, which reflected his background and his primary research interests. He was responsible for the fellowship that I got which took me to Germany in 1933. Both the intellectual stimulus which he provided and also the material assistance that he furnished had a good deal to do with the particular orientation that I developed.

Arthur N. Holcombe offered me my first job at Harvard as an instructor under rather unusual circumstances. He asked me at a tea that he gave at his house for graduate students in government what I would do if I had a Negro in class, and I said I'd try to teach him.

The next day I was offered an instructorship. He took the warmest interest in his students.

Now the same thing was true of William Yandel Elliott, under whom I also did some work. Bill Elliott and Friedrich were poles apart at Harvard and led divergent groups. In the department during those years, at times you belonged to one camp or the other. I always belonged to both camps. For example, Bill Elliott was the one who got me my job at Duke. Bill even included in his large entourage Henry Kissinger; indeed, he was the primary mentor of Henry Kissinger at Harvard. I was much more heavily intellectually indebted to Friedrich than to Elliott, but both were warm friends and mentors. I also benefited greatly from my early associations with Rupert Emerson and Pen Herring, among the younger faculty members.

The Texas Community in Political Science

BARBER: You say that there's a certain Texas community in the American Political Science Association. What does that mean?

COLE: Well, I suppose you've heard this expression: "The Texas Mafia." There were three presidents of the American Political Science Association within a reasonably short period of time who came from Texas. All of them were friends, V.O. Key, Emmette Redford, and I. The fact of the matter was that these people went in different directions when they left Texas, were in different fields, and were teaching at different institutions. But, somehow or other, that early Texas relationship endured.

But the point, I think, Dave, is that there was an extraordinarily stimulating atmosphere at the University of Texas during the relatively short period when we were students there—let's say, roughly, between 1922 and 1930. There were a number of young instructors and adjunct professors, most of whom had not finished their doctorates at Columbia, Harvard, Chicago, and other institutions. They were very, very stimulating, were adverse to being rigidified, so to speak, by local mores. They included Irving Stewart, Charlie Kneier, Frank Stewart, Malbone Graham, and others. There was a freedom and encouragement to move in directions which were novel and stimulating. And I think this atmosphere would be a fair way of explaining the background of, say, V.O. Key.

BARBER: You knew V.O. Key? You were a friend of his?

COLE: Yes, I knew V.O. Key quite well and worked with him over a period of time and saw him fairly often. Emmette Redford and I were contemporaries and roomed together at Harvard. V.O. came along, say, a couple of years later. I don't know of anyone in my professional career that ever was more genuinely honest in his letters of recommendation than V.O. Key. He had this reputation in the profession.

BARBER: How would you characterize his main impact on political science thinking at that time?

COLE: I would say that his approach was an important contribution during his earlier period. I think V.O. modified it somewhat toward the end. He did represent, I think, a certain traditional type of empirical behavioral approach, but less empirical than other contemporaries. The kind of research program that he adopted—calling for cooperative work with Alexander Heard and other extremely able individuals, with the support of Roscoe Martin—was followed by a lot of careful field research. His final books have been criticized, as you possibly know, on grounds he did allow for too much subjective evaluation. But I'd say his *Southern Politics* was his main contribution, given the time when it was written. His influence through his first textbook on political parties was also, of course, very substantial.

Let me add that there were other fellow students at Texas and at Harvard who probably had a greater influence on me than most of the professors. These included Emmette Redford, Roscoe Martin, and J. Alton Burdine at Texas, and Merle Fainsod, Fred Watkins, Hugh Elsbree, Norton Long, Bill Maddox, and others at Harvard. Long discussions with these friends opened many new vistas for me.

BARBER: Now there are some other names of professors that have come up in our conversations.

COLE: T.V. Smith I knew at Texas, I was always intrigued with his *Ethics of Compromise*. I still feel that, within politics, there is much to be said for the argument of the *Ethics of Compromise*. I would say that T.V. Smith would have approved the way that we went about integrating Duke University.

Bureaucracy and Reform

BARBER: Your interest in bureaucracy?

COLE: I suppose that my interest in bureaucracy started at Louisiana State University, where I did my first college teaching in 1926–27. One of my unusual students there did a master's thesis under my direction, the first one that I ever directed in my life (if "directed" is the right word, as I didn't know what I was doing). But the student was one of the members of the House of Representatives that drew up the first impeachment charges against Huey Long. My student told me a great deal about the Louisiana civil service and the way that appointments were handled. Everyone was aware of the abuse of patronage, but he gave me details that were revealing and that suggested possibilities of reform. I later helped write the first draft of the civil service law for Louisiana. It was adopted, to our amazement, with open arms by the Long crowd. We couldn't understand it until we realized we were helping provide a useful instrument for perpetuating the system. This legislation created some machinery that actually facilitated the patronage process.

This was my first interest and involvement in bureaucracy, and the applied side thus came before the theoretical one. I got to Harvard in 1929–30, and Carl Friedrich interested me for the first time in Max Weber—this was before Weber was very well known in this country. Weber's concept of bureaucracy was brought to my attention by Friedrich, and I got interested in the theoretical aspects of bureaucracy. Later, I did a good deal of field work on bureaucracy. I did a book on the Canadian bureaucracy. It actually was a study, to put it in more simple terms, of the Canadian civil service and public employees.

Then later, in 1948, I worked as a consultant to General Lucius Clay in the military government of occupied Germany. We were asked to see what we could do about the reform of the German bureaucracy, the theory being that the bureaucratic system in Germany had been one of the factors in the build-up of the Nazi regime. On the one hand, I started out with this skepticism that I developed in Louisiana, and, on the other, I felt that anything we imposed in Germany would be of short range. I wound up this experience with the conviction that the lasting way to reform the German bureaucracy was through the educational system. I later used some of this material in a talk on "The Democratization of the German Civil Service" that I gave before the Southern Political Science Association when I was president. In essence, what I said was the impositions from abroad would not only be of short duration but would be actually counterproductive in the long run.

Studies of Facism and European Politics

BARBER: Well, maybe we could move on to your initial interest in Fascism at Harvard and Friedrich's and your initial exploration of that.

COLE: Well, I have a feeling that my first interest in Fascism was of a general sort. Again, Friedrich was a factor in this. The history of Italian Fascism in the 1930s was in the air.

BARBER: I guess you were an assistant professor by then, weren't you?

COLE: Yes. John Hallowell did a study of German professors in his analysis of the decline of liberalism in Germany after he had spent 1935–36 there. I was able to help get him to Germany at that time.

BARBER: Oh, did you?

COLE: He was a senior at Harvard when I was a tutor in Kirkland House in 1934–35. His doctoral dissertation later at Princeton was thus in part a product of some of his own experiences in the Third Reich.

I felt that, when I traveled from Germany, as I did a time or two into Italy, despite the fact that there had been a longer period of gestation for Fascism, I was moving into another world. There were many excesses and abuses under Italian Fascism, but there was a much freer atmosphere there than in Nazi Germany.

BARBER: Among professors who taught about government in Germany, was there some resistance to the political system?

COLE: Yes, there was. I suppose if I were to pick two people who stand out, one would be a professor of law and another would be a professor of cultural sociology. The latter was the brother of Max Weber, Alfred Weber. There was still a Max Weber group in Heidelberg in 1933, and Max Weber's wife was still alive. But Alfred Weber, who maintained his distance from his famous brother, was himself quite a distinguished sociologist at the Institute of Social and Political Science. He had refused to run up the Nazi flag on January 30th, 1933, and was immediately dismissed as director. I saw a good deal of him then and also after the war. He was very much opposed to the Nazi regime and played a very important part in the postwar period, especially in the renovation and revival of the German universities.

BARBER: Out of your studies of Fascism, what do you most hope future readers will derive?

COLE: Well, I hope that they will look at the abuses. I would say that would be lesson number one. Of course, you could move on from there to so many other phases of National Socialism: the perversions of extreme nationalism leading to war. And as far as practical application to the local scene, the dangers to the universities, the prevention of freedom of speech and freedom of expression by professors and students.

BARBER: Now it sounds to me as if the studies of Fascism that you did represent a warning: watch out, this could happen again. The studies of federalism seem to be more hopeful.

COLE: I think that's right, Dave. In a general sense, I am a confirmed federalist. One of the books that I read early, I remember, was R.M. MacIver's book *Community*, and there was, in that early study, a recognition of the theory of mutuality of federal relationships in society as a whole. I found Carl Friedrich's study of federalism, as is his *Constitutional Government and Democracy*—the original edition—to be stimulating. I was later involved in research in countries where federalism has been applied. To start with, the United States. Later my research took me to countries with federal institutions—Canada, Germany, Nigeria, the British Commonwealth itself—which in my view could be viewed in federal terms.

Research and Experiences in Africa: Further Studies of the Bureaucracy

BARBER: We're sitting here in the Africa room in your house, and, of course, Africa became a whole new realm of interest for you. I wonder if you could talk a bit about how that happened, what you can say of that.

COLE: Well, my interest in Africa developed out of my interest in the Commonwealth Studies Committee at Duke, which I headed for a period of time. Nan and I went to Nigeria in 1959—the year before Independence—for several reasons. I was interested in the transfer of power; I was interested in the changes in the Commonwealth; I was interested in the Nigerian federal system. So we headed out with a grant from the Commonwealth program here for a period of study. I was never an Africanist in a real sense. To be one, you have to know some African languages; you need a respectable anthropological background; you must live long enough in some of these areas to understand their mores.

BARBER: When you went to Africa, was there anything that particularly impressed you at first?

COLE: Well, I suppose the low levels of standards of living were bound to be noticeable. I also found that some of their standards of conduct, in many respects, I thought were superior to our own.

BARBER: Such as what?

COLE: Well, the relations in their extended families, Dave. One of the things that interested me was their great feeling of obligation, not just to the immediate family but to the extended family. There was a high degree of commitment. There was a feeling of responsibility. The extended families included not only those with the same father and/or the same mother but also those from the same village from which they came.

BARBER: You were advising governments in that trip, I think.

COLE: I presented the opening paper on federalism in Nigeria at the Constitutional Conference in 1959 and later served for a dozen years as a member of the Council of Ahmadu Bello University in Zaria. I was asked in 1964 to go out one summer to advise President Nyerere in Tanzania shortly after he had almost been toppled from power in a coup. I did prepare a document containing a number of recommendations, a few of which were followed.

My most important recommendation was ignored. I opposed the formal legalization of a one-party state, which was a very controversial issue, and had a long discussion with President Nyerere on this point. He maintained that my position was that of a Western political scientist coming from a pluralistic system and accustomed to the give and take of political parties, whereas the "African approach" was a very different one of seeking consensus. In the end, the one-party system was legalized in the constitution, and I will have to say it worked better than I would have anticipated.

The Politics of a Modern University: Racial Integration at Duke

BARBER: In your comments about university life, you seem to see the university as a kind of community, and maybe even a political community, in which some aspects of federalism, for instance, apply there as in formal governments. I wonder if you'd talk some about the modern university—after all, that's where political scientists work.

COLE: Dave, I had some personal experience as provost at Duke University for about nine years in the 1960s, and I have done some research over a period of years on universities in the Commonwealth and Western Europe. From these two perspectives, I have a feeling that the university of today is marked by an inflation of functions, not only in the United States but abroad.

One of the things that I think we should do is to take a more restrictive view of the role of the university. I think, consequently, that restriction on the scope of the functions of the university ought to be one of the important moves. The university should cease to be a place to train hotel managers or cheerleaders or bartenders. I do think that this does not mean that we should completely ignore pressing social problems of the day, but that there is a rule of reason which we can follow. The university does not exist to cure all of the ills of society. If I could put it in a negative way, maybe I could say that what can be done well by General Motors ought to be done by General Motors, not by the university. Otherwise, you will destroy the basic intellectual purpose of the university.

BARBER: I wonder if you could go over a bit some of your own experience in integration at Duke, because that's the crisis you were right in the middle of as provost.

COLE: Well, the history of integration at Duke—and we were the first major private university in the South to be wholly integrated—dates back to the 1940s, when some of the divinity students took umbrage at our segregation policies at Duke. There was a period of mild protest in the 1950s. Hollis Edens, who became president in 1948, was himself personally in favor of admitting blacks to the university, but he was faced by strong opposition on the Board of Trustees. When he first broached the proposal for the admission of some blacks on a selective basis in 1954, the board did not respond at all. He talked to me a number of times in the 1950s about this problem. There was no question but that a large majority of board members would have opposed any type of resolution calling for the admission of blacks prior to 1960, the year when I was appointed provost.

Three of us in the administration drew up three documents in which we presented strong arguments—the strongest that we could muster—for integration. Barnes Woodhall drew up a document with his eye on health affairs, Marcus Hobbs drew up a document with his eye primarily on arts and sciences, the faculty, and internal developments, and I dealt with the other problems. I consolidated these documents. We initially proposed integration in the graduate school and professional schools only, as a starting point.

We concluded that we would present the proposal to the board in terms that we thought would be fully understandable to the board— the cost of segregation in terms of ability to keep faculty, the effect on the students, the attitude of our own faculty, the inability to bring professional associations to meet at Duke, and any number of other legal, economic, and educational reasons, all of which pointed toward the absolute necessity for integration.

We took this single document, with its three parts, with the full support of President Hart, and buttonholed almost every trustee that we could contact. We would leave this document, have lunch or cocktails and discuss it with them. We welcomed the opportunity to discuss orally the moral aspects of segregation, but we did not stress these in our written presentations. And the result was that, in 1961, we were able to get a motion passed by the Board of Trustees to permit the admission of blacks to graduate and professional schools. Then, with that as a background, we pursued the undergraduate side, and, in 1962, the Board adopted a resolution permitting the admission of blacks, undergraduates and graduates, without any consideration to race, creed or religion.

BARBER: Did the Duke example become somewhat contagious in the South?

COLE: I do not know to what extent our action had outside influence, but certainly Duke was the first major private institution in the South to be wholly integrated. Vanderbilt and Johns Hopkins, if you include Hopkins in the South, had earlier arrangements for the admission of blacks, but on a very limited basis.

Activities in the Southern and the American Political Science Associations

BARBER: Taylor, you've been an active leader in the professional affairs of political science all the way from the early days of the Southern Political Science Association to the creation of the International Political Science Association, and you've been Editor of our professional journals, the *American Political Science Review* and the *Journal of Politics.* So I wonder if we could go over some of that ground.

COLE: Dave, I attended my first meeting of the Southern Political Science Association in 1935, which was the year that I came to Duke University. It consisted primarily of a small group of friends who met socially. The professional emphasis was minimal, and the social aspects were rather dominant. There were few prepared papers. The development that took place between then and, let's say, 1945 or 1946, was amazing. And I think a very important part of that development was due to the establishment of the *Journal of Politics.* The *Journal* was established in 1939, especially under the instigation of a committee headed by Roscoe Martin, then at the University of Alabama, with the essential cooperation of Manning Dauer at the University of Florida. The *Journal,* although it was established by a regional body, never had a regional focus. I was very pleased to edit the *Journal* for nearly four years between 1946 and 1949, following Bob Harris, who was the first editor.

BARBER: In those early meetings of the Southern Political Science Association, didn't you meet at Gatlinburg or someplace like that?

COLE: Our first meetings were in Atlanta, and we later moved to Gatlinburg. The primary reason for the first move was the fact that the hotels in Atlanta would not take care of black members, whereas in Gatlinburg they would.

BARBER: Now, what did you try to do as president and as editor of the *Journal of Politics?* Did you hold both offices at the same time?

COLE: No, I was president of the Association, I believe in 1951 to 1952, which was three years after I resigned as editor of the *Journal of Politics.* I was interested in the *Journal* because it reflected the quality of the research work that was being done. It also represented an opportunity for me to apply my views on federalism, because I did decentralize responsibilities to a very considerable extent, as I did later with the *American Political Science Review.* We put a lot of emphasis upon certain things such as symposia, which I solicited. Solicitation is a very controversial matter, but it does offer a chance to secure contributions from individuals who would not normally submit them to go through the usual procedures of selection. I suppose that 40 percent of the articles which I published were solicited.

BARBER: Do you think that's a good practice to do now?

COLE: Yes, I do, although I can realize how difficult it is. Solicitation places an extra burden on the editor. It allows him to exercise a good deal of arbitrary discretion, which is open to criticism. There were two reasons for my early interest in solicitation. One was that I was interested in foreign contributions. Secondly, several of the symposia—and this means collections of solicited articles—were utilized in the *Journal of Politics* for purposes of republication and sale. We did make several thousands of dollars out of these sales, sums which were necessary at that time to help keep financially afloat. I feel that this experience with the *Journal of Politics* represented basically my experience with the *Review* later.

BARBER: With the same federal principles?

COLE: I mean, I had more division of labor, or decentralization. We added some sections to the *American Political Science Review* that we didn't have in the *Journal*. One of them was by Herb Simon on methodology and research, and this came at a time in the early 1950s when the behavioral revolution was aborning. I feel that, for two reasons, this delegation of responsibility was sound. One of them was that you did get active involvement by a large number of individuals with different ideas, as widely divergent in their views as, say, Francis Wilson and Herb Simon. And secondly, there was the financial aspect. When I took over the editorship of the *Review* in 1950 for a three-year term, the editor was not paid anything. I had one full-time secretary who served also as an editorial assistant and proofreader. I am consequently baffled at times by the size of the staff and the financial requirements of editing some of the present social science journals, including the *Review*. The number of articles and other demands have increased, but not proportionately to the costs.

In 1950, the Nominating Committee came in with a panel of nominations, members of the Association put up an opposing list, which was accepted by the business meeting, and the aftermath was the appointment of a committee which asked me to serve as the editor, or managing editor, of the *Review*. That's how I became the editor.

BARBER: What was the issue?

COLE: The reformers felt that the Association was not being managed in an imaginative and democratic fashion. The headquarters of the Association was not located in Washington at that time. In addition, F.A. Ogg had been editor of the *Review* for years and years.

Ogg was viewed by some as concerned primarily with political science in a legalistic and descriptive way. Ogg resigned, very agreeably and very gracefully, and was perhaps happy to have the excuse to do so. I do know that he proved to be an enormously helpful person to me. I am told that when Ogg was editor of the *Review* he didn't even have a paid secretary. There was the initiation of some training and internship programs. These programs were largely the result of the effective efforts of Evron Kirkpatrick, the executive director.

BARBER: What was the relation between the Government Affairs Institute and APSA?

COLE: The Government Affairs Institute was established in a modest way in 1947 by the American Council on Education, to encourage and to assist in the reception and training of foreign students to be brought to the United States during the early postwar period. Subsequently, the GAI was incorporated as a separate, nonprofit educational organization in Delaware. One of the key persons in this development was Ed Litchfield, who had previously been one of General Lucius Clay's collaborators in occupied Germany. He was also the key person in the Governmental Affairs Institute, originally conceived of as a sort of research arm of the Association and as one of the avenues for relationships with governmental agencies such as the State Department, the Defense Department, and various other organizations.

There were a number of presidents of the Association who served on the board at one time or another, including Jim Pollock, Luther Gulick, and Carl Friedrich. Ralph Bunche was one of the early board members. Evron Kirkpatrick, in his capacity as executive director of the APSA, was a member for a number of years until he resigned in 1964. During the early period, Ed Litchfield secured, through the assistance of Will Alexander, who lived very close to Durham and who was a key advisor to the Edgar Stern Foundation in New Orleans, a fairly large grant for the construction, or purchase, of a political science building in Washington. The title to the building was legally vested in the name of the Governmental Affairs Institute. The final agreement was reached in 1966 in which the GAI paid the Association $100,500 for its equity in the building and common assets. This fund was used as the primary source for the purchase of the present APSA headquarters on New Hampshire Avenue.

BARBER: Now, when you were president of the American Political Science Association, what were the gripping matters that you had to deal with there?

COLE: When I was president in 1958–59, we had a relatively quiet year. Our main concern during the year was the usual financial one.

The Origins of the International
Political Science Association

BARBER: Now, you also had to do with IPSA.

COLE: Yes.

BARBER: How did that work?

COLE: IPSA was founded formally in 1949 and was the product of the action of the Social Science Department of UNESCO. The first president was Quincy Wright of the University of Chicago. The first Congress of IPSA was held in 1950 and met in Zurich, with fifty or sixty people participating. The first meeting of the council of the Association—that is the governing body—was held in 1952, and, again, I think the membership was more or less handpicked or selected or approved by the Social Science Department of UNESCO. In other words, I was one of the participants there, along with Jim Pollock, who had been the past president of the American Political Science Association, and Edward Litchfield, who was the executive director of the Association at that time. At this council meeting there was an election by the council for the first time of a new president; William A. Robson of Britain was chosen for a three-year term.

The early history of the International Political Science Association, to repeat, was rooted in its relationships to UNESCO. The leading member from UNESCO was Alva Myrdal, director of its Social Science Department. One outgrowth of the Council meeting was the decision by Robson to hold a miniconference in 1953. The first miniconference after the Congress was the one that was held in 1953 in Paris on comparative administration, with Raymond Aron as the leader of a seminar discussion of Max Weber on democracy.

The prospects for IPSA didn't seem to be all that bright. The quality of the discussions and contributions weren't as exciting as they might have been, so that I'd have to say that the future promising development of IPSA belies its very modest beginnings.

Marian D. Irish

Marian Irish was born on May 29, 1909, in Scranton, Pennsylvania. She received her B.A. from Barnard in 1930, her M.A. from Bryn Mawr in 1932, and her Ph.D. from Harvard in 1939. After a year as research librarian in government and law at Lafayette College, she joined the faculty of Florida State College for Women (which later became Florida State University). She remained at this institution for thirty-three years until moving to the American University as the Charles O. Lerche Professor of International Relations in the School of International Service in 1966. There she remained until her retirement in 1974.

She served as head of the Division of Political Science at FSCW for fourteen years and as head of the Department of Government at FSU for another fourteen. During this period, she was an active consultant to leaders in Florida state government and played a key role in the development of higher education in the state. She also served on the Florida State Legislative Commission on the Economy and on the Florida State Merit Council.

Her research encompassed both domestic politics and international relations. She was interested in and wrote about the context and conduct of American foreign policy. She also had broad interests in constitutional law and public policy and spent considerable time studying the jurisprudence of Justice William O. Douglas. She wrote several textbooks, including books for both secondary education and university use. The Politics of American Democracy *(with James Prothro) has been used as an introductory text by hundreds of thousand of students in American government courses.*

She was an early activist in the Southern Political Science Association. As editor of the Journal of Politics, *she was the first woman to edit a major journal in the discipline of political science. She served as president of the Southern Political Science Association in 1957 and as vice president of the American Political Science Association in 1960.*

Marian Irish was interviewed in Scientist Cliffs, Maryland, in July of 1988 by Walter Beach, a senior staff member at the Brookings Institution, who served as assistant executive director of the American Political Science Association from 1967 to 1980 and who has played a significant role in the development of the Political Science Oral History Program.

Precollege and College Education

IRISH: I was born in Scranton, Pennsylvania, in 1909. And I was educated in the Scranton public schools. My first academic experience—that I recall—was Miss O'Malley's class in fourth grade. She required us to memorize President Wilson's Fourteen Points.

BEACH: That's a good beginning for a political scientist.

IRISH: My mind was beginning to set on international relations—peace, self determination, a League of Nations to make the world safe for democracy. That was a long time ago. At Central High School, I took the classical course, grounded in Latin, French, American history, ancient history, modern world history—enough to pass the college board exams which were required in those days. I was partly financed the first year by a college club scholarship on the basis of a competition that included comprehensive exams and an essay. The award was a year's tuition to the college of my choice, and I chose Barnard College because it was in New York. The address was 3001 Broadway, and I wanted to see all the plays on Broadway and to visit the art museums and galleries. That's what I told the registrar, and I asked how to arrange my schedule so I would have two afternoons free.

I was at Barnard College from 1926 to 1930. I took the honors program in government with Raymond Moley, who was then a consultant to Governor Roosevelt. Moley's major interest at that time was the administration of justice at the local level. His introductory course in American politics, however, was what started me into political science. He gave a course which was not at all the conventional American government course. It featured interesting and influential and offbeat politicians from Thomas Jefferson, Hamilton, to modern pressure groups. I remember doing a paper for him on the politics of agriculture!

The honors course at Barnard, at that time, was modeled after the Swarthmore plan, and that released me from all formal course requirements. But I was free to audit any courses at Barnard and Columbia. In the final semester, I had to take a comprehensive exam on government, prepared by the Columbia graduate faculty. This turned out to be multiple choice, true and false questions. Very disappointing to one expecting to write an essay with explanations and concepts and principles. At Columbia, I audited most of the big shots on the political science roster.

BEACH: Who were they at this time?

IRISH: Raymond Moley, who was to later head President Roosevelt's "brain trust." Howard McBain in constitutional law (as it was taught in 1926, it was not useful in 1937 when it was my turn to teach constitutional law). Philip Jessup in international law. McMann in public administration. From today's perspective, the best of my courses at Columbia was Robert MacIver's on the modern state, which dealt with ongoing concepts of government.

The most influential person in the Barnard experience for me was Dean Virginia Gildersleeve. I remember her often-expressed faith in the ability of what she called her "seven thousand Barnard daughters." She encouraged us to break through the barriers of sexism and to reach whatever goals we set for ourselves. It was not until I reached Yale graduate school in 1933 that I realized that political science was traditionly reserved for men only.

BEACH: Didn't she go to San Francisco as part of the delegation?

IRISH: I remember especially both what she contributed and what her friend Eleanor Roosevelt contributed to the idea and the ideals of the United Nations. Dean Gildersleeve, specifically, for her work on the preamble to the charter. That grand language comes from her.

Graduate Education and Early Career

IRISH: Graduating from Barnard in 1930, I put in one dismal year at the Kirby Library of Government and Law at Lafayette College. My title was high-sounding: "research librarian in government and law." The pay was $1,500 for the calendar year, more than most of my Barnard classmates made that first year. But the work was dull—cataloging and pasting labels in new books, and dusting the shelves.

I remembered a casual conversation in Professor Moley's office in my senior year. There I met Professor Francis Coker, who had shared an office with Professor Moley at Oberlin when they were both teaching there. Professor Coker had queried whether I would be inter-

ested in graduate study. And if so, would I consider Yale, where he
had just become chairman of the political science department. Well,
it turned out I took that conversation more seriously than Professor
Coker, because, in Easton a year later, when I thought I was ready for
graduate work at Yale, he wasn't ready for me. He wrote me a polite
letter suggesting that I try elsewhere, maybe Radcliffe or Bryn Mawr,
which was for ladies.

I was at Bryn Mawr only one year—'31–'32. I took constitutional
law and international law with Professor Charles Fenwick. His seminar consisted of three students, including me. We did a very thorough case study approach, no nonsense. Bryn Mawr offered me a
fellowship to continue doctoral work in political science, but Professor
Fenwick urged me to widen my academic experience out of the women's colleges. So I wrote another chatty letter to Professor Coker
and asked, "Do you remember me?" He did and came across. I was
given a Cowles fellowship in government at Yale for 1932–33. It was
for $1,200 and that, in 1932, covered not only the tuition, which was
then $300 but also covered my housing at the Graduate Women's
Club and living expenses.

At Yale I took a number of seminars including Professor Coker's
Modern Political Philosophy, which was always full of dissension, because he took delight in telling us that he himself was anarchist. As
you remember, he was a very gentle soul, Very kindly, very courteous
and far from our visions of a first-rate anarchist. I took a course with
Walton Hamilton in the Yale Law School, and there I became an expert on public utility rates.

BEACH: That was a big issue at that time.

IRISH: Oh, it was *the* issue. And I had a very special tutorial,
just a one-on-one, with Harold Laski, who was visiting from the Lon-
don School of Economics. I spent a great deal of time reading what he
assigned me—the yearbooks of the British Miner's Federation, from
the late nineteenth century. And I also spent quite a lot of time learning why Harold Laski was the brains of the British Labor Party. He
told me all about it. And that also was largely forgettable when it
came to my first teaching. You know, I wonder how much of what we
teach today is equally forgettable, don't you?

BEACH: Yes. But one can't be sure.

IRISH: Not forgettable was a conference with Professor Coker after the Christmas holidays. He summoned me to the office and informed me that the budgetary situation at Yale was very tight because
of the Crash and the Depression, and it made it necessary for the
department to drop one of the Cowles fellowships. Since I was the
lone woman, I was obviously most expendable. Sad, Yale was not very
kind to women graduates in those days. There was no discrimination

in the classroom, but graduate women were allowed to stay only in a slum called the "Graduate Women's Club."

BEACH: Could you speak a little bit about some of the other students who you were with in graduate seminars?

IRISH: I do remember Cecil Dreiber, who was a member of Professor Coker's philosophy seminar. I came to know Cecil Dreiber much better when I returned to Yale in '38–'39, and he was then a professor on the political science faculty, and I took his course in British government, which was first rate. I remember from '32–'33, David Fellman. But I didn't really get to know him much at Yale, because there was very little fraternizing with the one woman.

Now when I went back in '38–'39 I did socialize much more with my fellow graduate students, and I think maybe the bias against women students was perhaps abating. I was the first woman in the Ph.D. program. In '38–'39 I knew very well the other Cowles fellows. There was Dwight Waldo.

BEACH: He became a very good friend, right?

IRISH: That's right. Robert Dahl, Fred Cahill, and George Millikan, who you may have known at Brookings. He was there a while. We have kept in touch over the years, and we have been supportive one with the other. In the interim between my two years at Yale, I was teaching undergraduate courses at the Florida State College for Women in Tallahassee.

BEACH: Which is now Florida State.

IRISH: I was teaching American government, European government, public Administration, constitutional law, and international law.

BEACH: Five preparations?

IRISH: Well, not necessary all in one semester. And I found that all to the good in preparing for the comprehensive at Yale. In my spare time at FSCW, I chose my own dissertation topic, and I thought it wise not to consult with my Yale faculty. I chose social legislation in the South, 1932–38. After I completed the comprehensives at Yale in '38, I alerted Professor Coker, in February '39, that I expected to graduate in June '39. He didn't seem to understand what I was saying and did not contradict me, so I went ahead and completed the dissertation in time for the June graduation.

BEACH: So you basically had no help from the faculty.

IRISH: That's right. It was already written when I got there. I was nominated by the department for the Porter Prize. One of my readers on the committee was Professor Griswold, who later became President Griswold, and he liked the dissertation. He sent it to his publisher, which was then Harcourt Brace. Two years later, a new editor at Harcourt Brace returned it to me with regrets and apologies. The copy was partially burned and there was never any explanation of what happened to it. By that time, I was already publishing excerpts from the dissertation and expanded diversions from it. The first was "The Proletarian South" in the *Journal of Politics*. And I went on and did a number of topics on the South: "The New South" in the *Sewanee Review,* and another for the *Journal of Politics,* the one which you read in the *American Political Science Review.*

Early Years at Florida State

BEACH: It would be good to tell a little bit about what it was like to be a faculty member.

IRISH: Well, when I left Yale in '33, the prospects were grim. The Depression was ongoing. I spent that summer writing letter after letter to places across the country for jobs. I saw a news story in mid-August in the *New York Times* that Bessie Carter Randolph had just been appointed president of Hollins College. She had been a professor of political science at Florida State College for Women. So I dispatched a letter at once to the Yale Placement Bureau with this information. One week later I received a telegram from President Edward Conradi at the Florida State College for Women, that I had been appointed associate professor, salary $2,500, wire acceptance, and I wired acceptance within the hour.

I was expected to teach that first year three sections in American government. And as I taught three courses in American government, I also taught international law and international relations. Professor Speakman from Yale hastily sent me his course outline because, I think, he was a little panic stricken of what I might do in an undergraduate course. And then I was also asked to teach the introductory course in history.

BEACH: In history. American history? World history?

IRISH: Modern European History. It was a very interesting year. It was very difficult for a first year of teaching. And it remained fifteen hours of teaching until we became a university in 1947. I did recruit a second member of the faculty, and that was Victoria Schuck, who had a brand new Ph.D. from Stanford. And I found her—I still didn't have my Ph.D.—I found her a rather awesome partner. She used to tell me what Churchill had told her at dinner or what Eleanor Roosevelt had said one night. And, you know, it was a long time before I realized this is her way of telling me what she'd heard over the radio.

When I went off to Yale, Vicky was left in charge of the Division of Political Science. Victoria and I had one year together after I returned, and she felt that was plenty, and she lucked into an opening at Mt. Holyoke in 1940, and there she stayed until her retirement.

The third member of the department before 1947 was Daisy Parker, who had done her undergraduate work with us at FSCW and got her Ph.D. from the University of Virginia. When she came, she added the new courses in political parties and state governments. Daisy Parker went on up the ladder. She came in as an instructor, and, when she retired from FSU three or four years ago, she retired as vice president and dean of Academic Affairs.

BEACH: Could you talk a little bit about some of the students that you had? What were their kind of interests, and what did they end up doing?

IRISH: When I first went to FSCW, I really was struck by the quality of the student body, and I think that the best of our students could easily compete with the best of Barnard and Bryn Mawr. The poorest of our students would not have been admitted to either Barnard or Bryn Mawr. The poorest students did not stay the four-year course.

BEACH: In the South, of course, the state universities always were in highest of esteem, as opposed to the Northeast.

IRISH: There were private schools for women in the South, when I went there. There was Hollins and Sweet Briar, Agnes Scott. And Sophie Newcomb in New Orleans. But in Florida the girls were not inclined, or their families were not inclined, to send them north— that far from home—so we had very good students, as well as some very poor students, who we were inclined to call the "swamp angels." In the '30s, Florida was not very much developed, you know. So, the best students came from the few major cities. And those that came from the back country, the piney woods, they didn't have much of a chance to be good. The schools were awful.

BEACH: Did some of those early students go on to work in graduate school, or what was the pattern of people who studied political science and liked our field?

IRISH: Well, in the 1930s, most of them went to teaching positions. But in the '40s, especially during the war years, many of the political science girls went up to Washington. They found jobs quite easily in the government. In the time when I was teaching position classification and budget analysis, I could place those girls in Washington without any difficulty. But there was still a notable discrimination. For instance, I was inclined to get my best students to apply for the State Department, the foreign service, which was open to women.

BEACH: Yes.

IRISH: And the girls who applied for the foreign service were allowed to take the exam, but they always got discouraging letters from the personnel office pointing out that most of the positions in the foreign service were not suitable for women. But if the girls instead applied for the staff side of State Department, they got the most encouraging letters. One of my brightest students, a Phi Beta Kappa student, talked to me. I said, "Just try the foreign service instead of staff side." She said, "Miss Irish, if I did that I'd wind up like you." She said, "I want to get married." And she was right. I had any number of girls who did that, who went up to Washington and met much more interesting men there than they would have in their small town in Florida.

The Growth of Political Science at Florida State

IRISH: Well, at any rate, let me tell you about another person there who was quite influential in this period, and that is our friend Manning Dauer.

BEACH: Oh, right. Yes.

IRISH: See, Manning headed the Division of Political Science at Gainesville. And all during the '30s and the '40s, the '50s and much of the '60s, we were two conspiring partners. From the 1930s, we wanted to liberate our divisions, to get them out of the history departments. And we talked about it a great deal. After the war, we both were named departments of political science, equal status and both coeducational. So then we became rivals for the money for this. We were at the mercy of the state legislature.

BEACH: Which still had this background of favoritism towards the University of Florida?

IRISH: Yeah. But both departments flourished, burgeoning with G.I. enrollments. But the University of Florida got the best of them. It's a long time since that was true, but, at the beginning, the men students at FSU were called the Tallahassee base of the University of Florida. And that arrangement lasted legally about two years. Well, when we became a coeducational university, our president wanted what was necessary to attract male students. So, immediately, he went about the business of creating new instructional units—professional units that would attract the men. A school of Business, a School of Journalism, and a School of Public Administration. We were upset by this, withdrawing faculty from our department and moving them into the School of Public Administration. I was luckier than some of my female colleagues. I was made the head of the department.

BEACH: Since political science was growing as a field, the environment was friendly?

IRISH: We had a large Department of Political Science at FSCW. Among the new faculty that we added, one of the first of the males was Charles Clapp. James Prothro came from Princeton. And the first year he was there, he was finishing his dissertation. His wife . . . his first wife was typing it, like first wives were expected to do. It was called *The Dollar Decade* and was published. There was Paul Piccard from Texas, who is still a specialist in political science and science. You know, he came from that famous family of Piccards. His father and mother were balloonists.

Well, they were recruited, all of them, with an eye to giving the department a wide range of subject specialization and also various methodologies and approaches in the discipline. In '52–'53, I applied for and received a faculty fellowship from the Ford Fund for the Advancement of Education. Do you remember those plushy grants?

BEACH: I have to say I don't.

IRISH: Well, what I got was what I thought was a munificent fellowship. It was equal to my salary at FSU, which was then $7,000. And there was also a supplementary cost of living allowance taken into consideration. It cost more to live in Cambridge, Mass., than in Tallahassee, Florida. So I was on my way to Harvard shortly. My tuition was waived in both the graduate school and the law school. I was free to visit any class lectures or seminars of my choosing. I could use the law library and Widener but not, of course, the men's library for undergraduates. There were no fixed requirements. It was a wonderful year.

I remember from this experience Robert McClosky's very vivid lectures, and W.Y. Elliott's seminar in U.S. foreign policy. I had Arthur Sutherland's seminar in civil rights in the law school. I also like to say that in that seminar there must have been twenty-five or thirty students who were post graduates, post–law school. There were only two southerners, so we tried to explain the problems of civil rights. And I was one of the two so-called Southerners, and the other one was a black fellow who graduated from FAMU. Both of us pointed out that we didn't see any black students in Harvard Law School. But we had a whole big law school for blacks in Tallahassee.

It was also for me, personally, a very interesting year because V.O. Key, who had been a longtime associate with me in the Southern Political Science Association, showed up in midyear. He had just left Yale in a huff, and he was not yet assigned anything particular at Harvard. He was just sitting there in his office, and we were neighbors. So I saw a lot of Key and his wife, Louella. But the thing I think you might be most interested in, regarding what I got out of Harvard—it was there I started on my research on William O. Douglas. Senator Claude Pepper, who was an old friend of mine from Tallahassee, thought that I might be interested in doing a Douglas profile, and he manipulated the introductions, and for about a half dozen years afterwards I was still pursuing the life and works of the Supreme Court justice. He was always kind and friendly, helpful, almost enthusiastic. I met some of his associates in New York and I met quite a few of his law clerks. And one of things he did was furnish me with fascinating letters exchanged between him and President Roosevelt over quite a few years.

And I read these with such enthusiasm, and at the very end it said, "None of this material can be used for any reason as long as the participants are alive." Well, that was a little bit dashing. So I put the Douglas thing on the back burner. I did publish one article in the University of Florida Law Review on Douglas, "Judicial Restraint," and he came to the campus as a public lecturer. So, I wrote him and asked him if he would, aside from the public lecture, would he come to my constitutional law seminar. And he said, "Yes."

BEACH: And did—

IRISH: He did, and he gave them a fabulous two-hour seminar. I had told the students, "Be very careful because he doesn't really want to talk about his opinions or anything that is pending," and so on. So the first thing he said to them, he said, "I have no doubt that Dr. Irish told you to be careful." He said, "Ignore her." He talked about a lot of things—his judicial opinions and his political views and so on. He was very forthright. The only thing he said was, "I will not have anything I say here reported in the press."

I invited Jim Prothro, who was my closest colleague, to come to the breakfast. Otherwise, it was a closed session. And we drove him or Jim drove him to the airport. I sat in the back seat while they talked. We had decided to give him the first edition of Irish and Prothro, which had just been published, and we had gotten it about a week or so earlier. And that date, I think, is 1959, and the first thing he did was to open it to the index.

BEACH: Of course, and look under "D."

IRISH: And looked under "D" and, fortunately, I can report that at "D" in the index he found his name many places in the text. We quoted him on academic freedom, the Bill of Rights, the Communist party, the First Amendment, free speech, national supremacy in foreign affairs and so on. And he was very pleased.

Well, at Harvard in '52–'53, I learned a lot about grantsmanship from people like V.O. Key. And so, when I returned at FSU, I discussed with the department, which by then was fair-sized, the possibility of our developing a Ph.D. program in political science. Now, up to that time there were very few independent departments of political science in the South with the Ph.D. program. The only ones that come to mind in political science were the ones at Chapel Hill and

Duke. Now, there might have been such a program at Vanderbilt, but I don't think so. I think that one came later, too. I learned how we could get some federal financial assistance to develop it. And we applied for and got a sizable federal grant that enabled us to offer four three-year fellowships towards the Ph.D's.

BEACH: Were those NDEA fellowships?

IRISH: Yes. That's right. That was after the Sputnik. We had a well-rounded department where I thought we had respectable scholarship and we had expertise and so on. But what we didn't have was a reputation established nationwide. Nobody'd ever heard of us. So, to add some prestige in the department, we established a series of public lectures which would bring to the campus each year, not one but a group of distinguished scholars. Now the federal grant enabled us to offer a modest stipend for the lectures. Modest was $250. Then I asked my longtime editor, Jim Murray, at Prentice Hall, if he would consider publication of the lectures in paperback, if I would edit them. And he agreed to it, and so we were able to augment the authors' stipends with the promise of royalties to be shared equally.

We also promised to show each author the alligator's act at Wakulla Springs. And I think that for most of them who came down in the winter, they were more interested in the alligators than in the royalties. The first volume of the series was titled *The Continuing Crisis in American Politics in 1963.*

BEACH: I remember this very well. I remember you have McClosky, Robert Harris, Paul David, Steve Bailey, Clinton Rossitor, Alpheus T. Mason, Morton Grodzins, and Arthur Smithies. It's a very distinguished group of scholars.

IRISH: That's right. And we thought this was a chance for our students to meet these people—to talk with them about their methods. The paperback, by contract, had to sell ten thousand copies, and this particular volume sold, oh, I don't know, thirty or forty thousand. It did so well financially that Prentice Hall was willing to continue it. The next volume was called *World Pressures on Foreign Policy.* And look at that list.

BEACH: Sure. Henry Mayo, Roy Macridis, William Livingston, Merle Fainsod, Frederick Watson, Gwendolen Carter, Federico Gil, and Lucien Pye.

IRISH: We brought the scholars to campus, and they went back with some recollection of what we were doing. Now, after I left, the department continued the series and the books.

BEACH: It accomplished its function very, very well.

IRISH: Those three-year students that we brought in, see, they met at least thirty of the most distinguished political scientists in the country.

Enticement to Washington and American University

IRISH: I resigned the chairmanship of the Government Department at FSU, in 1963, in order to take a leave of absence in Washington. I received the Senior Research Award in American Government from the Social Science Research Council and a guest scholarship at the Brookings Institution. My intent was to examine what changes in the content or conduct of U.S. foreign policy took place at the presidential elections transition period. And I had barely begun on the transition from Eisenhower to Kennedy, when I was hit by the untimely transition from Kennedy to Johnson.

Actually, I was in the executive dining room of the State Department with Dr. Bernard Noble, who had been a history teacher of mine at Barnard. Isn't the network interesting? And we were sitting there just chatting, when he was summoned to the seventh floor for a conference on the funeral details. I can tell you, the State Department was in a shambles that day. If that had been an international conspiracy, it could have turned over the whole State Department. People were out in the corridors; they were weeping; they were sitting and glued to their little hand radios and so on. I went back to Brookings by cab, and there I got a bitter taste of public opinion. My cab driver turned around to me and said, "One down and two to go." And when I got to Brookings, it was closed.

I did continue with my interviewing on schedule and also additional research, because I was right there on the spot to talk at the time of this unplanned, unexpected transition. So, I had a lot of stuff on that. At the end of my year, I had not completed—that's the story of my life—I had not completed the whole project, and I put it on the back burner until I took the year and two summers at the Woodrow Wilson International Center for Scholars (1972–73). Harcourt Brace Jovanovich published the result of that study, and Elke Frank collaborated with me in the final preparation for publication. She felt I would never get it done. Well, I wasn't very happy on my return to Tallahassee after my year's leave in Washington. There was access to the top echelons in the bureaucracy at the State, the Pentagon, even the CIA, for an interview. I could read the *Washington Post* instead of the *Tallahassee Daily Democrat*. And there were the Washington good music stations instead of Tallahassee's local radio station, which was unbelievably awful. When I went back to Tallahassee the John Birch Society was over-active in the community, and I was one of their targets.

BEACH: Oh, really?

IRISH: I was also targeted by the KKK, for this was a time of racial unrest in Tallahassee, which was resisting all attempts at integration in the schools. Now this is '64. I was not only the professor of constitutional law, but I was also on the vestry of the Episcopal Chapel. And, it seemed to me, every Monday morning I went down trying to get bail for our students. They were bent on inviting black students over, and the police were bent on preventing black students from invading the white campus. It was a difficult time. I was receiving midnight calls at my house, and they were very disturbing. And so were the messages that were left overnight under the door of my office. And I was not the only target in town, of course. I wasn't happy in Tallahassee, and Kirkpatrick said, "Well, why don't you go where you want to live? If you like Washington, come back." I did write some notes, and both the University of Maryland and the American University invited me.

BEACH: Was that Charles O. Lerche then? Was he the dean at the School of International Service?

IRISH: He had just been appointed dean of the School of International Service at AU. I knew Charlie when he taught political science at Emory. And we had been very active, both of us, in the Southern Political Science Association. I can't remember the exact date that Charlie and I and Sam Cook . . .

BEACH: Samuel Dubois Cook, yes.

IRISH: Yeah.

BEACH: President of Dillard University now.

IRISH: Well, at that time he was at Atlanta University.

BEACH: And he had been a roommate, of course, of Martin Luther King as an undergraduate.

IRISH: Oh, I remember that because it was through him that I was able to invite Martin Luther King for a Southern Political Science Association luncheon. I remember that luncheon particularly because not only were the members of the Association at the tables, but crowded around us was all the kitchen staff from the dining room. They had come into the dining room and stood around, and they were simply entranced. And he was a great speaker.

BEACH: Yes. Of course.

IRISH: Well anyway, I was also offered the post of a professor to teach foreign policy at Maryland, and, at that time, I had half a dozen of my former students at FSU on the Maryland faculty. Well, getting back to American. Charlie wanted me to teach an undergraduate lecture course in foreign policy and a graduate seminar in foreign policy at AU, and he also wanted me to help direct Ph.D. dissertations. But, most of all, he wanted me at AU because I had just been named editor of the *Journal of Politics*.

I wanted to continue teaching constitutional law, and he said, offhand, that could be arranged with the then-separate School of Public

Administration. Well, it was sad parting for me at FSU in 1966. I had taught political science there for thirty-three years, I had headed the Division of Political Science from '33 to '47, and I had headed the government department from '47 until '63. And people simply could not understand why was I leaving, and I told them about the good music station in Washington. It was not for financial reasons, like my friends in Tallahassee thought. I found my eight years at FSU very interesting.

BEACH: At AU.

IRISH: . . . did I say FSU?

BEACH: Yeah.

IRISH: AU. Sorry. I do get them mixed sometimes. You know this is my eightieth year. But, you know, the academic lifestyle at AU in the latter 1960s was totally different from anything I had ever experienced before. I enjoyed the faculty, especially that first group that had been recruited by Ernie Griffith, because he had brought in those *Who's Who* types, who were topping their bureaucratic careers with academic appointments.

By the time I retired, all of those had disappeared by attrition. The mandatory age retirement requirement was sixty-five. And the faculty at SIS were gradually built on the basis of assistant professors who were less expensive. They were recent Ph.D.s, who were just beginning, rather than ending, their careers. While I was at SIS, I was also teaching at the Foreign Service Institute of the State Department. And there I did a series of seminars, over several years, on the discipline of political science, and the idea was to introduce middle-grade foreign service officers to new approaches and methodology in political science before they went off on an extended leave to Harvard or Yale or Princeton, where they would get advanced degrees. At AU, I also had a great many of my foreign policy graduate students drawn from the government, notably from the Pentagon and State Department and the Commerce Department. And I found these government students very interested, as well as interesting, and I'd like to cite as an example a navy man in the foreign policy seminar, who questioned David Easton's model of systems analysis. At the end of the seminar, this navy man asked me if I would phone Dave Easton in Chicago and see if he would be willing to submit to an interview in person. He explained to me, and he also explained to Easton over the phone, that he could take his plane up to Chicago on practice time, and there would be no problem.

BEACH: That's fascinating.

IRISH: Easton was a bit startled, but he did name a date, and the student kept the date. He flew up and back on the same day, talked to Easton in his office at Chicago and returned to the seminar that night to report how Easton had done on explaining and defending his methodology.

BEACH: Not your usual run-of-the-mill freshman?

IRISH: No. No. No, these military people had a sense of importance and responsibility.

Experiences and Research in the South

IRISH: Let me move into my experience in so-called research and writing. When I became editor of the *Journal of Politics* in 1965, I soon learned that most of the articles submitted to the journal came from recent Ph.D.s who were anxious to publish the results of their dissertation research. I observed that almost all the articles in the *Journal of Politics* came from assistant professors, who became associate professors and achieved tenure on the basis of their publication. I also observed that, after that, they didn't submit many articles.

Well, in my dissertation, which was my initial attempt at research, I developed my own methodology. As I told you, I was writing it fifteen hundred miles from Yale. And I was caught up in the New Deal and the New South, and I could observe the changing patterns in the economy. In Tallahassee, I could see the emerging political responses in the form of social legislation, which the South had never considered before. My documentation for this was not in books. I built up a regional network of correspondents, and among my so-called primary sources were William Green, who was then president of AFL; George Googe, who was southern representative of the American Federation of Labor; a grand lady called Lucy Randolph Mason, an activist with the CIO. And then I also corresponded with William Mitch, who was with the United Mine Workers. The footlocker that I took with me from Tallahassee to New Haven in the fall of 1938 was jammed with current government reports from the eleven states of the old Confederacy, with popular and not-so-popular literature of the day. In addition, I traveled to all of the eleven southern states in my Chevrolet. It was the first Chevrolet to have knee action. I was steeped in southern politics at the juncture of the Old South and the New South.

BEACH: Did you stay in what we would call motels?

IRISH: Well, believe it or not, in those days there weren't any motels. The motels don't come in until after World War II. Sometimes in a tourist cabin, but usually I found a correspondent who was hospitable.

BEACH: So you got more personal contact, which was useful for your research.

IRISH: Oh, yes. And it was a wonderful time, I thought. It was a time of great paradoxes, of sometime red clay roads and straightaway concrete highways, banks of jasmine and Cherokee rose and billboards of Bull Durham.

BEACH: And no air-conditioning.

IRISH: No air-conditioning. Oh, Walter, I didn't enjoy air-conditioning in Florida until maybe two or three years before I left in 1966. My home was not air-conditioned. My office was air-conditioned in the last year or two I was there. Class rooms were not air-conditioned. Well, as I said, a great contrast. I remember high church Anglicans and Southern Baptists and Southern Presbyterians and Holy Rollers. White lightning and Coca Cola and mint juleps. Well, a lot of this went into my dissertation, and that's what I called my research. It was published in various articles in the professional journals over several years. In the 1940s, I took advantage of the proximity of the college and the capital, and much of that research was done in public administration at the state level.

In 1943, in the administration of Governor Spessard Holland, I was appointed to serve as—this is the official title—personnel technician consultant. And I was charged to study the organization and personnel practices of the Florida state government, with the idea that the study might lead to the establishment of a Florida merit system. We sent out questionnaires to about 9,000 state employees, and we had a wonderful return because we sent the questionnaires to the office, under the cover of the governor's authority.

BEACH: It gave them the proper encouragement.

IRISH: Oh, we got about 7,500 returns. We used the data processing facilities that had just recently been installed in the Industrial Commission. That was my first experience with using the computer for research. We could not have done it without the computer, so I learned how the cards were cut and so on. A long, long way from today's computers.

I was asked to present the personnel study and to explain the draft statute in person to a joint session of the Florida legislature in 1945. And I can only tell you that I was fed to the wolves. Governor Holland, who had commissioned the survey and was most enthusiastic about the proposed merit system, had served out his term as governor and was about to become our U.S. senator. And his successor, who was Millard Caldwell, told the joint session that he was against the whole thing. The legislators thanked me, and Millard Caldwell said that, as far as he could see, any merit system was generally inefficient and only encouraged mediocrity and a laid-back performance. So, I did get a standing ovation, but I learned, at that time, that politicians like to use academicians for public relations, but politics is first.

Over the years I remained more or less in the academic background of Florida government. I served on the Florida Citizens' Committee on Taxation, and I also served, along with Manning Dauer as a consultant for two constitutional conventions, none of which resulted in any great reforms. I enjoyed telling my students what was going on behind the scenes.

Experience as a Textbook Author

IRISH: In my latter years in Florida, most of my academic work, beyond teaching was not in what my colleagues in the discipline called research. I became a textbook writer. And I did, over the years, produce four fairly successful textbooks. The first was *The People Govern*, which was a high school textbook in American Government for Charles Scribner. The second was *The Politics of American Democracy*, which was a college textbook, which I did with Jim Prothro.

None of these textbooks were written off the cuff. I refer to it from time to time as "years of bondage." Let me start with *The People Govern*—how this came about. I was teaching American government and constitutional law in a southern state capital. It was not a job for sissies any time and certainly not in the 1950s in the era of McCarthyism. Probably the most fruitful piece of writing I ever published was an article in the *Saturday Evening Post* dated February 20, 1950. And it begins, "Everyone takes a loyalty test these days, an act which seems to assuage the widespread apprehension that there are subversive agencies at work in our country." The title of my article is— was—"You Can't Make Them Loyal That Way."

I wrote, "It's a tragic commentary, too, that millions of Americans would willingly die to save their Constitution, but only a few of them will ever read it." And so, more brash then than I became later, I ended the article with a great clarion call, "We need most urgently a primer of democracy." It ends with, you know, an exclamation point, and it was a highly controversial article, and the *Saturday Evening Post* kept sending me hundreds of letters from all across the country.

BEACH: Pro and con?

IRISH: Pro and con. I was astounded, though, at the number of readers who took affront at my use of words like democracy and republic. And it was a shocking revelation to me that so many Americans feel that democracy is really a dirty word. And, in many a letter, I got the first principle that this country was founded as a republic and not a democracy. And many letters explained to me that we must remain a republic, and never surrender to democracy.

But there was one of the letters that I selected out immediately. It was a letter from the senior editor of the textbook section of Charles Scribner and Sons. I think his name was Mr. Boardman. He was very favorably impressed by the article, especially by the suggestion of a primer of democracy, and so he asked if I would be interested in coming to him in his office in New York, with all expenses paid, and he'd like to discuss the possibility of my writing a textbook in American government. So I flew up to New York to Scribner's on Fifth Avenue to meet Mr. Boardman and also a young high school teacher of American government and American history, Laurence Paquin. And he had just completed a high school text in American history. Mr. Boardman thought that together we might collaborate on a textbook in American government along the lines I had taken off in the *Saturday Evening Post* article. After we sized each other up rather warily, we decided, yeah, we could give it a try, and we would write a textbook that we thought was both idealistic and realistic. We wanted to give these high school students a sense of pride but also a more objective approach than they were likely to get in the contemporary textbook. Most of our collaboration was by mail. The book was published in 1954, and Charles Scribner, Jr., delivered the first copy in person to President Eisenhower in the Oval Office.

The People Govern was widely adopted across the country from Maine to Texas, New York to California, and, in the process of adoption, the authors learned a lot about the politics of pressure groups and special interests in American government. In deference to the states of the old Confederacy, we called the Civil War the "War Between the States" all through the text. For adoption in Georgia, we agreed to drop a picture of an integrated classroom in New York City in 1954. With an eye on the purse, we agreed to a special edition for California statewide adoption, to drop the chapter on "The United States and the United Nations."

BEACH: Senator Knowland was looking over your shoulder.

IRISH: *The People Govern* sold very well, and, in 1958, we updated a second edition. And this was my first experience with a need for continuous revision of textbooks. And I tell you, to this day, I remember that neither Plato or Aristotle ever revised their volumes. However, the Irish and Prothro work on *The Politics of American Democracy* ran to seven editions. And textbook writing, I found, becomes continuous bondage.

The first edition of Irish and Prothro, *The Politics of American Democracy,* was published by Prentice Hall in 1959. Jim Prothro had joined the FSU faculty as an assistant professor in 1950, and he came straight from the graduate school at Princeton. For the first year he was busy finishing the dissertation. It was published in 1954 under the title of *The Dollar Decade*, and it was a study of business ideas in the 1920s. He was recruited for FSU to teach American government, American political thought, and American political behavior. And that third was a new addition that we were glad to have at FSU. We were both teaching American government, two sections of it. Well, we used to have our coffee breaks together at the college soda shop, and there we would frequently deplore the textbooks that were available then in American government. And Jim was also impressed by the royalties I was collecting from Scribner's on *The People Govern*, and he suggested that we might fruitfully collaborate on a textbook of our own.

Well, Jim contacted a friend of his from Princeton days, Donald Hammond at Prentice Hall, who was immediately interested and quickly signed a contract with us. We were very lucky to have Prentice Hall assign their top textbook editor for the book. That was Everett Simms, who always insisted that the book be enjoyable to read as well as educational. Ev Simms later left Prentice Hall for Harcourt Brace. Meantime, however, Jim Murray had come on board at Prentice Hall, and it was he who saw us through five editions of *The Politics of American Democracy*.

BEACH: Let me come back a little bit there and ask about adoptions and about how it was different than the high school text.

IRISH: Oh, very different. We were certainly much more free to write what we thought we should. For the most part, I don't think these special interests have much luck in the college and university publications. Well, the second edition was published in 1963, and it followed basically the same format as the first, but we tried to upgrade the text generally, and we tried to make the students more aware of the tools of political science that would enable them to understand the values and concerns in American politics. That's a way of saying we were sort of edging into political behavior.

We did expand on political opinions and voting behavior, and, again, we used the 1960 election, which, you remember, was a great election. And we talked about the transition from Eisenhower to Kennedy. Anyway, whether we wrote a better book in the second edition, or whether the tides of political opinions were changing, or whether there was this emerging revolution in political science, the second edition sales simply soared.

In the third edition published in 1965, we determined to try a radical revision of the contents. We were going to try and give the undergraduates the sense of excitement about politics as well as basic knowledge in American government. Instead of speaking of the Congress, it's the legislators. Instead of speaking of the courts, we were doing the judges, and we're looking at them as personal actors rather than pawns in a structure.

BEACH: It's not an institutional examination.

IRISH: That's right. And then, we examined what we called "the outputs of the system." And there we did individual rights and liberties and general welfare and common defense and national security. And again, the sales soared, and our royalties rose, and, under prevailing U.S. income tax rates, we were making substantial contributions to the support of the American system.

The Southern and the American Political Science Associations

IRISH: Now, besides the textbooks, I wrote a good many articles in the professional journals. But one in particular stands out in my mind. This appeared in the *British New Statesman* in December of 1957, under the title "The Cypher in the White House." It was my presidential address to the Southern Political Science Association in November of 1957, and it just happened that a reporter from the BBC was present when I delivered this speech, and he caught me after the meeting and asked if he could have a copy of it, and I gave it to him. And several days later, when I was back in Tallahassee, I had a cable from the *New Statesman* requesting permission to print the entire speech with no change in the text. Weeks later, when I got the printed copy of the December 7th issue, I was appalled at the title which the *New Statesman* editor used. They did not change the text, but what I had titled "The Organization Man and the Presidency," they called "The Cypher in the White House."

Well, I did publish the address, as is customary, in the *Journal of Politics*, and I did publish it under "The Organization Man and the Presidency." Now, I thought it was a carefully researched analysis of the growth of the White House following the Brownlow report of 1937. You remember that contained the famous line, "The president needs help . . ."

BEACH: Help. Right.

IRISH: . . . and what he needed were those seven bright young men with "a passion for anonymity." But since that time, there was a continuing increase of the White House staff. In 1951, President Truman's White House staff had grown to nineteen assistants, and most of them did not have any passion for anonymity.

The initial organization of the presidency, as Brownlow presented it, was not intended to substitute managerial efficiency for executive leadership. But, in the context of 1957, it did appear that the decision-making and the presidency was being handled largely by administrative management and public relations. And, some place in the text, I sort of intimated that, like the British monarch, the American president was becoming a symbol of unity, a significant cypher, as one British political scientist, Walter Bagehot, has once depicted the British Queen.

Let me do a little more now about the Southern Political Science Association and a little bit about the American Political Science Association. My association with the Southern Political Science Association goes back to the fall of 1933. My predecessor at Florida State College for Women was Bessie Carter Randolph, and she was supposed to give a paper on international law. As president of the Hollins College and newly inaugurated, she didn't have any inclination to honor the commitment. So I was asked to substitute. And I talked to my boss, Kathryn Abby, who was head of the history department, and she advised me, I think most prudently, to decline the invitation to deliver the paper, but to attend the meeting. I think that was pretty good advice. In the 1930s and even into the 1940s, the Southern Political Science Association was not much more than a section of the Southern Historical Association. And the section, when I first was a member, was very small. The membership grew very slowly, thirty to fifty is what I remember in those early days. I attended the annual meetings. As my department enlarged, I brought along my entire faculty with me, so we had quite a few women, Victoria Schuck, Lucretia Ilsley, and Daisy Parker. Now, among the members that I remember in those early years, there was Cullen Gosnell from Emory in Atlanta. There was Bob Harris, also from Princeton.

BEACH: And he was Hubert Humphrey's teacher too, at LSU.

IRISH: Carl Swisher was there from Johns Hopkins. He became president of the Southern Political Science Association and later president of the American Political Science Association.

BEACH: Yes. And the famous biographer of Chief Justice Roger Taney.

IRISH: That's right. Roscoe Martin was there with his Ph.D. from Chicago. When I first knew him, he was at the University of Texas. He moved on to the University of Alabama, where he established the Southern Regional Training Program for Public Administration. V.O. Key was one of the early members of the group. He was a longtime book review editor for the *Journal of Politics*, and I succeeded him in that assignment in 1962. Lee Green was there, a Ph.D. from Wisconsin. He stayed at the University of Tennessee all of his career. He was a distinguished professor there, and he was the third editor of the *Journal of Politics*.

Taylor Cole did his master's at Texas, his Ph.D. at Harvard. He was the second editor of the *Journal of Politics*. He was president of the Southern Political Science Association in '51 and president of the APSA in '58. I happened to be on the APSA nominating committee that debated and decided it was time—that is politic—to recruit a president for the APSA from the South. That was a very interesting debate, but I won't go into that. Charles Hyneman was there. And it was to Charles Hyneman that Kirk wrote to say he had this wonderful student at Minnesota, and he suggested that maybe Hyneman could help him get into LSU and to get a scholarship, and that was Hubert Humphrey.

There were not many women in the Southern Political Science Association in the 1930s or 1940s. One was outstanding. That was Gladys Kammerer with her Ph.D. from Chicago, another protégé of Charles Merriam. You know, it's interesting to see certain political scientists of one generation produce the bright stars of the next. She got her first grounding in political science with Louise Overacker at Wellsley. And I first knew Gladys when she was at the University of Kentucky and she later moved to the University of Florida.

I was book review editor of the *Journal of Politics* from 1962 to '64, and in that office, I learned more about the human nature of academicians, at least fellow political scientists, than I cared to know. "Dog eat dog" seems to be the motto in the ruthless arena of "publish or perish." Colleagues in the same field of specialization, I soon learned, are liable also to be cutthroat competitors. I became editor of the *Journal of Politics* in 1966; I lost some of my best friends in the discipline. Editing is not a job for sissies. While my commitment to the Southern Political Science Association was wholehearted in the years between 1933 and 1974, I moved up the escalator from the merest member, to member of the council, secretary, vice president, program chairman, president, book review editor, and editor of the *Journal of Politics*.

Now, I'll shorten my remarks on the APSA, of which I have been a member since 1940. There I was part of the organization but in less personal association than with the southern—it's much larger. But with three degrees from the Ivy League, a longtime southerner by adoption, a professional activist at the SPSA and withal a woman, I was a bargain token for the APSA. I served on the official escalator, a member of the council, secretary, vice president, and I also served, over the years, on countless committees, but I always knew I was a token.

At the time I was at AU and rather close to the national office under Ev Kirkpatrick, I was invited to a luncheon at the Dupont Hotel along with Valerie Earle and Ev's wife Jeane Kirkpatrick. Now this luncheon was Jeane's idea. She had experienced some of the discrimination against women in her own academic career, and she thought we might do something about it, at least set up an APSA committee to survey the situation. And so I came to serve on the first Committee on the Status of Women.

BEACH: And since I served as staff person, I was right there helping you.

IRISH: As I recall, the chairman was Josephine Milburn from Simmons College, later from the University of Rhode Island. She was married with young children. Other members of the commission included Vicky Schuck from Mount Holyoke. Joyce Mitchell, then assistant professor at the University of Oregon, married.

BEACH: To a political scientist, Bill Mitchell. They met on the APSA Congressional Fellowship Program.

IRISH: And we also had one empathetic male representative, Philip Converse of the University of Michigan, who later became also a president of the APSA. The Committee on the Status of Women investigated how contemporary graduate women students felt about the status of women in political science. We interviewed many of them, and their responses were quite different from what I expected. I had thought that the discrimination existed in hiring, in salary schedules. I thought they would have some genuine gripes about promotions. I thought they might be concerned about tenure. But actually they were more concerned about women's rights per se, not about political scientists' rights. They were interested in leaves of absence for pregnancy. They were interested in child care arrangements.

Remembering Some Students

IRISH: And now a few words about my outstanding students. But, truth to tell, at this point in my life, I'm not sure what makes a distinguished professor or an outstanding student in political science. I still have, in the bottom drawer of my oversized desk, grade books that date from 1933 to 1974. I can't bear to part with them because they are the symbols of my lifetime enterprise. Should I refresh my recollection of political science students, with the grades they made in American government, constitutional law, U.S. foreign policy? Should I refer, rather, to their present occupations, their current political views, their autobiographies in *Who's Who in America*? What makes them unforgettable people in my dimming mind? How shall I judge how well they've done for themselves or for others?

One of my best students, grade "A" in constitutional law at FSU in the 1960s, I recommended for Harvard Business School graduate work where he was very successful. He returned to Tallahassee to a prestigious job in the State Planning Commission, and then he left Tallahassee to join the American Nazi party, where he reached the top echelon. He was front page news the day he marched across the Memorial Bridge in Washington carrying the Nazi banner, the day Martin Luther King delivered his famous message, "I have a dream." I watched Carl in horror and pain on my TV set that night in northwest Washington. What kind of teacher was I, you know?

But then there were others, many others, who joined the Peace Corps in the 1960s, and they went to India or Afghanistan or Paraguay. Some stayed in Florida, put their political science into practice. Reuben Askew became the governor of Florida. He's a very good man and an outstanding student. Most of them are unforgettable people, outstanding, but outstanding for different things at different times. I would not be willing to say this is number one and down there is number eighty seven. There's Daisy Parker, who was one of my undergraduate students at FSCW in the 1930s, one of my colleagues at Florida State. Miss Mary Lepper, my last doctoral student at FSU, who got her Ph.D. in my last summer in Tallahassee—1966. I think her greatest feat: she was director of the civil rights section in higher education at HEW, where she was determined to implement the principle of affirmative action, to the great distress of her superiors in office.

BEACH: And the Women's Caucus for Political Science has an award named after her.

IRISH: And there is Deborah Snow, who did her undergraduate and master's work at FSU, on the staff at the Civil Rights Commission in Washington, where she headed the big study on the status of women under civil rights legislation. Among the men, Paris Glendenning, who took his bachelor's, master's, and Ph.D. all at FSU, now is a professor at the University of Maryland in the Department of Government, a longtime activist in local government, and county executive of Prince George's County.

BEACH: One of the largest counties in America.

IRISH: Well, he's definitely, I think, on the way up the political ladder. Then there is Ron Walters, who took his Ph.D. with me at AU, and he is now head of the Department of Political Science at Howard.

BEACH: And has also been a very central advisor for Jesse Jackson.

IRISH: I go back and look at the grade books—there he is, grade "A." Bradley Canon. Do you know Brad?

BEACH: He is the president-elect of the Southern Political Science Association.

IRISH: Well, as an undergraduate, he was the editor of what was known as the *Flambeau*, that was the student newspaper, and as long as he was editor it was inflammatory. He took con law with me. He's been, I know, a long time in the political science department at Kentucky.

BEACH: Those are wonderful examples of people who have surely been inspired and learned at your feet.

C. Herman
Pritchett

Herman Pritchett was born on February 9, 1907, in Latham, Illinois. He received an A.B. from Millikin University in 1923 and a Ph.D. degree from the University of Chicago in 1937. Early in his career he worked for the Department of Labor and worked for three years for the Tennessee Valley Authority. In 1940, after a year in England on a Social Science Research Council fellowship, he joined the Political Science Department at the University of Chicago, where he remained for thirty years, serving as chairman for thirteen years. In 1969, he moved to the University of California, Santa Barbara; he became professor emeritus in 1974, but remained active in both teaching and research.

The multiple editions of Pritchett's book The American Constitution *served as the standard work on constitutional jurisprudence for graduate students, along with many undergraduates, for over two decades. His* Courts, Judges, and Politics *was the first collection of readings in judicial politics and remains widely used as a text in American judicial process courses. His book on* The Roosevelt Court *(1948) was a pioneering analysis of the judicial behavior of the Supreme Court and was followed by* Civil Liberties and the Vinson Court *(1953). Pritchett is viewed as the founding father of the behavioral approach to public law.*

Pritchett was president of the American Political Science Association in 1963 to 1964 and was also active in the American Association of University Professors.

He served as a political adviser to Encyclopaedia Britannica, writing a yearly summary of Supreme Court decisions.

Herman Pritchett was interviewed in Santa Barbara, California, in
March of 1980 by Gordon Baker, a colleague who has taught at the
University of California, Santa Barbara, since 1952. Baker is an expert
on legislative reapportionment.

The Chicago Experience: Student

BAKER: You entered Chicago in 1926.

PRITCHETT: The following year, I developed tuberculosis and
had to drop out of the graduate program. For almost four years, I was
not in the university. I was recuperating, and I didn't resume my
graduate study until the spring of 1932. I resumed work with Charles
Merriam, Leonard White, Quincy Wright, and, rather importantly,
Harold Gosnell, as well as Harold Lasswell and Fred Schuman. Since
Lasswell came from Decatur, Illinois, as I did, he took a special interest in me when I first came to the department, visited me in the
sanitorium, and maintained fairly frequent contacts when I returned
to Chicago. It was a small but very distinguished department, which
was beginning to open up some of the most important fields as we
know them: Lasswell, psychopathology; Gosnell, the mathematical approach; White, the field of public administration. At that time, the
Chicago department was the cutting edge of development of the field
of political science. The students who were graduate students when
I was became the leaders of the profession. V.O. Key, Albert Le-
pawsky, Victor Jones, Herb Simon, Bob Walker, David Truman, Gay
Almond—that group supplied some of the most distinguished leadership for the political science profession in the next decade or two.

BAKER: In those days, I suppose graduate students ordinarily
would take the whole gamut and there wouldn't be as much specialization as there would be today.

PRITCHETT: That's true. Charles Merriam had a seminar that
met on Wednesday night, and every graduate student was expected to
attend. Anyone who had written a chapter of a thesis or prepared a
paper would read it, and there would be general criticism of it. It was
a small operation in the sense that everyone could attend the same
seminar. You were aware of what was going on in the other fields of
the department. And Merriam, being a fountain of universal knowledge, could handle the general input of the work that we were all
doing. That was an interesting experience.

BAKER: Was there much interaction with other departments?

PRITCHETT: A fair amount. The social science building was
dedicated in 1929. It was the first social science building on an American campus. The idea in that building was to mix the departments
up. You didn't have the political scientists all on one floor, the histo-

rians on a separate floor and so on. In later years, my office was on
the same floor with Milton Friedman and Theodore Schultz. I didn't
realize I had two future Nobel Prize recipients next door at that time.
Moreover, in the 1920s and 1930s, there was a Social Science Research Council, which had money to sponsor studies of the local community. These studies were sociological studies, economic studies,
political science studies, and the guiding committee was drawn from
the social science departments. Merriam had published *New Aspects
of Politics* in 1926, and the whole theme of that book was relating
political science to the other social sciences. So we were propelled
into an acceptance of the fact that political science was a social science
and was obligated to use the methods of the other social sciences.

Getting Started in the Profession

PRITCHETT: I had always planned to teach, so I applied at a
number of institutions and was rejected unanimously by all of them.
My rejections ranged all the way from Smith College, the University
of Massachusetts, and Syracuse, to the Illinois Institute of Technology
and Southern Illinois at Carbondale.

BAKER: So you were turned down by the high and the low, re-
gardless of standing.

PRITCHETT: Yes. Marshall Dimock had gone to Washington as
second assistant secretary of labor and one of his responsibilities was
the Immigration and Naturalization Service, which at that time was in
the Labor Department. He offered me a position, and I went there in
July 1939 and got the experience of being a bureaucrat in Washington.
At the end of that year, Dimock, who had been on leave from Chicago, decided he wasn't going to go back, at least for quite a while,
and his courses needed to be taught. So Leonard White offered me a
six-month appointment at the university to teach public administration. We had just moved to Washington five months earlier, but the
prospect of going to Chicago even for six months was attractive
enough so that we packed up and went to Chicago for six months. I
stayed for thirty years.

The Chicago Experience: Faculty Member and
Chairman

PRITCHETT: Charles Merriam reached retirement age in 1940,
six months after I got there, and Leonard White became chairman.
Robert Hutchins had been president of the University since 1929. He
was a very forceful person, with his own ideas about what a university

should be doing, and one of the things he didn't think a University should be doing was studying administration or writing textbooks. So, when Leonard White became the choice of the department as chairman, Hutchins wouldn't give White the satisfaction of being chairman. He said we'd have to have an administrative committee in the political science department, and he appointed a troika to run the department.

BAKER: This was not so much a personal dislike by Hutchins, but more of a field dislike?

PRITCHETT: I think so. So Leonard White was the chairman for eight years. They dropped the facade of the administrative committee before long, and he became the chairman in fact. During the war, most of our department was off somewhere, and the department was down to four people between about 1942 and 1945. There was Leonard White, Jerry Kerwin, Hans Morgenthau and myself. We taught the entire field of political science.

It began to be built up again by Leonard White after the war was over, but, in 1948, he was diagnosed as suffering from glaucoma. He immediately resigned as chairman because his doctor told him he should get rid of any obligations that were causing him pressure. I was selected as acting chairman since I had been involved as more or less secretary to White and had somewhat more contact with the paperwork in the department than anybody else. That was a temporary arrangement. The selection of a permanent chairman was worked out in a rather haphazard fashion. Quincy Wright was directed by the dean to go around and talk to everybody and see who they'd like to have as chairman.

Anyway, at a department meeting, Wright reported that I was the majority choice for chairman. Hans Morgenthau spoke up and said he didn't think I should be chairman, he thought he should be chairman. Herman Finer made the same statement; he thought he should be chairman. So I got off to a good start, as you can see, with the opposition of two of the important members of the department.

Well, I was launched then, in, as it turned out, two three-year terms as chairman. We had some building to do, obviously. For example, Ed Banfield was appointed to the department. One of our brightest students was Jim Wilson. Before long, Banfield went off to Harvard. We didn't mind too much because Wilson had worked with Banfield, and we regarded him as an extremely capable replacement. But then Banfield had Wilson come to Harvard to give a lecture, and, as soon as they saw Wilson, they said, "Oh, we want him, too." So we lost Wilson after one year. That's the problem about being number two. Invitations from Harvard are seldom turned down when you're number two in the academic pecking order.

BAKER: Let's talk about Leo Strauss for a moment. If I recall correctly, his appointment was an interesting phenomenon.

PRITCHETT: That was 1948. We had never filled Charles Merriam's theory position. But then we began to hear about Leo Strauss at the New School in New York. It was agreed that he should come out, and we should have a look at him. He came out in the summer of 1948. Hans Morgenthau, who was acting chairman that summer, took Leo over to Hutchins' office and left him there. By the time he came out, a half hour later, Hutchins had appointed Strauss as a member of the department, full professor, with a salary more than anybody else in the department was getting. It was somewhat of a surprise to us, as most members of the department didn't even know much about Leo. In fact, Charles Merriam, who still kept his office in the department as an emeritus professor, said, "Who is Leo Strauss?" It was very interesting that the man whose chair was being filled hadn't even heard of him. Of course, their approaches to theory were entirely different. Strauss was a value theorist and a textual analyst of the classics, whereas Merriam was historical and more interested in the application of theory to current problems.

BAKER: Was there any resentment in the department about the procedures Hutchins used?

PRITCHETT: I don't think so. There was rather amazement. Later on, there were personality clashes, with the three most powerful newer members of the department—Finer, Morgenthau, and Strauss—rather at odds with each other. I think one of the reasons I became chairman is that none of these other persons would have been satisfactory. I was the lowest common denominator because I was more or less acceptable to everyone, which was not true of all the other members of the department.

My term expired in 1955, and Morton Grodzins became chairman. In 1958, Morton left for a year in Palo Alto at the Behavioral Sciences Center, and so the chairmanship was open again. The department decided—although there were some who didn't agree—to ask me to be chairman again. So I took it on for what turned out to be another six-year period.

BAKER: Did anyone publicly denounce this?

PRITCHETT: Well, yes, there was some opposition. Leo Strauss, who was a very gentle man and one of my closest friends, came into my office one day and said, "I signed another letter against you today."

BAKER: No personal offense.

PRITCHETT: Nothing personal.

BAKER: You chaired the department for about thirteen years in all. And, during that time, you had people like Strauss and Morgenthau and Finer, other persons of considerable stature. Did you feel a little bit like a lion tamer in a three ring circus, trying to keep the peace with these very strong personalities?

PRITCHETT: Yes.

BAKER: How did you manage to do this?

PRITCHETT: Well, there were undoubtedly some difficult periods. I had a very able administrative assistant, Doreen Herlihy. I was rather regarded, I think, as being a member of the Strauss group, or at least favorable to it, although, of course, I had really no ideational connection with them; it was a matter of personal relations with Leo Strauss. Morgenthau, I think, simply tolerated me. Herman Finer—after all, I had worked with him for a year and knew his family very well, so he didn't carry any grudges, and we got along well. We had a difficult period in the '50s and '60s, when we seemed to have trouble recruiting people to come to Chicago. We used to say they've got the climate on the West Coast and they've got culture on the East Coast and nobody wants to come in between to Chicago. We had one very depressing period when six offers we made were turned down in a row.

We had one success that turned out not to be a success. It concerned Henry Kissinger. Along about 1957, I think it was, Kissinger had let it be known that he might consider offers from elsewhere. We thought that was an interesting possibility. I took a trip to New York and had an interview with him, and I was very much impressed. He had admirals and generals and so on coming in and out of the office and on the telephone. So we asked him to consider appointment at Chicago, and he accepted. He came out to Chicago, in the spring of 1958, and had dinner with us at the Quadrangle Club, and that was the extent of our experience with Henry because Harvard promoted him. So we had Kissinger signed up for about three months as a member of the department, and that was all it amounted to. As I say, people who were well-established on the East or on the West Coast were not at that time ready to come to Chicago. Later on, that situation eased and a lot of the younger people who are now at Chicago or have been there recently accepted appointments.

BAKER: In the late 1940s, you started to rebuild, and, by the 1950s, it was certainly again one of the best departments in the country, a different kind of department from the '30s, more diversified, I suppose, in approach, in methodology.

PRITCHETT: Yes. Everyone more or less went his own way. There was no effort made to dictate. There was no problem with respect to the courses one was going to teach.

BAKER: Is this part of the secret, do you think, of the department's success? Commitment to quality, both students and faculty, and a high degree of energy, or at least a good deal of letting one do his own thing?

PRITCHETT: I think so.

Illustrious Colleagues

PRITCHETT: Charles Merriam was a great man. He was great in the sense that he knew directions in which political science ought to be moving, and he started people in those directions, like White and Wright and Gosnell and Lasswell. He had this conception of the interrelationships of political science and the other social sciences. And he was such a genial person, with great personal force. Later on, he was adviser to FDR, a member of the National Resources Planning Board and the President's Committee on Administrative Management and was, for a considerable time, quite obviously, the most important figure in American academic political science.

BAKER: Also, he had very extensive ties in the community, didn't he?

PRITCHETT: Yes, as a matter of fact, he was alderman from the Fifth Ward and he ran for mayor. He was a Republican in those days; later on he changed his registration to Democrat in the New Deal period.

BAKER: He chaired the department for what period of time? A long period, wasn't it?

PRITCHETT: Until 1940. He joined the department in 1900, with the rank of docent, but he didn't become chairman until 1923. Then he was chairman until 1940.

BAKER: He certainly carried a lot of portfolios, though, if he was chairman of the department, stimulating the interaction of the social sciences . . .

PRITCHETT: Going off to Washington when the New Deal came along. Going off to Washington every weekend or so.

Leo Strauss had a tremendous impact, not only in our department but on the teaching of value theory throughout the country. His method was primarily reading the texts. He would take the classic texts and simply go over them with his seminars, line by line. He engendered a most remarkable loyalty and interest—I could almost say fanaticism—on the part of a very substantial number of our students. They formed an organization; they contributed money to tape his lectures. And after they had left the university, his lectures would be typed and sent out to his disciples throughout the country. A good third of the students in our department were Straussites. In his seminars, people sat on the floor since we didn't have a seminar room big enough to accommodate the students who wanted to work with him.

He was one of the great experiences of that department, and he kept on for a couple of years after his retirement age had been reached before he went to Claremont.

Chicago Politics

BAKER: In 1960, you became involved in a local Chicago problem. Would you like to go into that a bit?

PRITCHETT: My friend Herman Finer had developed a contact with Mayor Daley which pleased both sides. Herman Finer, an English scholar, was flattered to be taken in by this rough-and-tumble American big-city mayor. And Mayor Daley, on the other hand, was flattered to have this distinguished professor. So he appointed Finer to the Port Authority or something of that kind; gave him a nonpaid job. Well, Mayor Daley was very much distressed by the publicity on the 1960 election, charges that the election had been stolen for John Kennedy in Chicago. Newspapers were full of allegations of that kind. He asked Herman Finer if Finer could suggest anything that would help to dampen that kind of publicity. He said, "Get some of your colleagues together out at the university." So Herman Finer got Jerry Kerwin and me to go down and have lunch with Mayor Daley while Daley outlined his problem and asked us to see if we couldn't turn off this abusive publicity that Chicago was getting. Very rashly, we agreed to try to do something.

BAKER: No such thing as a free lunch.

PRITCHETT: What he did was to have his press secretary turn over to us all the collection of clippings that the Chicago papers had printed, all of their allegations, and we undertook to go through those and analyze them to see how much there was of value, of really solid fact, in there. And, of course, there were a lot of stories that didn't really bear up under examination. But that was all the material we had. We were in no position, obviously, to analyze the conduct of voting officials in Chicago. But the newspapers got hold of the fact that there was a University of Chicago group that was working for Daley. They began calling us up, asking us what we were doing and so on. They even camped outside Herman Finer's door in the Social Science Building. We were trapped in there. We couldn't get out.

BAKER: Hostages.

PRITCHETT: The newsmen wouldn't leave. Eventually, we wrote a report that wasn't too bad, turned it in to Mayor Daley, and he had it printed. A report by three distinguished political scientists, he said, on the press coverage of the 1960 election in Chicago. The Chicago *Tribune* referred to us for some time as the "three blind mice of the Midway," who could not see what everybody else could see, that the election had been stolen.

That was my most direct contact with Chicago politics and Mayor Daley. It was interesting to get a sense of the power exuding from that man. We met him in his office, we walked out of his office, down the elevator, and down the street to the Bismarck Hotel for lunch. People would line up and bow to him just to have the privilege of saying hello to the mayor. We got a picture of what the influence of the mayor is in that situation.

APSA Politics

PRITCHETT: One of the most interesting jobs I had as president of the Association was to be on the platform with Barry Goldwater at the 1964 convention of the Association in Chicago. It was not the intention of the Association to invite either of the two candidates to speak to the convention, but the Goldwater people invited themselves. They were interested in getting Goldwater to have a chance to talk to political scientists, who were not regarded as generally favorable to him. And so once they had asked to have a platform, the Association could not refuse and we felt, well, we'll have Hubert Humphrey come and talk for the Democrats, and so we'll be preserving our bipartisan character.

Johnson, of course, was the candidate, but he wasn't available, and it turned out that Hubert Humphrey wasn't available either, so we were left with just the Republican candidate speaking to our convention. Something had to be done to make clear that we were not sponsoring Goldwater. What happened was that I, as president of the Association, introduced Don Herzberg, and he, in turn, introduced Goldwater, so in that way there would be no direct link between the officers of the Association and Goldwater. Moreover, I was given a speech to read in introducing Herzberg, and it pointed out how the Association was nonpartisan and how we had often heard from members and candidates before. I said, "Why, only in 1960, Lyndon Johnson spoke to our convention," and there was a tremendous roar from the audience at mention of the name of Lyndon Johnson. Then I said, "And last year, Hubert Humphrey talked to our convention," and there was another roar. You see, this was very clever. It gave the audience a chance to express their views before Goldwater made his speech and took the edge off any resentment that might have been felt on the part of the membership that Goldwater was going to be speaking. As a matter of fact, David Broder, in a column, commented on the "heckling" that Goldwater had received at the convention. I didn't feel there had been any heckling. They laughed at the wrong places sometimes, but I didn't regard that as heckling.

BAKER: It may have been the fault of the speech writers.

PRITCHETT: Yes. And this speech was one in which Goldwater attacked the Supreme Court. He used the opportunity to make his point against the Court quite effectively. Well, that was an interesting experience; having lunch with Barry Goldwater in the midst of a presidential campaign. And he was just as relaxed as he could be, pleasant, noncontroversial, saying nice things about Hubert Humphrey, and so on.

BAKER: Perhaps also the campaign wasn't sufficiently close at that point to make him tense in any event.

PRITCHETT: Perhaps not.

Studying the Court

PRITCHETT: I'm not good as a theoretician at all, so I chose to go into the field of administration. I really was not very well trained in the field of public law, constitutional law. My training was primarily in public administration. I'd always had this residual interest in constitutional law, but it wasn't taught as a graduate subject in our department. I went to the law school of the university and took two quarters of constitutional law and one quarter of administrative law, but it was taught in traditional law school fashion. Consequently, I wasn't well-trained. So, when I got the opportunity to get into the field of constitutional law, I had really to teach myself. I learned along with the students.

BAKER: Well, at least you had a good professor.

PRITCHETT: I can remember, for example, that in one of the early constitutional law courses I taught, the problem of double jeopardy came up, and I didn't have the slightest idea of what the general principles were in the field of double jeopardy. So, in a way, I was a self-made scholar of constitutional law and that may have had certain merits, but obviously it also had some demerits. As the opportunity was available to start teaching in constitutional law, I was struck by some things that perhaps wouldn't have occurred to someone who was better trained in the field, and I began to think about these personal aspects of the judicial experience, and that led me into the work with the dissenting opinions of the Supreme Court, which was the basis for *The Roosevelt Court.*

I had always had a secondary interest in the field of constitutional law. In fact, when I was an undergraduate at Millikin, judicial review was one of our debating topics. So I was interested in following up in this area. I began to subscribe to the *Supreme Court Reporter* and keep up with the decisions of the Court. One day when I was reading one of those opinions, I was struck by what seemed to be an unusual combination of justices in dissent. I wondered what it was that made them join in this rather illogical combination. So I started to approach the problem mathematically—very simple mathematics, of course, simply a study of the dissenting records of the justices in the preceding few terms. This was more or less incidental to my teaching, since I was primarily teaching public administration.

For several years, I did an annual study of the dissenting record of the Supreme Court and published the articles in law reviews. Arthur Krock, in the *New York Times*, picked up one of these reports, and I got publicity in his column of the *New York Times* every year for several years. And, eventually, after having done an annual survey of the Supreme Court for about five or six years, I began to put the materials together—in 1946, I think—and *The Roosevelt Court* was published in 1948.

BAKER: Now, *The Roosevelt Court* made your professional reputation, but was it not treated with a little bit of skepticism in the lay public at the time? This was a very new approach to the Supreme Court.

PRITCHETT: Not only the lay public but also the judges and lawyers. Justice Frankfurter was very vocal in opposition. In fact, I was told by Ed Levi and others that, for a time, everyone who went in to see him was treated to scathing denunciations of my book, and you can read in his published diaries what he thought of that "silly stuff" that Pritchett was doing out in Chicago. On the other hand, of course, the book struck fire with a number of our colleagues. People like Glen Schubert and others regarded this as something that could be followed up, and, of course, this has been done. The whole field of judicial behavior is often dated from the publication of *The Roosevelt Court*, even though those who have gone into that field are much better equipped, technically, than I was and may have carried the studies further than I regarded as profitable.

BAKER: But, at that time, it was something you put on the map, whether it was Frankfurter's map or the professional map.

PRITCHETT: Yes, that's true. It was regarded as a breakthrough in the sense that it treated the decisions of the Court as value statements which could be examined as votes on public policy issues. Consequently, I undertook to line up the votes to see what kinds of blocs were present on the court. This was very low-level mathematics, and it simply enabled one to say with a certain amount of assurance what the alignments were on the Court. These were, perhaps, rather evident, but you couldn't document your findings as fully as you could when you did this kind of research and voting analysis. I didn't have statistical training to go much further as other methods of studying the Supreme Court were developing.

I have reservations about how far you can carry this kind of analysis. For my purposes, it was sufficient to be able to speak with a little more assurance about the relationships on the Court. That was too much for some people, of course. Wallace Mendelson wrote an article in the *American Political Science Review* accusing the entire school of judicial behaviorists, of which he regarded me as the dean, of losing all interest in law. We were not dealing in law at all, we were accusing all of the members of the Court of simply voting their preferences.

On the other hand, I think there are some who were disappointed I didn't propose to go any further in this direction. In *The Vinson Court*, I didn't use quite as much of this mathematical approach as I had in *The Roosevelt Court*, and I subsequently haven't explored it any further. I undertook the rather more traditional task of constitutional analysis. I had a period of three years when I was not chairman at Chicago, and I retired to an office on a different floor during that period and proceeded to turn my notes and my class lectures into a book on the American Constitution, the first edition of which was published in 1959.

BAKER: *The American Constitution* is a very impressive kind of summing up and synthesis of a vast range of materials, and it does draw on a variety of approaches, but it's largely so-called traditional or analytical, or whatever you want to call it.

PRITCHETT: It is, yes.

BAKER: It seems to me this indicates that your general approach to the field has been somewhat eclectic. You have used a little bit of behavioral or quantitative methods when you felt they would answer certain questions, and then you have used other, more traditional methods when you felt that would be more appropriate.

PRITCHETT: Yes. There's one other approach. We can speak of the approach of the Roosevelt and Vinson Court books as judicial behavior and of *The American Constitution* as traditional constitutional law. But there's also what's been generally called the field of judicial process, which has been developed by political scientists who are not satisfied simply with teaching what the Supreme Court says the law is, or with statistical studies of voting behavior. The judicial process approach endeavors to put the judiciary in the political process, to examine the judicial branch in the same way that the administrative branch is dealt with in terms of how it's appointed, what the background is of the judges, how they proceed to develop the reasoning on the basis of which they make decisions, what the problems are in enforcing judicial decisions, and so on.

That entire field of judicial process was of interest to me, and I kept thinking that I really would like to give a course of that sort. Then Walter Murphy, my former student, who had gone to Princeton, proposed that we do a book together on the subject. Consequently, we did write the book *Courts, Judges and Politics*, the first edition of which came out in 1961, and I finally had a book for my course. We've maintained that interest through three editions now. I think it is a very common approach in political science departments today, but ours was really the first and helped to establish the outline, the framework of courses of that sort.

One other thing that I did along this line was the book on *Congress versus the Supreme Court*, dealing with the efforts to limit the Court in the late 1950s. Both Walter and I wrote books on that subject—his is somewhat more extensive than mine—just about the same time and dealing with the same period.

BAKER: There is a relative dearth of scholars of public law at established age level—say their 40's, 50's, at this point—and the result seems to have been that some major institutions have, in the departments of political science, decided not to offer it. Do you think that, like the South, public law will rise again?

PRITCHETT: Well, of course, my answer is affected by my dedication to this field. I certainly hope the field is a live one, and it has seemed to me that the interest in the field of judicial behavior and judicial process has had the effect of tying the public law work more closely into the ongoing programs of departments. Back in the days when political scientists were just reading Supreme Court opinions and not much else, public law was a kind of backwater. But it has been stirred up by the more recent interest, which has endeavored to demonstrate that the Supreme Court is a very important contributor to public policy.

The Changing Discipline

BAKER: You have had a professional involvement as a political scientist for about a half-century now. I think it might be worth your looking back over that rather substantial and interesting period of years and perhaps just contrast what has changed in the discipline.

PRITCHETT: Perhaps most obvious is the matter of scale, the size of the profession. When I went to Chicago, there was just a handful of graduate students, twenty-five or thirty. Political science was such a small operation. Our conventions were small, regional affairs that drew just a handful of people. We met in the lodges in Indiana state parks, so far as the Midwest was concerned. Well, that's obvious. We've gotten much bigger now. The second thing, I suppose,

would be the behavioral revolution. Charles Merriam had a good bit
to do with this. But before long, everyone was undertaking to use
survey methods, teach students statistics, and all the things we more
or less now take for granted. The American Political Science Association had no national office. The president was appointed and had no
staff or responsibilities except to see that a convention was held.

BAKER: The convention and the *Review*, that was about the Association.

PRITCHETT: It's hard to understand how the Association really
got any work done at all when it didn't have a Washington office and
an executive director and so on. The Association is quite a different
kind of experience now.

Gabriel Almond

Gabriel A. Almond was born in Rock Island, Illinois, on January 12, 1911. The University of Chicago provided both his undergraduate and his graduate education. He received the baccalaureate degree in 1932 and the Ph.D. in 1938. His first teaching position was at Brooklyn College, where he taught from 1939 to 1946. He then joined the faculties of Yale (1947–51) and Princeton (1951–59), then returned to Yale (1959–63). He moved to Stanford University in 1963 and served on the faculty there until his retirement in 1976. He served as executive head of the Department of Political Science at Stanford from 1964 to 1969.

During World War II, he was employed by the Office of War Information, where he interacted with a number of other social scientists, including Bernard Berelson, Angus Campbell, and Renis Likert. Throughout his career his major research interests were in comparative politics, both European and the developing nations. His work (with Sidney Verba) The Civic Culture, *attracted attention within the discipline to the possibilities of true cross-cultural approaches to the study of attitudes and behavior, while identifying concepts that have continued to play a pivotal role in the discipline. His early works* The American People and the Foreign Policy *and* The Appeals of Communism *(with James Coleman) demonstrated the value of some of the new methodologies on international politics.*

He served as president of the American Political Science Association in 1965–66, following a term as a vice president and a term on the Council of the APSA. He was also active in the Social Science Research Council, serving in several capacities, including member of the Board of Directors. He has served on the editorial board of sev-

eral major journals, including Public Opinion Quarterly, World Politics, Comparative Politics, *and* Comparative Political Studies.

Gabriel Almond was interviewed in Stanford, California, in September of 1978 by Richard Brody, a colleague who has taught at Stanford University since 1962. He has written extensively on public opinion and voting behavior and has been active in the planning of national election surveys.

The Chicago Experience

ALMOND: I was at the University of Chicago from 1928 until 1938, when I got my Ph.D., with one year out for field research. My original aspiration was to be a journalist, a writer. Right in the middle of my undergraduate career, the Depression hit. It began to get more and more difficult to get any kind of job, and the career of a journalist and writer was much more chancy than the career of a teacher, so I began to think in terms of teaching. Around that time, I happened to take a couple of courses, one with Fred Schuman in international politics and one with Merriam. I got very good grades on my papers, and so, in a sense, that decided me for political science.

That would have been the period of the development of the Department of Political Science at Chicago, the flowering period. The core group consisted of Merriam, Wright, White, Lasswell, and Gosnell. The department was small, so that would represent half of the full-time equivalents of the department. Now, if you're thinking of how much of the time of these five scholars was going into the innovative research that we associate with the Chicago school, you'd have to say that Harold Lasswell was involved full-time in this kind of creative work; Gosnell, similarly, was involved full-time in teaching and research of this kind; Merriam mainly played the role of the mobilizer of resources and the picker of talent; and Quincy Wright and Leonard White had research interests of a conservative, solid, creative sort, but they were also open to new ideas and possibilities.

You can't really understand the political science part of Chicago without the whole social science enterprise. The late '20s and '30s were the period in which the Social Science Research Building was built. It contained all the departments except psychology—all the social sciences, including a substantial part of history. Economics, sociology, political science, and anthropology were all in this five-story building. There must have been roughly forty professors in that building with offices. It would be typical of a graduate career that you would get to know, at least by sight if not for purposes of actual acquaintance or friendship, the economics, anthropology, and sociology faculty as well as the political science faculty. There was a lounge on the second floor, and every afternoon tea and cookies were served, and most faculty members and graduate students made a practice of going to these teas. So the physical setting was such that you thought of yourself as being both a political scientist and a social scientist. Graduate students weren't necessarily housed only with colleagues who were in their field. I think that this relatively intimate setting contributed to the development of the social sciences at Chicago. Also, it was the first university to acknowledge the unity of the social sciences by building a building. But, on top of that, there was the faculty.

While I suffered a bit at the beginning of my career because a Ph.D. in political science from Chicago was a little unconventional, I got an enormous advantage out of it in the period after World War II, when I discovered that I was about a decade ahead in terms of my training as compared with colleagues in my age group. I've often wondered why Chicago turned out to be such a creative place. There are some obvious structural conditions, one of them being that it was a new university that started off with a lot of resources. It didn't have a tradition to buck, it could be selective in deciding what lines to pursue. In addition to that, there were the accidents of just who were the people who were brought in, like Merriam and Park, Burgess and Ogburn in sociology—all very ambitious, imaginative men in a situation in which the institutional limits on what they could do were relatively loose. So it was a combination of an open situation and aggressive, enterprising scholars.

There were also a couple of inventions, as far as the social sciences were concerned. One of them was the organized research umbrella. I think it was the first one that supported social science research. It wasn't a foundation far away, it was a source of funds right there. Another innovation was the relation between research-oriented faculty and graduate students—the research assistantship as a typical part of a graduate student's training, a period of apprenticeship doing actual grown-up research with a creative scholar. That wasn't true of the social sciences in other parts of the country.

Illustrious Political Scientists

ALMOND: Charles Merriam had all these different interests, and he saw how it all fitted together. He was concerned with what he thought of as the professionalization of the public service and thought of bringing to bear on the training of public officials and on their professional standards the knowledge that would be accumulated through the social sciences. This was very much the central theme of Merriam's life. It was science, and it was civic activity; it was moral, not only in the local context but in the national and international context. And he also saw these developments of an empirical and a practical sort in continuous relationship with the history of political theory tradition out of which he came. It was his ambition that somehow he'd pull all this together when he retired, but when he thought, "Now I'm going to sit down and do the *Gemeine Staatslehre*," it just didn't come. In that sense, he felt that his life wasn't fulfilled.

Merriam really had an enormous need for affection, and his relationships with graduate students and with his younger colleagues and his older associates were as whole people. He was concerned about people like myself who came from immigrant families and had to work our way through college. I think it gave him particular pleasure to see these young men and women moving into mainstream careers. And he was concerned about your family. He would go to the weddings of people and get to know your parents if they were around. It was Prohibition for most of the time, and he always had a couple of bottles of Scotch in his filing cabinet. With close friends, he would take a bottle out and have a drink toward the end of the day. There was an air-conditioned bar in Hyde Park at the Shoreland Hotel, where he had a table, and whenever one of his graduate students had, in a sense, made it—passed his prelims or finished his dissertation or got his first job—it was the mark of having made it for Merriam to invite you down to the Shoreland bar and give you a drink in this wonderful, dim, whiskey-smelling atmosphere.

Harold Lasswell was somewhat isolated. He didn't have a lot of graduate students. Most would take one of his courses, but what he was doing, even at Chicago, was a bit on the high-risk side. The impression that somehow Lasswell and Gosnell and that kind of behavioral tendency was the central or mainstream tendency of graduate training and research in the department during those years is not really correct. There may have been half a dozen people who were doing their Ph.D.s under Harold's direction, but there were considerably more whom he influenced and for whom the kind of work that he did legitimated that kind of research.

When I first encountered Lasswell, his was the only door in the Social Science Building that wasn't half glass. It was a solid wooden door, which was symbolic of what he was doing and the kind of mystery that was associated with his work. He, at the time, was a lay member of the Chicago Institute of Psychoanalysis. He was doing psychoanalytic interviewing. He was very much out in front. The things that went on in his laboratory, where he had real machinery and the door that didn't have a glass pane in it, and the kinds of issues he dealt with, and his lack of inhibition—in that Victorian era you just didn't talk about processes like toilet training, specific kinds of sexual activity, homosexuality and the like—all had the effect of making him seem like a somewhat dangerous kind of person to be associated with, and he suffered somewhat from that. I know that the people who did work with him got a lot of his time, and he was extremely generous, both in time and support.

Harold Gosnell was a very shy and gentle soul, who was quite undervalued at the time. The fact that he was so preoccupied with quantitative analysis was viewed as a purely technical kind of accomplishment that didn't really compare with the kinds of research that was done by other members of the department. He was just solidly productive, one book after another, but he wasn't really taken seriously. He wasn't really viewed as a figure of great creative and seminal importance. You can see what a tragedy it was, what happened to the University of Chicago. Somebody as ingenious and as creative as Gosnell, and somehow his quality wasn't appreciated, and there was a conservative reaction, in a methodological sense, that affected the department and really pretty well brought to a close the University of Chicago's contribution to the development of political science.

Research Apprenticeship

ALMOND: After graduating, I had to accumulate a little more money before I could go to graduate school, and I got a job at the Unemployment Relief Service. This was a very exciting place; there were all the various ethnic groups, including blacks and Mexicans, in this area, and they were very angry, sullen, or passive. Lasswell had told me that these things were important for politics. So when I had been doing that job for a couple of weeks, I called Lasswell and said, "Gee, I think there's a chance that we can do some research." We planned it out, that I would try to interest the other complaint aides to make records of the way in which they were approached by people seeking assistance. It was possible to get demographic and other kinds of data on them from their case histories. After six months, I must have had data on a couple of thousand individuals, and it was obviously going to be impossible to do them all. At that time, I didn't know anything about sampling, but Harold Lasswell did, and he said, "Well, look, you take every Nth case." And so I learned about "Nth" just as the King of Siam learned about "et cetera." I learned about Nth, and for me that was a big jump. We ended up with maybe a hundred cases selected according to the way in which they behaved. We wrote that up, and it got published in Ogg's *American Political*

Science Review. As far as I was concerned, it made me because it was unusual to have anything published in your first or second year of graduate work.

A Dissertation Saga

ALMOND: Lasswell was just beginning to write about elites and suggested that I do an elite study. Around this time, Merriam was involved as an entrepreneur in getting the Social Science Research Council established, and they were offering, in 1935, for the first time, a predoctoral field fellowship for the social sciences. I got recommended for one of those. What I proposed to do was utterly fantastic: I was proposing a comparative study of the elite in New York City and Charleston, South Carolina, to get the opposite, premodern extreme, insofar as anything premodern persisted in the United States. I went to New York, bringing my University of Chicago culture with me. I was going to study, not just as a political scientist but as an anthropologist and as a sociologist. But what that meant was that I had to look at New York City as an anthropologist would look at it—a field site. Making contacts with the New York City elite presented some problems because it meant that I had, in some sense, to give false credentials so that I'd get invited to a dinner or a social occasion. And I'd come there as a graduate student working for a Ph.D., but what I really was interested in was encountering these people and seeing at first hand what their attitudes and values were.

Well, my effort at being a participant-observer as a way of researching the elite in New York City lasted until Christmas, as I remember. I just couldn't take it and at the same time do a full day's work at the New York Public Library, which had a whole room on New York. So after my experiment at participant observation, I went fully into this business of really putting together the data for an analysis of the transformation of the elite in New York City from the Revolutionary period to the modern period, by taking temporal crosssections. I collected an enormous body of material. It was quantitative, and this was pre-IBM cards and precalculators. I had each biography on little slips of paper, and I just calculated it myself by hand. I think I ended up with a dissertation that had about 150 major tables. I don't know how many ideas there were in it. When it was finally presented to people like Gosnell and Lasswell and Merriam, they had to acknowledge that I'd accumulated an enormous body of material.

BRODY: You didn't do the South Carolina side of it?

ALMOND: No. That was hopeless. I bit off more than I could chew. I finished the dissertation in 1938 and took my first job at

Brooklyn College. For the first couple of years there, I didn't have time to do anything but go from one class to another. In the first three years of my teaching career, I taught government 130 times, and, just to keep from dying of boredom, I exhausted all the secondary literature on American government. It was possible to do that in those days—everything on parties, everything on legislatures, constitutional law, political theory as it bore on the constitutional system, and all the rest. We had to publish, and for me to get a book out was the most important thing. I had been encouraged by Lasswell and Merriam to see if I could turn the dissertation into a book.

So, in whatever spare time I had in my first three teaching years, I began to accumulate biographical material on New York businessmen, prominent corporation executives, entrepreneurs, corporation lawyers, men who were on the margin between economic power and political power. I collected a couple dozen of those biographies to see if I could explain what kind of propensity they had, ideologically speaking. Was there anything in their psychological development that could illuminate the choice of a reactionary or a conservative or a liberal option on the part of people who, roughly speaking, came from the same economic stratum? So I added three or four major chapters to my doctoral dissertation introducing this psychological dimension. In 1944, I presented the dissertation to the University of Chicago Press. They were very excited about it—wealth and politics, the kind of book that both can be represented as scholarly and might sell.

Merriam, around this time, had become increasingly melancholy. Hutchins had taken over the university. The whole thing that Merriam had built looked as though it was on shaky foundations. Hutchins was ridiculing it. Mortimer Adler ridiculed this kind of crude empiricism. Merriam was perhaps somewhat frightened at the time, too, and, when I went to talk to him about the book, he said, "Well, take that psychological stuff out." What he was concerned about was that I had done some psyching of John D. Rockefeller, who was the founder of the University of Chicago and the source of its funding; and I had gathered material on Carnegie, and the Carnegie Corporation was becoming an important source of research funds. Merriam probably thought, "Here's this little snip. It isn't enough for him to do this dissertation on wealth and politics, which is a risky thing, but he wants to get all this stuff about their family life and how nasty their parents were to them." So, he said, "Take it out," and just gestured with a sweep of his hand. The parts he wanted to take out were the ones I was proudest of—the stuff I had just lovingly put together. When I got back after working on the Strategic Bombing Survey, instead of taking the chapters out, I rewrote them in the form of an article, which was the only part of my dissertation that got published. It's called "Political Attitudes of Wealth," and it was published in the *Journal of Politics.*

So that's the story of my dissertation. In a sense, it tells the story of what had happened to that wonderful department. I think political science took the worst beating of the major social science departments. Hutchins, I think, was resolved not to approve of full professorships for Gosnell and Lasswell. Both of them left around this time, and Merriam was on the margin, so the department went into a period of mediocrity. It was just at that time that Merriam was sitting in judgment of my doctoral dissertation. It might have had a different outcome had it been completed earlier.

The American People and Foreign Policy

BRODY: How is it you came to secondary analysis in *The American People and Foreign Policy?*

ALMOND: Well, why didn't I make a sample survey of attitudes toward foreign policy? I don't think the time was right for it. When I was doing *The American People and Foreign Policy,* I still had the problem of convincing people that the social sciences had something to offer. I was trying to demonstrate the relevance of a whole body of social science methodology and of substantive findings for the study of foreign policy and international relations. I was about five years off from the time when people would say, "Okay, we'll back you up. You go to Carnegie or Rockefeller and ask them for $150,000 to do a survey." They didn't think in those proportions, and they weren't ready to do that. They had to be sold on the relevance of sociological and psychological kinds of research and findings for the study of foreign policy and international relations.

And that's what *The American People and Foreign Policy* did. In the first place, I introduced the notion of the foreign policy elites, which comes from Harold Lasswell. I dealt with mass opinion and its relationship to foreign policy. I took surveys that already had established certain series of questions that allowed me to make some very general statements about the nature of mass opinion in relation to foreign policy. In that connection, I developed the concept of attentive publics and the moodlike character of mass opinion. It had to be a kind of demonstration, and it was successful. People would lift their eyebrows when they looked at one of Lasswell's books, but, when they took my book, which was a much more simpleminded rhetorical presentation, they could see that opinion surveys or even psychoanalytic and psychoanthropological material was useful. There was enough conservative material in there, too, so that it was what the traffic would bear at the time.

The Appeals of Communism

ALMOND: *The Appeals of Communism* study came at the time that McCarthyism was beginning to develop in the United States, and I was hoping to establish what kind of a movement American Communism was, from the point of view of internal security. It offered me the opportunity to use the whole battery of methodologies I had learned at the University of Chicago. I had a psychologist working with me who did some of these more clinical types of interviews. It also involved the interviewing of psychoanalysts and psychiatrists who had Communist patients. It also involved content analysis as a means of establishing the characteristics of the interior culture of a political movement and its peripheral culture. I think that the thing I'm proudest of in *The Appeals of Communism* is that it was the kind of architectonic methodological approach that I was excited by.

The SSRC and Comparative Research

ALMOND: My contacts with the council first go back to the fellowship I got to carry out my doctoral dissertation research in New York, and the values and the criteria reflected in the council had an enormous impact on me. From that point on, I had a sense of identification and involvement with the council. It wasn't clear from the outset what the scope of the Committee on Comparative Politics was going to be. Should it include the Third World? After all, this is after World War II, and you're getting the national explosions in the Middle East and in Africa. Or should it be confined to Europe? At that time, comparative government substantially was European government. It seemed to make sense to have a Committee on Comparative Politics that would deal with more than the Western and the developed areas. But how to do that? How to relate to the prejudices existing in the profession, and, at the same time, set up a committee that could take some initiatives?

When I was appointed chairman of the committee in 1954, I was given a committee that didn't consist of the heavyweights in comparative government. If we had, for example, appointed Friedrich and Finer and men of that stature and commitment, it would have been rather difficult. It was deliberately decided to cut below them in age, to include, among the more conservative members, those who seemed more open to new ideas and also to include people who represented areas outside of Europe. We were also very interested in getting kind of a range of social science interests. We looked at the agenda of the committee as a mixed question of intellectual standards and intellectual politics. That is, what would the traffic bear? As a new committee, we had to establish contact with the practitioners in the field, we had to win the respect of, or at least avoid being attacked by, the more conservative members of the profession.

We picked two kinds of activities in the very beginning. The one was the training of personnel—postdoctoral research training. The second was interest group studies in the extra-American context, not only in Europe, but in other parts of the world. If you looked at the European situation, there was no work at all being done on interest groups and lobbies and pressure groups. As a matter of fact, many European political scientists denied that there were pressure groups in Europe, or they thought of them in Marxist categories.

I think we got our first support from the Ford Foundation for grants for the study of political groups abroad, and we had something like a quarter of a million dollars, which was rather substantial in those days. The idea was that we would invite people in all the area studies to make applications. We made fifteen or twenty awards for field research. We also wanted these studies to be done in such a way as to enhance their cumulativeness, since we were concerned not only with increasing knowledge but also with developing theory. To develop theory, the use of the comparative method was appreciated, and we built into this program a means of encouraging this kind of cumulativeness.

We held three or four research planning conferences at which the people who were going into the field met with their colleagues and with members of the committee. Research plans were discussed and a common conceptual vocabulary exchanged. I think we had unrealistic expectations. We thought that it might result in some theoretical product as well as important monographic studies. Well, it certainly resulted in important monographic studies.

We thought that it was our job on the Committee to make area specialists into political scientists and social scientists. We brought them together by giving them grants and by bringing them to our conferences, so we would meet for a whole summer, and these people would come through for a week of discussion. We gave them a sense of obligation by stressing the importance of comparative work, the development of theory, the relevance of the other social sciences, the understanding of political processes.

The Politics of the Developing Areas

ALMOND: The problem was how to encourage the development of theory, and I suggested it was really through individuals deliberately setting problems for themselves. I think the first crack at this was a conference that we held at Princeton, in 1955, at which I wrote a paper applying Weberian and Parsonian categories to the problem of comparative study. Let me say something about the origins of that paper. I spent a year at the Center for Advanced Study in the Behavioral Sciences. I guess I was beginning to get intrigued by the possibility of doing a little more of a theoretical nature, and what I thought I needed was interaction with anthropologists. I felt that I had a tremendous amount of information about modern, advanced, complex industrial societies and political systems, and what I needed was to interact with somebody who had an equivalent mastery of the small-scale society. It happened to be a very good year for anthropologists. We set up a little seminar on comparative political systems, looking for categories that could come to grips with the problem of the varieties of societies that political scientists were encountering.

Well, before we were through, we developed the categories that were used in *The Politics of the Developing Areas*—interest articulation, interest aggregation, and rule making, rule application, and rule adjudication, instead of law-making, and so on; that was because the anthropologists felt more comfortable with a concept like "rule" than "law." Socialization they understood very well. The notion of political culture was easy for an anthropologist to accept. I convinced the Committee on Comparative Politics to join with the Center of International Studies at Princeton, where I was then doing my research, in a collaborative venture of commissioning the ablest area specialists we could find to work along with me (and Jim Coleman, as time went on) in putting out a book on the new nations, the developing areas.

The first version of *The Politics of the Developing Areas* was *Politics of the Underdeveloped Areas*. It didn't strike us as being a pejorative term; it was a descriptive, analytical one. I remember receiving a letter from Dan Rustow, who was in the Middle East. He said, "It's absolutely impossible. You cannot call this book *The Politics of the Underdeveloped Areas*." And it suddenly occurred to us that it just couldn't be done. Charlie Wilson, who was secretary of defense under Eisenhower, made a speech around this time and he used this wonderful euphemism, "developing areas." And so a brilliant thought occurred to me—let's call them "the developing areas."

The idea was that my paper would be circulated to the people who would author analyses of the politics of the countries of their particular areas of the world, in terms of those categories. Looking back on it, it's easy to exaggerate the naïveté of the people who were doing that work. We knew that this was going to be a very first approximation, but it was better than nothing. It was looked upon as a demonstration. The theoretical part was looked upon as a demonstration and so were the applications of the theoretical parts to the various parts of the world; you might say it was an effort to push the field ahead theoretically by showing what it's possible to do.

BRODY: Thinking about that framework, would you agree that the research that follows seems to have difficulty employing the model? I wonder, as you reflect back on this experience, whether you feel that the enterprise itself is procrustean or whether the people who knew something about these countries simply weren't flexible enough to adopt social science categories.

ALMOND: Well, I think both. If you're going to be a classifier, you've got to be prepared to overlook some uniquenesses; you've got to massage things a bit. I've often been bemused at some of the critics who have taken cracks at classificatory or typological activity. I've always felt that one has to be very tentative about it. It's quite crude in the beginning, but, over time, as you develop more and more powerful means of discriminating significant differences, classification improves. I think it's best done the way we did it, in a movement back and forth between the examination of cases and then efforts at codification and classification. I've never blushed when someone would come along and say "Well, here's this classification scheme back in 1956, and look how crude it is." Of all the things I've ever written, I think *The Politics of the Developing Areas* gave me the most joy. Somehow things came together. It was a case of my sociological, theoretical background intersecting with my comparative politics, political science background, and the intersections were even more complex than that.

The Civic Culture

ALMOND: *The Civic Culture* was an effort to apply modern social science to the collapse of democracy and the totalitarian experience of the 1930s and World War II, with all its horrors. Why did Germany and Italy develop this grotesque form of politics? German science was as far as we had gotten, and Italy had the culture of the Renaissance and the church. How to explain this kind of barbarism, or, on the other side, how to explain why Britain survived what looked like superhuman kinds of pressures and threats, with its institutions largely intact and with a minimum of denial of judicial process and the like. The idea of studying what we later came to call political socialization had been an aspiration during my graduate years. In the back of my mind was the notion of doing a kind of civic training study, and it was the most natural thing to apply it to questions we were asking in comparative government at that time. From the psycho-cultural part of my memory came hypotheses and theories about family authority patterns, differences from one country to the next.

In general, it was an effort to discover how much explanatory power one could get from political culture. By political culture we meant propensities, values, beliefs, conceptions of how to go about functioning effectively in politics, and the like. So there met in *The Civic Culture* the kind of traditional interests and hypotheses coming out of comparative politics, the psychoanthropological part of my background, and the sociological-theoretical part of it as well. In addition, I had in Sid Verba an unusual collaborator. I had originally thought we would have to collaborate with a social psychologist because I didn't think that, between the two of us, we fully commanded social psychology and survey methodology. But Sid was bound to master and to learn as much as could be learned. So we pretty well did it ourselves. Both of us had enormous chutzpah, and we enjoyed the whole undertaking. It was an innovative thing to do, and it had a substantial impact in comparative government, in the study of political behavior, and it rapidly was assimilated into course work not only in political science but in the other social sciences. The data from the study were cleaned and made available through the Survey Research Center Consortium, and, for several years in the 1960s, I think it was the most frequently used body of data for purposes of all kinds of analyses.

We were concerned with the relationship between political culture and political structure. When we wrote it, both Sid and I would have imputed more persistence to those attitudes than turned out to be the case. That is, I don't think that either one of us would have predicted the rapid decline, for example, in Germany of the indicators of democratic indifference or that there would be the sharp decline in trust of governmental institutions in Britain and in the United States. We discovered that, while a civic culture helps explain democratic stability, these attitudinal tendencies are a good deal less stable than we had assumed and that they can be acquired and lost, at least in part, more quickly.

Crisis, Choice, and Change

ALMOND: That book really reflects my intellectual style, which is essentially as a synthesizer. I've gotten the greatest mileage when, for example, I've combined sociological theory, let's say, with emerging theory relating to the democratic infrastructure in the nineteenth and twentieth centuries, as occurred in *The Politics of the Developing Areas* or in *The Civic Culture*, when I could synthesize some problems in the field of comparative politics with sociological theory and with psychological and psychoanthropological theory. And again, using as rigorous a methodology as we had available. That's really the way I work. In the case of *Crisis, Choice and Change*, I was kind of the ultimate last-ditch compromiser. I had never given up history as an approach to explanation, and so it was obvious to me that even though I had moved in a sociological and psychological direction, ultimately, if I were concerned with explaining change, I would have to use historical case material as a test of their validity and utility. That's what we did in *Crisis, Choice and Change*. We took four distinctive approaches to development and used them in historical contexts, not so much to generate a theory but to demonstrate that these approaches had to be used together to get an adequate explanation of the historical outcome.

David Truman

David B. Truman was born June 1, 1913, in Evanston, Illinois. He received his B.A. from Amherst College in 1935, and his M.A. in 1936 and his Ph.D. in 1939 both from the University of Chicago.

After two years in a temporary position at Bennington College, he joined the Department of Government at Cornell University as an instructor. In 1942, he took leave to work with the Foreign Broadcast Monitoring Service of the FCC. A year later, he became deputy director of the Division of Program Surveys, which did opinion and attitude surveys for a variety of war agencies. In 1944, he received a commission in the navy and was assigned to planning and survey divisions for the remainder of the war and in the early postwar period.

After the war, he served as a visiting lecturer at Harvard and then joined the faculty at Williams College, where he became the first director of the Roper Public Opinion Center. In 1950, he moved to Columbia University on a visiting appointment, joining the Columbia faculty on a permanent basis a year later. In 1962, he became dean of Columbia College and, in 1967, vice president and provost of Columbia University. In 1969, he moved from Columbia to Mount Holyoke College as president of that institution.

As a staff member of the SSRC Committee on Pre-Election Polls and Forecasts, he was a key figure in the committee's report on the failure of the polls in the 1948 presidential election, The Pre-Election Polls of 1948. *His book* The Governmental Process *was a thorough examination of group politics in America, and in* The Congressional Party, *his examination of behavior in Congress, he used extensive computer analysis of aggregate data, exploring methods that were new to political science.*

He is a fellow of the American Academy of Arts and Sciences and served as president of the American Political Science Association in 1965.

David Truman was interviewed in New York City in March of 1979 by Donald Stokes, who has taught and held administrative positions at Princeton University since 1974, after many years at the University of Michigan. He was a pioneer in the development of the American election surveys and co-author of a number of major books and articles on voting behavior.

Early Interest in Politics and Political Science

STOKES: Dave, I suppose the first line of questioning that would be of interest is how you came to have an interest in political science.

TRUMAN: I had an early interest—a kind of boyhood interest—in politics, which an awful lot of us have had, the same way you get interested in baseball— as a spectator sport. But interest in political science as such I didn't get until I was in college, simply because, prior to that, I wouldn't have had the remotest idea what it was all about. But I did have an interest always in what was going on on the political scene; always from maybe about the age of eleven on. I guess my first political memory was listening to the radio broadcast of the 1924 Democratic Presidential Convention, the 103 ballots. In fact, that was the first one that was on the radio. And, of course, the LaFollette candidacy of that year was something that was big in the Middle West, and I remember hearing my parents and their friends arguing about the pros and cons.

STOKES: Were there major family influences?

TRUMAN: It really was at college that the thing developed. I took a minor in political science. The department at Amherst College then was, I think, two persons. Phillips Bradley was the senior member of the department, and Phil took a very active interest in me. We were really good friends as teacher and student, so that I had a fairly substantial minor in political science, and the real choice came along at the point where I was deciding whether I'd go to law school or to graduate school in political science.

STOKES: What would you have read in those days for political science as a minor?

TRUMAN: Well, I'm afraid one read fairly conventional kinds of things. It was a strange kind of minor in that I never had a course in American government in my life, either at the undergraduate or the graduate level. D.W. Brogan's book on American government first came out, and it was influential, and Laski's *Grammar of Politics* was read pretty actively still at that stage of the game. And, of course, some of his more contemporary things that were more controversial at that stage, like *Democracy in Crisis*, which was based on his Weil lectures.

When I was turned down for a fellowship at Harvard and was given a scholarship at Chicago—and thought my life had come to an end—in fact, that was the greatest advantage I could have had. Chicago was the right place to be in the '30s. You couldn't be around that department for very long without having the questions of definition, of delimitation, of concept, of method, as just a part of your daily living all the time. That was when I first became aware of the field. The challenge has been one of: how do you bring some orderly meaning into this mess of unruly data? How do you bring meaning at a level somewhat above a purely descriptive, formalistic kind of thing? How do you get a handle on things?

And this was Merriam's genius, I think. He was a very unsystematic guy himself, but he was stimulating and challenging, and he attracted the characters around him like Harold Lasswell and Fred Schuman and others of that sort because they were offbeat. Even Harold Gosnell, at that stage, because Harold was doing what was regarded as very screwy stuff. You know, coefficients of correlation and stuff like that. It wasn't what was supposed to be done in political science.

The University of Chicago and Graduate Studies

STOKES: Well, coming back to Chicago and your entry into Chicago, I'd be interested just in having you reset that scene for us. What did it feel like as you went there as a new graduate student?

TRUMAN: Terrifying.

STOKES: How did you spend your days, weeks? What was a course?

TRUMAN: It was terrifying. Everyone has that experience, that change, when you go from, particularly, a small undergraduate college to a university, a sense that now you're playing for keeps, and everybody around you is smarter than you are, and you're not going to survive more than a couple of weeks. But at the same time there was an enormously challenging kind of atmosphere. Most of us spent an awful lot of time simply catching up—reading, reading, reading.

Some of the courses were really very conventional. It's interesting that Merriam's lecture courses were just in the history of political thought. I think, in some ways, they were very little more than the notes he'd taken from William Archibald Dunning when he was at

Columbia, who in turn had copied them out of a then-untranslated French history of political thought. I don't think that's quite fair, but there were certain similarities of points, shall we say. Other people there had unusual things in the way of courses. Harold Lasswell, of course, and Harold had a series of courses that were offbeat in content and strikingly offbeat in title. Nonrational Factors in Political Behavior. And Gosnell's studies, which were basically then studies of voting behavior from the aggregate voting statistics, and so on. You didn't find many courses like that around in other universities.

Among the most stimulating teachers in that department was Quincy Wright, whose course in international law I still think is one of the finest courses I ever took from anybody in my life. Leonard White was another one. Leonard, of course, was doing his public administration then. Public administration was the big field in that period.

STOKES: You were studying administrative decentralization?

TRUMAN: Yes. White ended up as my sponsor on that dissertation, although the initial idea, curiously, came from John Gaus. He was an Amherst graduate twenty years ahead of me. And we happened to have been in the same undergraduate fraternity. And Gaus, wonderful man that he was, had a certain slightly sentimental streak to him. He kind of took me under his wing. He made one of his many visits to Chicago to give a series of courses, and I was detailed to be his assistant, and we became very good friends. John said to me, "You know, why don't you consider doing something dealing with this problem of field offices, and maybe I could, out of my grant, give you a little help, so you could come down to Washington and maybe do a little bit of interviewing."

STOKES: How many graduate students were there in that department?

TRUMAN: About one hundred. For those days, it was quite a large department. But there were in that social science building at Chicago—which itself was an important thing because they had the departments all mixed up; they didn't have all the political scientists in one place—research assistants all over the place. And this made for a whole culture all by itself in that building, and you talked shop with everybody around; that was the center of life. If you were lucky enough to be a research assistant or a fellow and had quarters in that building, you lived in an almost English college atmosphere, although you didn't reside there. The last three years I was there, I was a research assistant. I made the magnificent sum of $86.11 a month.

STOKES: Looking around the profession or the discipline at that time, there was Harvard, and there was Chicago. And what other places were there?

TRUMAN: There was Berkeley, of course, and Stanford. And Michigan had a good department, a recognized department, at that stage. There were good people at Penn and scattered around various places. But Chicago was the place that had to be reckoned with. It was a very offbeat place. Harvard was a good solid department. They were just doing fairly conventional things.

Bennington, Cornell, and Early Thoughts on Interest Groups

STOKES: Dave, now let's get on the train for Bennington. You went initially in 1939, for one year.

TRUMAN: One year, and then I was invited to stay for a second year, which was nice. And two years was about the right length of time to be there, because it was so pleasant and congenial that, if I'd stayed much longer, I think I would have drowned in the lotus blossoms.

STOKES: What sort of teaching did you do?

TRUMAN: Well, it was the easiest teaching in some ways that I ever did, because the numbers were so small. The largest class I ever had at Bennington, I think, was about six students. The hard part was that I was covering the waterfront, and they also had a practice then that you didn't announce necessarily ahead of time what the courses were. You waited till the students came and asked you what they'd like to have you teach.

STOKES: What were you reading in those days and writing?

TRUMAN: Well, I did have to revise the dissertation for publication, which took a fair amount of time. The other thing, actually, that I started on at that time, with my wife's assistance, as I usually did have—always did have, I should say—was something that then didn't come to anything. I started playing around with roll call votes in the House and Senate.

STOKES: Did you really?

TRUMAN: Yes. Because, again, I had read Stuart Rice when I was in graduate school, and I'd always thought more could be done by a considerable measure than he had succeeded in doing. It's a good thing I didn't pursue it because there weren't any computers then, and if I'd tried to do anything without even the kind of rudimentary computer I used in the early '50s, I never would have gotten there. So I had, until a few years ago, a whole bunch of work sheets that we had developed and started doing some coding on, and I finally junked them because obviously they weren't going to do any good for anybody.

STOKES: And were you heavily into Bentley at that time?

TRUMAN: No.

STOKES: You weren't.

TRUMAN: No, that didn't really happen until I went to Cornell in 1941, where I taught a course in the department on—I think they called it lobbies—and I was talking then with Leonard Cottrell, who was in sociology at Cornell, and he was kind of annoyed with the stuffiness of the government department at Cornell, with reasonable basis. He said to me, "You know, you really ought to use some of that Bentley stuff." And he said, "As a matter of fact, there's a book to be written in that area." He was the one who kind of reintroduced me to it, and I had to come—again, I had to come to grips with it, because I had to teach a course. Cornell was a marvelous place.

STOKES: How large a department was it?

TRUMAN: It was quite small. I would guess, if my recollection's right, it was maybe five or six, not more than that.

TRUMAN: But the thing that was really kind of startling about it was the scale. My first class I walked into in the government department was 125 students.

STOKES: Did you do some graduate teaching yourself?

TRUMAN: No. No, because I had this upper junior-senior level course, the one that scared me to death because of its size, and then I had two or three sections of this interdepartmental course, so that was my load. I think I sat in on a few doctoral exams, that was about all.

Wartime and Government Employment

STOKES: Dave, Pearl Harbor did come, and, presumably, as the year went on, you were increasingly aware you'd be doing something else. How did that all work?

TRUMAN: It was only a few days after Pearl Harbor, I think, when a couple of kinds of inquiries began to come in. One was from the Civil Service Commission for a job down there and another was from a friend of mine in the Office of Price Administration. I decided to go with OPA, and during the whole of that second semester, I commuted down to Washington and put in a couple of days a week and then back up to Ithaca. But as the spring went on, I got an inquiry from Goodwin Watson at the Federal Communications Commission asking me if I were interested in taking a job there. Which I did, in June, and transferred over from OPA and went to Washington full time then.

STOKES: Well, now, that went on till March '43. And then you shifted over to the Division of Program Surveys?

TRUMAN: Well, I had gotten Angus Campbell a bit, because he came over to talk to us about some aspect of what was going on at Program Surveys and whether they could help us. I can't remember what it was. I got acquainted with him. I think it's not unfair to say that Ren Likert was one of the most imaginative people I've ever known and was a great promoter, but he wasn't the world's best manager. They had built their division up to the point where it was quite sizable, and, in order to keep it going, it had to get a certain number of contracts, transfers of funds, from other departments of the government. And frankly, many times he'd sort of underprice the product and so on, and so—things were getting a little messy. And so I think Angus sold Ren on the idea that I was—that, one, he needed somebody to be the deputy and the administrator and, two, that I was the one to do it.

Well, Ren could sell refrigerators to Eskimos and fur coats in the tropics. The biggest first client that the division had, I think, outside of the Department of Agriculture, was the Treasury Department, in connection with the sale of war bonds. Ren persuaded some Doubting Thomases over at the Treasury that, in fact, this sample business was really something. I remember the thing that really convinced them was when Doc came in and, on the basis of a relatively small sample—I can't remember what it was, it was long before probability sampling, by the way—told them within a very small margin exactly how many war bonds they had outstanding in people's hands. And they checked it against the Treasury records, and he was right. They were damned impressed.

So they made that leap of faith that was involved. So we were, in effect, doing market research for them and quite a lot for OPA. It was a strenuous year. But, again, I learned an awful lot. But Doc Cartwright, Angus Campbell, Dick Crutchfield, Burt Fisher, a whole bunch of those guys, were there around that shop, and I learned some of the lore about sampling, about questionnaire construction, about nondirective interviewing—again, I was sitting in on a seminar for free.

STOKES: And you did that for just a year.

TRUMAN: I also increasingly got a feeling of unease, of being my age, male, civilian in Washington, just riding the buses. Not that anybody did anything, but you know you couldn't help feeling: am I doing what I ought to be doing or the most that I could be doing? I decided that I was going to volunteer for the navy. I had great ideas about being a fighter director on a carrier or something like that. They changed my clothes and cut my salary in half and put me behind a calculating machine in Washington.

STOKES: One of the things to be said about your war experience is that, just as your early experience in that social science building had had multidisciplinary aspects, so in Washington you were thrown in with real social scientists.

TRUMAN: Yes.

STOKES: But they were from all over the lot in disciplinary terms.

TRUMAN: Right. I was still, in a sense, engaged in that quest that had started way back when I was a graduate student in Chicago, that Merriam used to plant, namely, can you find some tools here that will help you to get a better grasp of your own substantive field of interest? I was still doing that, without necessarily knowing I was doing it. One of the things it did was make my first real acquaintance with V.O. Key, whom I'd not known at Chicago. And the other one was that, when I went to Harvard after the war, to that department—which was a strange year's experience—I found myself to be the only member of that department who, for example, had any interest in talking and getting acquainted with the people in the Department of Social Relations.

And I used to sit down and talk with Sam Stouffer, and I was welcome in the halls of the social relations department. Key was starting his career by the time I got to the University of Chicago. I had had one brief bit of correspondence with him in the fall of '41, when the first edition of his textbook came out, and I was teaching the course at Cornell. I remember writing him a fan letter, because that book was like a breath of fresh air.

The next time, when I got really acquainted with him, was—after I left the Division of Program Surveys, I wrote a piece for the *Public Administration Review* on the use of public opinion surveys in public administration, and V.O. wrote me a note and made a very characteristic V.O. gesture, as you know, because he was famous for those little five-line notes. He wrote a little note, saying, "I enjoyed your article. I hope perhaps we can get together for lunch sometime." That was the start really of the fact that my book that I wanted to write was published by Knopf. Because V.O. became the editor—consulting editor—for Knopf, right after the war. He sent their representative up to sign me up to write the book. That was the year I was at Harvard. So that, in a curious kind of way, the fact that I'd been writing up what—some of what—I'd learned at Program Surveys in the *Public Administration Review*, started up a friendship with V.O. that lasted as long as he lived.

I think now political science is in a better shape to accept that kind of influence than it would have been back in the early '40s, when, in fact, most political science was legal formalities, rather pedestrian institutional description, and exhortation. And it was pretty dreary. It really was pretty damn dreary.

Time at Harvard and Organizing the Roper Center at Williams

STOKES: Maybe that's the bridge line for us to get onto Harvard.

TRUMAN: That was an interesting year at Harvard, actually. And I went there because they were the only place that would offer me enough to go. I had to have $4,000, I figured. And Berkeley offered me $3,600, and Cornell offered me $3,600, and Harvard offered me $4,000. So I went to Harvard.

It was a rugged year. I said earlier, I made some very good friends with people like Sam Stouffer. I made some good friends in the government department, too. Especially Merle Fainsod, who was chairman of the department that year. The thing that made the year rugged, of course, was simply that I had been away from any teaching for four years, and I had huge classes. My God, I gave a course the second semester in politics and voting behavior and parties that had 250 students, and I shocked all the government department by teaching things out of *The People's Choice*. Nobody believed that political science had anything to learn from Paul Lazarsfeld, for heaven's sake. Pretty silly.

I taught two sections of gov one and one lecture course of my own and I had twenty tutees, and I sat on doctoral exams and so on. I didn't like Harvard, quite frankly. There was a kind of rigidity, falseness. And, as I say, the reason I'd gone back into teaching was, I had a book I wanted to write, and I had a feeling that was not the atmosphere in which I'd be able to produce. So, at the middle of the year, when Merle said the department had recommended me to a regular appointment as an assistant professor, I told him that if something came up that had more meaning to me, I wanted to feel free to resign and take it.

Well, it did. Elmo Roper had given his collection to Williams. And they were considering whom they should appoint as the first curator of the Roper collection. And Julian Woodward remembered that Dave Truman had been working with Ren Likert, and he was now at Harvard. So that's why I got there. I was brought to start the Roper collection, and the Roper collection then was a lot of boxes and a card-counting sorter and a couple of file cases and Ellie and me.

We devised the indexing system and the means of repairing the cards and getting them in shape so people could use them. And I did teach a course in public opinion and made the kids do some analysis, pretty crude, using a card-counting sorter. But the damn thing would jam, as you know how the old ones used to do. We weren't even far enough along so that we could afford to have a tabulator. We had just a card-counting sorter. That was a slow way of doing analysis. This was the horse and buggy stage, but it was good. But the main thing was that it gave me an atmosphere—not a great deal of time, but it gave me an atmosphere in which I could begin to get going on my book. I'd outlined it during the year I was at Harvard, outlined in the sense I had a series of chapter headings. And I began to—actually began to write in the summer of '48. Most of it was written in summers.

STOKES: And it would have been about three years in the making?

TRUMAN: I finished it in the summer of '50, just before I went to Columbia. I mean, the actual writing.

STOKES: Well, Dave, how did your conception of that book change over time, and how did you see it fitting into the field as its intellectual development then was?

TRUMAN: I was attracted by the sociological and psychological insights that I had been exposed to. The most fundamental difference between what I was trying to do and what Bentley did is that he was afraid of psychology, and for good reason. And the important change that had occurred, really, was that attitudes had become something that could be dealt with empirically. I remember it being exciting during the course of writing the book. That excitement of feeling, from time to time, as you went along, there's a piece that fits in here. Maybe this isn't right, but, by God, it makes more sense in that way than it did previously. Of course, I was teaching a course in this kind of thing, or using it in the course, all the time I was at Williams, so there was that useful sort of interplay between my writing and what I was saying in class. It was a very interesting, very satisfying experience. I must say I get a great kick out of that book still even being read.

STOKES: Dave, that feeds into the next question that I would like to ask: what was your sense of where it fitted in forcing sense into the field as it then was, and what flowed from that?

TRUMAN: I think I had the feeling that one has with a young child. Hope and apprehension and a kind of prospective, tentative pride. I remember, when I was writing it, I sent it chapter by chapter to V.O. as it went along, because he was the consulting editor for Knopf, and he read every chapter and wrote comments for me. And I remember at one point, about halfway through, he wrote me a note, and he said, "If you keep it up this way you've got a minor classic." I had hopes for it but a good deal of anxiety. When you get it out there, and people start reading it, it may just turn out to be a real turkey, and people say, well, this hasn't got anything new in it. So I had hope but apprehension.

I remember saying to my wife when we were talking about it— well, she asked me once, "You're working awful hard on this. What do you really want out of this thing? Do you hope you're going to make a lot of money?" And I said, "No, I don't think I will" (and of course I haven't because it hasn't sold that much) but I said, "I would like it to establish me as a political scientist." And for it I hoped that it would help to give a few graduate students and young scholars who were coming along a base from which they could take off to do something different.

STOKES: Before we leave Williamstown, where had the Roper collection got to by that time?

TRUMAN: We improved the thing physically, but it was very little used by members of the Williams faculty or by Williams students. And at that stage, we were getting comparatively little use from others outside. The location was an almost insuperable handicap because it was relatively inaccessible. Frankly, it was not terribly valuable in many ways, as it stood, when I got it. Not only because it hadn't been organized but because of the technical quality of the sampling. You never knew, for secondary analysis purposes, whether you could trust it or not. I don't mean there was anything dishonest in it, but you know of the problems that happened in '48 with the Roper sample.

STOKES: Sure.

SSRC Works to Legitimize Survey Data and Political Behavior

STOKES: Let me draw you out a little bit on that '48 episode.

TRUMAN: V.O. Key was a member of the overall SSRC committee that was concerned about the matter when they decided after the debacle in November of '48 that some group ought to do a study of why it happened, not just for history, but because the fear was that the acute embarrassment of the commercial polls would handicap the development of support for the sample survey instrument in more serious fashion.

Pen Herring was by then president of the SSRC, and he was, of course, the key figure. Sam Stouffer was very much concerned about it. Sam was on the committee. I came in as a member of the staff, not as a member of the committee. It was a very interesting bunch, because we wrote that book in the period from about the fifteenth of

November to the first of January. I know about the beginning date because I remember spending Thanksgiving, including Thanksgiving Day, in Princeton, with that staff, working all day Thanksgiving Day, and there was Fred Stephan and Fred Mosteller, who was chief of staff, and Herb Hyman, and Eli Marks, and Phil McCarthy, and me, and we just slaved right straight through.

STOKES: And that helped create a climate of support for that sort of thing?

TRUMAN: Yes, I think it really did, because I'd already been doing a certain amount quietly for Pen, at the SSRC. The Bureau of the Census had published some election statistics, and there was Robinson's collection that was made out at Stanford, and that was just about it. The whole business of trying to get the equivalent of *America Votes*, which now everyone takes for granted, was just hell. I wasn't the only one involved. V.O. and Alex Heard came up with some of the same conclusions when they were doing *Southern Politics*—that we have these among other bodies of data—because one of the things I'm convinced that has speeded up the power of the economists is that the society has generated their data. They have a good, long, pretty reliable time series, for most of what they need, and we really got virtually nothing. I think the '48 experience persuaded a lot of people who otherwise hadn't been persuaded that this was in fact critical. There were other things that came out of it, like the importance of the technical things in the surveys that were so deficient.

STOKES: Did that give a substantial thrust forward to the interest of Carnegie and in funding, through the SSRC committee, the '52 study?

TRUMAN: Yes, it did, I think. The sequence ran something like this. There was that '48 group, and then, in '49, came V.O. Key's *Southern Politics*, which was the document around which a very lengthy conference on political behavior was held on the Ann Arbor campus. And then the establishment of the SSRC Committee on Political Behavior, and the sponsorship of the '52 study by the Michigan group. They were all sort of sequentially and otherwise connected with one another. V.O.'s *Southern Politics*, I think, has got to be recognized as a landmark piece in that area.

He had to be framed into doing that *Southern Politics* job because Roscoe Martin, who had been with him in the Budget Bureau and had known him in Texas, wanted him to do a job on the southern one-party system, and V.O. kept saying no, he had other plans. Roscoe worked it around through V.O.'s bosses at the Budget Bureau and at Hopkins and had him out on a limb where he couldn't say no. But he didn't want to do it.

Comments on Columbia University

STOKES: Well, now, Dave, I would like to turn back to your move to Columbia and pick up the story there.

TRUMAN: All right. That was an interesting case of the man who came to dinner, because I went down there in the fall of '50 for a one-year visit and stayed for nineteen years. I loved the undergraduate teaching in the college at Columbia as I have not any other that I've ever done.

STOKES: Really?

TRUMAN: That was the most exciting group of undergraduate students I've ever had.

STOKES: It was just primarily the quality of the students?

TRUMAN: Not that they were necessarily a lot brighter than the ones I've had, say, at Bennington or at Harvard or at Williams, but they were hungrier, and they therefore kept one on one's toes.

And the other thing was that there was a marvelous group of men in that faculty who were wonderfully generous and a kind of democracy of the intellect about Columbia, which I enormously respected. One was not what your credentials were. One was what one had to say. You knew you were being listened to if you had something to say, and if you didn't have anything to say it didn't make any difference what your rank was, you were going to be ignored. It was a place where one worked very hard. That was partly, of course, because Columbia has always taken its pace from this city. There's a pulse about the place that's just like the pulse you feel down in midtown Manhattan. And, in that respect, it's unlike any other campus I've ever spent any time on. It's not—the pace is not that of New Haven or Princeton or Cambridge or Ann Arbor. And that can be very exciting. It also can drive you insane if you don't dilute it a little occasionally.

STOKES: You also had some remarkable figures, in what I'll call loosely your own generation. Wally Sayre, Dick Neustadt—

TRUMAN: Yes. Dick came along later. Bill Fox, Herb Deane. It was a marvelously interesting bunch, and Dick Neustadt and Wally Sayre came along later, but they belonged in that group and belonged quickly. There were some absolutely first-rate, very exciting people who, because of the structure of what Columbia calls the Faculty of Political Science, were involved with one another in examinations and so on.

STOKES: There was inherent in the organization of at least the social science disciplinary departments there more cross-fertilization than would ever have been true at Harvard.

TRUMAN: I think so. I think so. Departmental lines were still fairly strong at Columbia, despite that structure, but I think there was more cross-penetration as a consequence of the tradition of the Faculty of Political Science having grown up as a school back in the early days of its organization.

The "Behavioral Revolution"

STOKES: What you've just said is a natural lead-in to the behavioral revolution, so-called—where it came from, what it really was, what has happened to it. I'd be very interested to hear you go over that sort of ground, Dave.

TRUMAN: Well, I think it came out of a lot of the threads we've already been talking about. But I think it would be—it's a mistake to overstandardize the definition of what it was. It was a kind of multifaceted expression of dissatisfaction with the constraints and the formalities of the conventional political science, which we had inherited.

STOKES: Exactly the sort of delight you felt in reading V.O.'s text.

TRUMAN: Right. That kind of freshness, or certainly when he did the *Southern Politics*. Frankly, the excitement that I felt the first time that I read Paul Lazerfeld's book *The People's Choice*, which I read just before I went up to teach at Harvard. That feeling that here's a piece of something that sets an awful lot of otherwise disparate, jackstraw bits of data into some kind of framework where it sings a little bit. And I think that thrust, that impulse, was the only thing that was in common among really a quite diverse series of efforts.

The reaction against it is—I guess it's as hard to characterize as the thing itself. The reaction has been as multifaceted as the original. On the other hand, I also think the reaction has been perfectly understandable, because there has been a tendency to get so fascinated with the gadgetry—particularly as sophisticated, quantitative techniques and the computers and even, I must say, the sample survey, have become more readily available—with what Lasswell used to refer to as the systematic elaboration of the obvious, a minute dissection of things that don't make any difference. I remember V.O. used to worry about that, and, good gracious, he's been gone fifteen years, but he would say, you know, one of the things we ought to watch out for is these guys are going to stop asking any good questions that are worth trying to answer. I wish, and I suspect that the power of the tools that we have and the increased sophistication of some of the means of insight that we have now could be harnessed to some of the big questions. Of course, then, the politicization of the profession, not only ours but most of the others, in the wake of the late '60s and Vietnam is just terribly distressing to me.

Discussion of His Own Research

STOKES: Let me ask you something more about the continuity in your own scholarship. What stood between *The Governmental Process* and *The Congressional Party*? Does one connect with the other?

TRUMAN: Well, one connects with the other in a certain way. Having gotten—subsequent to *The Governmental Process*—having gotten a bit noisy about the importance of empirical research and good, hard data and one thing and another, I decided that it was high time I put my money where my mouth was.

I said earlier that I'd been convinced way back, as early as '39 and before, that there was more that could be done with roll call data, and, when we had a seminar, an SSRC summer seminar, out in Chicago in the summer of '51, I did some planning on that at that time, and my concern, of course, was with party structure and leadership in the Congress, but I had a notion that the careful use of the roll call data would throw some significant light on that. And besides, it seems funny now to think back on it, but the emphasis on the presidency and the executive branch in that period was overwhelming, and the amount of literature that there was in the middle '50s that was available that dealt with the Congress, with the legislative branch, was really very slight and very poor. And I proved one thing to myself, and that was in fact one could use roll call data to find out quite a lot of interesting stuff, not about individuals necessarily, but about structures.

STOKES: If you're putting your finger on the two or three most interesting things that you felt came out of that, what would they be?

TRUMAN: Well, one was the thing I really stumbled on, about the business of the tendency for delegations from the same states to vote the same way. I would be interested to check it now because, with the decline in the party system that has occurred in recent years, you wonder whether maybe that's become more fragmented. The other was, I think, that—the rather obvious point, perhaps— what I was able to show about the origins within the pattern of the two parties, both in the House and the Senate, of the individuals who were likely to become the key leaders. That is, they were middlemen, structurally. Then, more as a consequence of the interviewing that I did than of anything else, I began to get some sense of the nature of the power relations that flowed within the Congress and between the Congress and the White House. But that's not something you do through the roll calls.

Of course, it's mechanically interesting, too, when I think that, at that stage, we were using one of the grandfathers of the modern computer. I remember going to the professor of celestial mechanics at

Columbia, who was head of the Watson Lab, and persuading him to let us have some time from the Watson Lab on their computer in order to do this job. He thought I was crazy as hell, but he thought it was kind of an intriguing thing, so he let us have the time. All the light bulbs would flick on and off, and, at that stage of the game, it was almost impossible for us to have a system that was sophisticated enough to really go beyond the basic tabulation problems.

Yeah, we had our run-in with the computer. The thing would have been impossible without it, namely, to be able to compare on every roll call within the part that we were looking at, the vote of every legislator with every other legislator. But the business of building the bloc structures, which you could do now with a computer program, didn't seem to be easily within reach, so we did it manually. But, of course, that was one of the reasons I discovered the thing on the state delegations. I wouldn't have noticed that had I not been doing it by hand. We would have built the program to look—to get you the answers to the questions you wanted to ask—and it wouldn't have been as likely to throw back to you some questions that hadn't occurred to you. The problem of the apparatus dictating the insights and restricting them is a very serious problem.

Role as APSA President and as University Administrator

STOKES: I'd like to cover your presidency of the APSA and the Association as an organization of the discipline. The other thing does have to do with your—the insight you get into careers lying outside academic teaching proper with your movement into academic administration.

TRUMAN: I'd be glad to talk about both. I think the first one, my period as president of the Association, came, I think, at a kind of boundary point, and I think I was almost the last president who lived in another era. Civility was still possible. There was a kind of willingness to trust one's colleagues. I did not have to go through a major constitutional crisis every time I wanted to make an appointment. Curiously, I've never been—I've never regretted the decision I made back in 1962 to go into academic administration.

STOKES: Was that when you became dean?

TRUMAN: When I became dean of Columbia College, yes.

STOKES: How long had you been department chairman before that?

TRUMAN: I had been chairman of the department since—just three years—'59 I took it over. I've been almost glad that I did it at the time I did because I have the satisfaction of having made some modest contribution to my own discipline, and at the same time, have stepped aside before I became threatened by the bright young men and women coming along who, in fact, could outdistance me. But it was really—even though I stayed in the same institution—it was like a whole new career. I keep telling myself, in a way, that something in my own discipline assisted me in academic administration. We were saying informally earlier, why was it that so many political scientists went into academic administration? I think I do know. It seems to me tha: the political scientist, whatever his particular approach to the field may be, has, if he's learned anything, become sensitive to institutional shaping and the way in which institutions adjust through time. But I think that awareness of institutional change and growth and movement that one can get in political science stands one in very good stead, and it is as good preparation for academic administration as anything that I can think of.

STOKES: What were some of the main problems that you worked on?

TRUMAN: I was concerned about a problem that had persisted at Columbia since the days when John W. Burgess founded the Faculty of Political Science, namely, that the undergraduate college, Columbia College, tended to be a stepchild of the university. Of course, when I decided to accept the opportunity to step up to the vice president and provost position, I did it, in part, because I was still working on the same problem, and I'd have more leverage from there than I would from the college level. I would have, if I'd had a little more time.

STOKES: What year was that?

TRUMAN: '67. So I'd been in that job for less than twelve months when things blew up. If you had to do things, you had to do them rapidly, and you had to make up your mind. If it was the wrong thing, it was too bad. But the ability to sit back carefully and think a thing through—uh-uh—there wasn't time for that.

I think that was one of the things I learned, again, about politics. I can be very compassionate about a president or a governor on the hot seat, even if he does badly, because I think I know what some of the limitations just inevitably are. You know, this is one of things that I suspect has been a gain for my generation of political scientists from the depression and the war. A little more sensitive, a little more understanding of the complexities of institutions, and we get an awful lot of simplified explanations of the complex world these days from some of our colleagues, it seems to me.

STOKES: Well, Dave, let me just say, for the typist's benefit, that I think this is the end of a marvelous interview.

Robert Martin

Robert E. Martin received his B.A. and M.A. degrees from Howard University and his Ph.D. (1947) from the University of Chicago. His first full-time teaching position was at the A&T College of North Carolina, where he served on the faculty from 1939 to 1947. He moved to Howard University in 1947 and remained there until retirement. During his career, he was a visiting faculty member at several institutions, including Columbia University, Atlanta University, and New York University.

He served in the U.S. Office of War Information in 1942 and 1943. He was the director of the Peace Corps Training Project in Gabon in 1963 and 1964. He served as chairman of the Division of Social Sciences at Howard University in 1960 and 1961 and as an associate dean of the College of Liberal Arts from 1969 to 1971. As a long-term member of the District of Columbia Board of Elections, he has arranged for hundreds of college students to work in a variety of capacities in electoral administration. His research interests focused heavily on the voting process and on civil rights. He did extensive field research in collecting data for his work Negro Disenfranchisement in Virginia.

He served as president of the District of Columbia Political Science Association in 1967–68 and served as vice president of the American Political Science Association in 1972.

Robert Martin was interviewed by Russell Adams in Washington, D.C., about 1985. Adams is a colleague who has taught at Howard University since 1971. His academic interests include public policy, ideologies, political parties, and political socialization.

Early Life and Education

Note: Discrepancies between this interview and the recorded oral history occur because of changes in the transcription provided Dr. Martin.

MARTIN: I was born in Abbeville, Alabama, on November 29, 1913. However, my mother, when she came north, did not wish to be ridiculed by northern Negroes, who often teased black migrants from the South by calling them "'bama." So she selected Hartford, Connecticut, to be our pretended point of origin. She chose Hartford because there was a small city named Hartford near Abbeville. So all of my educational records show Hartford, Connecticut, to be my birthplace. On the trek north, my mother and stepfather—Oscar Martin— lived for a while in Lanes, South Carolina, where they ran a small store and restaurant.

ADAMS: What kind of work was he pursuing?

MARTIN: Part of the time in South Carolina he worked as a cook with a railway roadbed repair crew. After a year or so in Lanes, we moved to Selma, North Carolina, where my parents operated a small hotel, and my stepfather also worked as an auto mechanic. He was a fine mechanic and bought a few old cars and then repaired them and sold them. He was also a skillful gambler and frequently won money gambling. He was such a good poker player that wealthy white men used to play cards with him to learn from him. The handyman who worked at our hotel often met incoming trains—Selma was located at a junction for trains going north, south, east and west—and call out "Martin's hotel, Hotel Martin."

ADAMS: Do you remember any of the school situations at that age—grammar school experiences?

MARTIN: I attended a large wooden school in Selma. I think it was a consolidated school because a lot of the children came from the nearby rural area. Each room had a potbellied wood stove. We kids used to start the fire each morning in cold weather. I was a born "ham"; whenever there was a play I sought a part and usually got it because many of the kids had stage fright. I remember being given the assignment of reciting Patrick Henry's famous speech. I borrowed an older boy's overcoat that came down to my ankles and a derby hat and then gave a spirited rendition of the great speech, which ended with the dramatic peroration, "Give me liberty or give me death."

ADAMS: Your first introduction to political science!

MARTIN: In 1928, a couple of years after my stepfather had left home—never to return—my mother and I moved to Washington, D.C. I entered Shaw Junior High School, named in honor of the white officer who commanded black soldiers in the Civil War. While taking printing as my shop at Shaw, I became so engrossed in printing that I was declared the outstanding student in printing and was awarded a prize at a special assembly in 1929. I published several articles in *The Torch*, the school newspaper. So I decided to pursue printing as a career. However, in high school, instead of having a fine, personable, inspiring printing teacher like Mr. Baltimore at Shaw, my teacher had serious personal problems such as excessive drinking. Within the year I changed my mind about becoming a printer. Fortunately, this high school, a few years earlier, had established a college preparatory program, so I took the work necessary to qualify for admission to college. My experience in working on the student paper at Shaw and serving as editor of the Armstrong student paper and my longstanding and active interest in photography helped to make up my mind to pursue a career as a newspaper reporter and photographer. However, by the time I entered Howard University, I had decided that greater financial success would be more likely to result from the study of business and law. But, soon after entering Howard, I came under the influence of some great social scientists and became excited about ideas and phenomena in the social disciplines.

Education and Howard University

ADAMS: What year did you enter?

MARTIN: I enrolled at Howard in September 1932 and took classes with Alain Locke—

ADAMS: The philosopher?

MARTIN: Yes, the philosopher, author, and first black Rhodes Scholar. I also studied with Ralph Bunche in political science, Abram Harris in economics, E. Franklin Frazier in sociology, Harold Lewis in history, and other excellent teachers. Fascinated by all the social sciences, I began taking courses in each department and eventually decided to become a political scientist.

ADAMS: What pushed you toward political science?

MARTIN: Several factors. Most decisive were the ideas, personality, and teaching of Dr. Bunche. He became my main role model. I was deeply impressed by his views about politics and society: that most decisions in our society—in most societies—were made in a political context and are usually made by politicians, and that, if you want to have influence, you need to be well informed about the political process and know it can be manipulated in favor of your group, etc.

ADAMS: And you were what—a sophomore—when you heard this?

MARTIN: Yes, I was a sophomore at this time. That year, it began to come through to me in a very meaningful way. Also, I decided to become a political scientist because it would give me a chance to teach—and I had decided to be a teacher because I wished to help shape young minds, influence their values, and I was particularly interested in the politicization of students. I wanted to excite them about the political process, to help them to understand that process. I wanted to expose the political process to them, to show them what it has done to our people and to convince them that we had to learn about it in order to be able to change it, to improve it. And that led me into political science. Speaking of "exposing the system," you will not be surprised that the title of my M.A. dissertation was "Negro Disfranchisement in Virginia." It took two years to get the master's degree because there were not enough teachers in the department to offer the number of courses required for the graduate degree in one year. Since the graduate sequence of courses in political science was spread out over two years, I was able to take courses in economics, sociology, and history. Indeed, my teachers felt that, to comprehend adequately any one of the social disciplines, it was necessary to be well-grounded in the others. So I came out with a major in political science and at least a minor in economics, sociology, and history—and some courses in philosophy.

ADAMS: In terms of Howard and the organization of the disciplines at that time, were political science, sociology, and economics regarded as separate departments then?

MARTIN: Yes. The division consisted of separate departments of political science, economics, sociology-anthropology, history, and philosophy.

ADAMS: What was the size of the political science department?

MARTIN: Ralph Bunche founded the department in the late 1920s, and he brought in Emmett Dorsey, fondly known as "Sam," and there were two other younger teachers. So, basically, it was a four-person department, with another part-time instructor at times.

ADAMS: One was William R. Robinson, late of Norfolk State?

MARTIN: Yes. Let me say a little more about Howard and my time as a student there. Each year the Division of the Social Sciences sponsored a conference of national significance. Outstanding regional and national leaders and other figures were invited to the campus. To name a few: W.E.B. DuBois, A. Philip Randolph, Norman Thomas, Earl Browder, etc. Each conference had a theme, and the proceedings were published. Another program of the division was an annual competition to select the two best M.A. dissertations, which were published. I am pleased to say that my dissertation, "Negro Disfranchisement in Virginia," was one of the first two published by the Division.

ADAMS: That was when?

MARTIN: 1938. Incidentally, Russ, in those days, the master's degree was the highest granted by our graduate school. In those days, none of the historically black colleges offered the Ph.D. And many of the master's dissertations were, on the average, far superior to those of many of the larger institutions—where a teacher often supervised six, seven, or more, theses. I discovered this years later, while serving as visiting professor at some of the top universities. Some indication of the quality of Howard master's dissertations is the fact that many of them were in considerable demand in interlibrary loan. Mine was reviewed in two or three publications and was used by the Virginia WPA Writers Project. Some of the writers liked it very much. Finding that it related the dramatic struggle of blacks in Virginia politics, they requested a brief biography to be used with some excerpts from my thesis. However, when some of the top white officials said that my essay documented the highly discriminatory treatment of black Virginians' legitimate political efforts, I received merely a footnote in the book published by the Virginia Writers Project.

ADAMS: Now, after doing the M.A. were you able to continue grad school or was there a digression?

MARTIN: By that time, I was married and expecting a baby— and needed a job.

ADAMS: We're talking depression years here.

MARTIN: Yes, depression years—and I had to take responsibility for my education. My mother had given me room and board, but I had to pay for my education, buy my clothes and books, etc. I worked my way through school doing a variety of jobs. I worked as an usher at the Lichtman movie theaters on U and Seventh Streets during my last year in high school and first two years of college. I received seven dollars a week and worked from 5:00 P.M. to 10:00 P.M. and still found adequate time to study and get good grades. Indeed, after securing a tuition work scholarship at Howard University my freshman year, I raised my scholastic average further, made the dean's list, and enjoyed a tuition scholarship the next five years while securing the bachelor's and master's degrees. My work as an usher was ended because of a jocular remark I made to a white official of the theater company that owned the chain of theaters in black neighborhoods. It was not a bad remark, but he did not like it and directed the black manager of the Lincoln theater to fire me. I then got a job as an elevator operator at a white apartment house, working from 4to 11 P.M. six days a week and received forty dollars a month. I found it possible to do some studying during most evenings.

First Teaching Position: The Difference between North Carolina A&T College and Howard

ADAMS: Now, after leaving Howard, you said you faced the situation of finding employment.

MARTIN: Yes. While working for several months with the municipal social services department, I applied for a Julius Rosenwald Doctoral Fellowship and for a teaching position. I think you would be interested in how I went about seeking a job teaching. Now, I knew I couldn't get a position teaching only political science because very little of this discipline was being taught in black colleges—for obvious reasons. So I would have to teach primarily in the other social sciences. Secondly, I recognized that I might have to teach in high school at first, so I took several courses in education—even though members of the social science faculty tended to frown upon education because they felt that department placed too much emphasis on how to teach rather than what to teach—subject matter. These were two additional reasons why I took courses in all of the social science departments.

Now, here was my strategy in deciding to which colleges I would apply for a job—and, of course, I could expect to be hired only by a black institution. So I went to the library, accompanied by a student with a master's in economics, and examined reference books containing information about the curriculum and annual budgets of the black colleges. We decided that we would apply to those colleges with a well-developed social science curriculum *and* a sizable annual budget. This narrowed the number of applications down to about a dozen. In those days, you know, there were institutions where a teacher might not be able to depend upon receiving his full salary after six or seven months of the academic year. One teacher told me that there were times when he even dickered with students about turning over to him money that they otherwise would give to the bursar for tuition.

ADAMS: And that was regarded as proper by the administration?

MARTIN: If not proper, perhaps, at least, acceptable.

ADAMS: Or tolerated.

MARTIN: Tolerated in budget crises.

ADAMS: So where did you finally accept?

MARTIN: I was offered a position at A&T College in Greensboro, North Carolina. And I was also fortunate enough to receive a fellowship from the Julius Rosenwald Fund. I accepted the job at A&T after the Rosenwald Fund agreed to allow me to teach for a year before beginning my doctoral studies, and A&T agreed to hold my position while I was pursuing the Ph.D. degree—a great moment in my life!

ADAMS: You were in their social science division?

MARTIN: No. There was a social science department rather than separate specialized departments. I must say that I was impressed by the recognition I received at A&T. At that time, Howard University was regarded as "the capstone of Negro education," and Howard graduates were generally highly respected.

ADAMS: While we're talking about the quality or the expectations of the place, what was the thrust of the poli sci curriculum when you were coming through Howard?

MARTIN: I think the faculty had two major objectives. First, to do the best a small department could to give students a good view of political science as a discipline, not with highly specialized courses but an appropriate sampling or introduction to the basic major fields: government—national, state, and local—public administration, foreign relations, political philosophy, international law, comparative government, constitutional law. Dorsey was regarded as a specialist in political philosophy and Bunche in the international field.

Secondly, they wanted to help us understand the black political experience in the United States. So, frequently, when the books would give data and illustrations of the general course of American politics, we would also get data and illustrations dealing with the black political experience, wherever it was relevant. Reconstruction after the Civil War, the long struggle of black Americans to exercise their political rights, the barriers to the franchise, the attack on the poll tax, and the white primary, etc., were also emphasized.

ADAMS: Now this was in the early thirties, right?

MARTIN: Yes, the early and mid-thirties.

ADAMS: At A&T, did you find yourself doing what Bunche and Dorsey were doing?

MARTIN: I reflected many of their ideas and values, but it took place in a very different type of course offering. At A&T, there was only one course in political science—the government of the state of North Carolina—and it was taught by the dean of the college. There were courses in sociology, but I taught economics and history, and these provided an opportunity for weaving in data about the socioeconomic and political role, status, and problems of black Americans. The teaching load was twenty hours a week—four courses. I taught four courses the first quarter, four different courses the second quarter, and repeated one course the third quarter—twelve courses for the year, eleven of which were different. With a fairly good grounding in the social disciplines—and assiduous preparation for my classes— this was a useful experience, especially to grasp interrelationships. However, one should have a chance to narrow one's focus and become more specialized soon thereafter. This opportunity came to me only after moving to Howard University. Incidentally, my classes at A&T were quite large—thirty-five, forty, and, often, near fifty. When I spoke to the president of the college about this, he informed me that as long as the students could fit into the room, he did not see any problem. And I was a firm believer in essay-type exams!

ADAMS: How long were you at A&T?

MARTIN: I was at A&T from '39 to '40—one year. Then I went to the University of Chicago on a Rosenwald Fellowship. When I went to A&T, one of the things the president did the first day I got there was to call me in to meet with the chairman of the Board of Trustees, who was a white gentleman, a part of the power structure in North Carolina. His family had produced a couple of governors. And I never will forget—this man said to me, "Mr. Martin, you come from the north, and you may not like some of the things you see around here, but we feel we're making progress, and if you look around here and think about it, we think you will find that it's slow but it's steady, and you should be satisfied." What he was telling me was "don't start rocking the boat down here." After hearing this, I recalled what Bunche and some others had said to me: "Bob, just remember this. You cannot bring about any revolution down there, but you can do some real good. You can plant some ideas, you can sow some seeds on fertile soil that will grow and eventually mature and bear the kind of fruit that will help to bring about ultimately some of the things you'd like to see." As you know, years later the militant student protest movement was to originate at A&T. Any connection—!

ADAMS: You were at A&T for—

MARTIN: For one year. Then I went out to the University of Chicago in September 1940 to work on the doctorate.

Experience at the University of Chicago

ADAMS: What is your estimate of two things: your academic experience there, and how do you assess that in comparison with what you had experienced at Howard?

MARTIN: I had applied to and had been accepted at Chicago and Harvard. I enrolled at Chicago because it had the only teacher-scholar in the United States who had expressed long-term interest in black politics. He was Harold F. Gosnell, who had written the books, *Negro Politicians* and *Machine Politics: Chicago Model* and several articles on urban politics. I found Chicago very much to my liking.

ADAMS: You were a pioneer.

MARTIN: Well, I was the first black person to get a Ph.D. in political science at the University of Chicago. Being very much interested in American history, I decided to pursue a mixed doctoral program. I was permitted to do an outside field in United States history since the Civil War, the period of my greatest interest, the era of black American citizenship. I enjoyed my courses in history but was amazed to find that one of my three teachers in that department— Professor Craven—supported the view that slavery was not really so bad, that the slaves were generally satisfied and that most of them loved their masters. I had to challenge this idea, so I asked him, "If slavery was all that agreeable to the slaves, how do you account for the large numbers of slaves who deserted the plantations and followed the Union armies when they came through the South?" Can you believe this? His answer was, "Well, Mr. Martin, everybody loves a parade."

There were about five or six other black students in this class, none of whom ever joined me in challenging this self-appointed defender of the values and peculiar institution of the South—a man who was married to Wade Hampton's granddaughter. One of them informed me that he knew the professor's views and also knew that he was not going to change, so why antagonize a man who was going to sit in judgment on his work. However, I persisted in challenging the teacher, until one day he tired of it and said to me—not wishing to be too abrupt, "Mr. Martin, look, I understand your concerns but I cannot delay the work. We have a lot of work to cover. So hold your questions until after the reading period." He was aware, of course, that there really would not be time for discussion then. I was quite pleased to find that at the comprehensives Professor Craven's questions were quite straightforward and appropriate.

ADAMS: Leonard White—was he there?

MARTIN: Yes, he was chairman of the department. I took two classes with him and found him to be a very interesting person and an excellent teacher. He had a reputation for being tough in grading students. I'll never forget that, as we prepared for his final exam, a student moaned, "Oh, if I can just get a C." I responded, "A C? I expect an A in this course." Another student explained that, "Man, listen, his C's are equivalent to any other teacher's B and his B is like an A." Here is what happened to me. On the first exam, which I felt very good about, I received an eighty-seven. So I decided to dig in and raise my grade several points on the next exam. However, I again received an eighty-seven, so I went to Dr. White and explained that I would like to go over my exam with him. I assured him that, "I do not question the grade at all; I'm just interested in knowing where I lost the thirteen points, because I want to improve." He replied, "There is nothing wrong with your paper, but there are places where your statements are not quite as complete as they might be." He smiled but displayed no disposition to point those places out specifically. So I said, "Well, all right. I'm going to do an outstanding research paper for your class." Aware that he was the American expert on the British public service, I wrote on the unique role of the British Treasury Department in supervising the government service there. I dug deep in the bowels of Harper Library for in-depth research data in preparing that paper—so I was sure it was an excellent essay. Later, when Dr. White returned our term papers, he did not give me mine. He said, "Oh, yes, Mr. Martin, you did a very fine paper, an excellent job. As a matter of fact, there are some things in it that I'm interested in, so I'd like to hold on to it a little longer. I'll give it to you in a few days." Shortly thereafter I came across an article he had just published, and it contained some of the information from my paper—and I got no footnote either!

However, although my paper was graded A, I received a B in the course. There were only four or five Bs—and only one A. I don't believe Professor White had any racial bias, but he may have had a little class bias. Incidentally, Russ, White's exams always called for information from references he had mentioned the day before the exam!

ADAMS: Bob, what was the political science department like in the terms of its general orientation?

MARTIN: First, let me say a word about Professor Charles Merriam. The grand old man was capping his long, notable career with a seminar on bibliography. It met in a hotel where we could relax with a cocktail and enjoy his informal lectures. I had read just about everything he had written and knew his views, so it was delightful to be exposed to his personality and hear him reminisce about the people he had known and his experiences over the many years when he was sort of growing up along with the development of the discipline of political science.

Professor Jerome Kerwin was holding forth ably in political philosophy but not stimulating much discussion during his lectures. C. Herman Pritchett, one of the youngest members of the department, was an effective teacher, interesting and easy to approach and always willing to continue the discussion with a student after class. Harold Lasswell was on leave, but Nathan Leites was presenting rapid-fire lectures in the developing field of propaganda and quantitative analysis. Isola de Pool, a young graduate student and part-time teacher, was also working in the field.

Harold Gosnell was presenting courses in politics, parties, and democracy. He was a fine teacher, though not a very exciting lecturer. He was well grounded in the political process and quite knowledgeable in the area of black politics—I learned a lot from him. Dr. Gosnell was also into quantitative methodology. I will never forget how he would come to class at times with a black globe and proceed to draw angles, triangles, etc., on the globe to illustrate his discussion. I doubt that more than half of the class was able to follow him and fully comprehend his points. I had no idea then that I was destined to be the first black political scientist to do a doctoral dissertation in political science with heavy emphasis on quantitative methodology—my study of the AAA referenda, which produced hundreds of statistical tables and numerous graphs.

Field Research in the South

MARTIN: My dissertation was a study of voting in the cotton and tobacco referenda to determine whether farmers wanted compulsory limits on the production of these crops in order to prevent overproduction and lower prices. I wished to compare participation in terms of race and tenure—owners, tenants, and sharecroppers. I got the idea for the study from the fine research Ralph Bunche did while working on the Myrdal project that produced the classic *An American Dilemma*. Bunche believed that the participation of black farmers in the AAA voting may have been an important factor in stimulating their growing desire to take an active part in the regular political process. So that became the major hypothesis for me to test. I worked out a carefully constructed research proposal and submitted it to the Social Science Research Council. They found it promising and awarded me a field fellowship, amounting to my annual teaching salary and funds for the extensive travel necessary to do the interviewing in North and South Carolina. I covered more than seventeen thousand miles in interviewing hundreds of black and white farmers in Wilson County, North Carolina and Darlington County, South Carolina. The interviews were intensive, lasting from forty-five minutes to over two hours. And I worked out a neat technique to help insure that the respondents would relate to me when approached and talk candidly about politics: I dressed casually, talked like a southerner, found something to compliment them on—the yard, the garden, the flowers, the house, or something—and let them know that I was a student seeking information that only they could provide, etc. Responses were typically like the following statement: One farmer said, "Yes, sir, you can study a stack of books as high as that tree yonder and all you'll get is a headache. If you want to know 'bout farming, you gotta ask the man who follows the plow!" After this came a long, informative discussion.

Now, previous experiences as a fair-complexioned person suggested that the white respondents were not likely to recognize that they were talking to a Negro—like DuBois, Bunche, Frazier, Harris,

Locke, and others, I use the terms Negro, Afro-American, Black American, in referring to our people. This was important because politics was a highly controversial topic of discussion between blacks and whites, especially back in the 1940s. Although blacks usually recognize light-skinned Negroes easily, I found that my role—a man conducting a study—caused blacks to mistake my racial identity. As one respondent said after being informed who I was, "When you see a man going 'round asking a whole lot of questions and doing a lot of writing, that's a white man. We ain't been writing insurance long."

ADAMS: How many interviewees did you end up with?

MARTIN: I spent four and a half months in each county, interviewing all day, doing several interviews each day, six days a week, and ending up with more than eight hundred respondents. There was a great sense of relief when the interviewing was completed because, at times, the statements of some white respondents left me rather tense. For example, this is the kind of response some whites made to the question "How do people around here feel about colored people voting?" "Colored people" was the operative term for most southern whites. Answer: "Colored voting? We ain't gonna' have it! Why, if a nigger came to a polling place and I was there, I'd break his head." Another response was, "No, no we can't allow coloreds to vote, man. If they voted they'd run the country." After I suggested that this could hardly happen, since Negroes made up only about twenty percent of North Carolina's population, he inquired with a frown, "Where'd you get them figures?" That study provided some interesting experiences—enough for a good book.

ADAMS: What was the reception back at the university of the results of your work?

MARTIN: It was well received, indeed. They told me that probably more miles—over seventeen thousand—were covered in obtaining the data than in any other study. Dr. Pritchett, then chairman of the department, wrote that "it was one of the best dissertations in the recent history of the department." Dr. White was gracious in his praise. However, he may have been surprised that I had completed the study because, years earlier, when I was leaving the university after doing the formal work, passing the comprehensives and the exams in French and German, he said to me in his farewell, "Do keep in touch and let us know about progress on your dissertation—if any."

Let me say a few words about the language requirements at Chicago. Exams in two languages were required. The exams lasted three hours and assumed that there had been two or three years of preparation for each—and I had studied only Spanish! That the exams were tough is indicated by the attrition—only nine out of forty-eight passed when I took the German exam, and only twenty-two out of ninety-five passed when I took the French exam. I taught myself French in the summer while taking one course in political science and I taught myself German in two quarters, while taking a full program in political science. Believe me, mastering these languages—especially German—in such a short time, gave me the greatest thrill of my academic career, far greater than passing the five-day comps in political science.

Participation in the War Effort

MARTIN: I went back to A&T after two years at Chicago and one year in government service in Washington, D.C. With the war on, I was anxious to have a hand in the war to save democracy from the fascist onslaught. Convinced that I could make a better contribution doing something other than carrying a gun, I looked for civilian work in the war effort. Dr. Locke said he would talk with his friend, Lymon Bryson, who was the head of the Bureau of Community Services in the Office of War Information.

ADAMS: The eminent philosopher, Alain Leroy Locke?

MARTIN: Yes, the philosopher, distinguished author of *The New Negro*, chronicling the black renaissance in the 1920s. After being interviewed by Dr. Bryson, I was appointed as associate field representative in the Bureau of Community Services, the function of which was to serve as a linkage between the national government and community organizations across the country so as to provide more effectively information necessary in strengthening the war effort. Although OWI [Office of War Information] made a solid contribution to the country's morale and wartime activities, it never fully achieved its goals. This was because of the opposition of conservatives—especially in Congress—who accused that agency of "harboring a lot of damn liberals." Many racist conservatives especially disliked the OWI booklet "Negroes and the War," which was aimed at boosting the morale of Black Americans who were being denied jobs in defense industries during the time of acute labor shortages and while the U.S. was fighting a war "to save democracy." As you know, Russ, this disgraceful situation finally resulted in A. Philip Randolph, Walter White, and other black leaders threatening to organize hundreds of thousands of people to march on Washington in protest, which forced President Franklin Roosevelt to establish the first Fair Employment Practices Commission in American history. This OWI publication contained pictures showing black and white people working side by side in some employment and Negroes making significant contributions to the war effort wherever they were permitted to work. This was anathema to segregationists who regarded this as a liberal attack on southern racial policies and which, they felt, would encourage blacks to believe that they were going to get equality in American society.

ADAMS: Subversive, subversive, subversive.

MARTIN: Right. And Congress began making substantial cuts in the OWI budget, which resulted not only in aborting the agency's ongoing plans for future activities but also necessitated serious curtailment of existing programs.

ADAMS: So this is what, 1943?

MARTIN: This is 1942–43. So, frustrated by this turn of events, I resigned the position with OWI and resumed teaching at A&T in September 1943, which meant taking a cut of one-fourth in salary, as I had been earning $4,000 a year in government. It was at this time that I applied to the Social Science Research Council for a field fellowship to enable me to do the study "Negro-White Participation in the AAA Cotton and Tobacco Referenda," which I have discussed. Incidentally, Russ, I had to take off a quarter and a summer from teaching in order to analyze the statistical data and write the dissertation which amounted to two volumes and over four hundred pages. This financial hardship probably would not be necessary today because often a university will give a teacher in this situation leave with pay, or at least a reduced teaching load. But not back then, so I had to depend on meager savings and my wife's salary.

As the dissertation neared completion, I received a letter from Professor Dorsey advising me to finish the study soon, as he wanted me to join the faculty at Howard as an assistant professor of political science, which required the Ph.D. So I finished the thesis, defended it at Chicago in the summer of 1947, and moved to Howard in September, where a new, exciting academic experience awaited me.

Robert A. Dahl

Robert A. Dahl was born on December 17, 1915, in Inwood, Iowa. He received the A.B. degree from the University of Washington in 1936 and the Ph.D. from Yale University in 1940. In 1946, after working in government agencies and serving in the army during World War II, he was hired at Yale University, where he spent his entire academic career. He chaired the political science department from 1957 to 1962 and retired as professor emeritus in 1986.

His first book was Congress and Foreign Policy, *published in 1950.* Who Governs? Democracy and Power in an American City *(1961), his study of the community power structure in New Haven, attracted a great deal of attention in the profession. The publication of* A Preface to Democratic Theory *in 1956 established Dahl as one of the leading contemporary democratic theorists, and his interest in this topic has continued throughout his career. Major books have included* After the Revolution: Authority in a Good Society *(1970),* Dilemma of Pluralist Democracy: Autonomy versus Control *(1982), and* Democracy and Its Critics *(1989). He has had a long-term interest in opposition parties in democratic societies. He edited two volumes on this topic,* Political Oppositions in Western Democracies *(1966) and* Regimes and Oppositions *(1973).*

He was president of the American Political Science Association, in 1966–67, and president of the New England Political Science Association in 1951. He became a fellow of the American Academy of Arts and Sciences in 1960 and of the National Academy of Sciences in 1972. He was a trustee of the Center for Advanced Study in the Behavioral Sciences from 1974 through 1987.

Robert Dahl was interviewed in North Haven, Connecticut, in May and December of 1980 and in April of 1981 by Nelson Polsby, who has taught since 1967 at the University of California, Berkeley, after starting his academic career at Wesleyan University. Polsby's research and writing cover a number of fields, but he is particularly known for his work on American political parties and elections and the U.S. Congress. He served as managing editor of the *American Political Science Review*.

Populist Roots

DAHL: My interest in politics probably comes from my father. He grew up on a farm in North Dakota and recalls his father coming home from a Populist meeting at which William Jennings Bryan spoke. My grandfather became a Populist, and my father, throughout his life, was a kind of Populist. He was passionately interested in politics. My mother was relatively conservative in a Middle Western Republican style not dogmatically so.

I grew up in Iowa. Within four or five years after my birth, the land boom collapsed and whatever small savings my father had had been invested in land. He never had much sense about money—less than I, I think, which means he had almost none at all. He had a very considerable medical practice in the countryside, but, when the agricultural boom collapsed, the farmers didn't have any money, and, as a result, we didn't have any money. We might have a whole hog that would be butchered and delivered to us, but it's very hard to buy shoes. Even if you're eating high on the hog, you can't buy shoes. So we were very poor, except sometimes for lots of food.

One of the people dad had gone to school with was practicing medicine in Skagway, Alaska, and it was arranged to take his practice. There was some enormous retainer like $250 a month, which just seemed like a million. We arrived in this little town of Skagway, population of five hundred. My class in the eighth grade had perhaps twelve people in it, and, by the time I got to my senior class, it had six.

Growing up in a small town, at that time and in the kind of town it was, had a very powerful effect on me. I mentioned my father and grandfather as kind of a Populist spirit, which I have both wrestled with and absorbed. It's a part of me at the same time that I often quarrel with it. Now there's something of the same kind of thing about small towns, I think.

POLSBY: You knew you were not going to stay there.

DAHL: My brothers and I—we had no sisters—knew from the beginning we were never going to stay there, much as we liked the town. I knew I was going out to the university; I didn't quite know what I was going to do, but I was going out to the university. There wasn't any future in a town like that for us. There were really two categories: those who stayed, though they might migrate somewhere else; and those who assumed they would have to leave. The second almost coincided with those who went on to the university (which would almost always be the University of Washington) and who, then, characteristically, didn't return because they believed there was nothing for them to do. My brothers and I knew from a very early age that we were going to be in the first group. Even in our utmost, direst poverty, we always took it absolutely for granted that we would go on to college. My parents were always interested in argument about a variety of things, more politics than anything else. They were "readers."

POLSBY: So you went down to the University of Washington. What did you major in?

DAHL: I was going to be a lawyer, so I chose political science and did a lot of work in economics as well. There were faculty members there who certainly had some influence on me. One was Kenneth Cole. He was interested in legal theory, jurisprudence, things of that kind. I think that's probably where I first encountered pluralism, believe it or not.

There were various left currents there. I was invited to join a discussion group, which was either Socialist or fellow-traveling Communist. At that point, I was probably too naive to detect the difference. One of my instructors in philosophy was later fired for Communist activities but was finally reinstated. The Spanish Civil War broke out in 1936, and a friend of mine went over as a volunteer.

I had thought, until the fall of my senior year, that I was going to go to law school but decided I didn't want to be a lawyer. Probably, I had some picture of the legal career as being narrow and crabbed and concerned not with justice but taking on small cases. So I didn't know what I was going to do. I went to talk to Kenneth Cole, for whom I had great respect. And he said: "Well, why don't you go to graduate school?" My memory is that, in effect, my response was "Graduate school, what's that?" He explained what it was and suggested that I apply for fellowships. Yale came through with the biggest fellowship, which may have been $350, so I went to Yale. Even then, my aim was not to be a scholar and not to go into university teaching. It was to do something in politics or in public administration.

Graduate Studies at Yale

DAHL: At Yale it was the government department. I've often regretted that the name was changed over to political science, which seems to one a somewhat less apt term than government. When Jim Fesler came as chairman, he felt that it was more appropriate to be called the political science department.

POLSBY: He with his Harvard Ph.D. in government.

DAHL: Yes. The department was very strong in international relations, and for a while the department came to be known as the Department of Government and International Relations. And it had people like Arnold Wolfers and a young, obscure instructor whom Arnold once said had no future there, named A. Whitney Griswold, later the president of Yale. The government side was comparatively weak. It was not as distinguished a department as Columbia, Harvard, or Chicago.

Dwight Waldo and I and two other fellows formed a study group toward our final year that met once or twice a week and did précis of works and of topics. It was enormously productive and a powerful learning experience, where you would digest into a set of propositions the argument of the book, and then we would argue over whether we'd gotten them right.

POLSBY: Were the seminars heavily populated?

DAHL: I suspect that one of the biggest seminars I attended had maybe ten people around the seminar table. It was a small department, a very small department.

POLSBY: How did you pick a doctoral dissertation?

DAHL: The title of it was "Socialist Programs in Democratic Politics." It was terribly ambitious, as I look back on it; I don't think I would allow a student to do it. It was a survey of socialist programs in the perspective of democratic processes. I suppose I had the hope that the United States would move through a kind of second New Deal that would not be all that far away, in the direction of a democratic socialist order.

POLSBY: That's not far from the commitments you've maintained ever since.

DAHL: I've had that commitment throughout all this time, which has often been missed by readers of *Who Governs*. In the opening chapter of the dissertation, I laid out five or six criteria that a program would have to meet in order to satisfy the requirements of a democratic order. Then I tested each of these.

POLSBY: So it's all there.

DAHL: I've been writing on it ever since.

POLSBY: Your dissertation wasn't published per se, although in a sense it's been published in about twelve books of yours.

DAHL: That's exactly right. Spinning out. Even now there are bits and pieces of this that I see coming out here and there in things I do. It's only midway through my career or later, looking back, that I began to see that I was really writing the same thing over and over again.

POLSBY: Was writing the dissertation hard?

DAHL: It was hard but rewarding. I finished it in that academic year, believe it or not. As I look back on it, it was a prodigious achievement. I worked every day from morning till midnight. It flowed pretty easily. I think the organization of it, with these five or six criteria at the beginning, gave me a kind of an organizing technique, and I knew a lot of the stuff anyway. It was mainly a question of reading it and fitting it against these criteria and then writing it. Right at the last moment, somebody said, "But you haven't said anything about Austro-Marxism." Good God, I didn't know anything about Austro-Marxism and my German was never that good. I had to go back and plow through Austro-Marxism, part of which was in German. That was a painful period right at the end.

POLSBY: It was a library dissertation?

DAHL: It was a library dissertation.

POLSBY: I guess most people's were then.

DAHL: They were. I don't think we had even a conception of how you'd get out in the field and do a dissertation. Anthropologists might do that, but political scientists didn't do things of that sort.

POLSBY: I suppose not at Yale particularly.

The National Labor Relations Board and Socialism

DAHL: The National Labor Relations Board was an embattled agency, fighting the good cause, perhaps the best cause of the whole New Deal. It naturally attracted all sorts of radicals.

POLSBY: And that made you a Socialist rather than a New Deal Democrat?

DAHL: You're absolutely right. The economics division was headed by a man by the name of David J. Saposs, who was a conservative, right wing Socialist, bitterly anti-Communist, as only a conservative, right wing Socialist could be.

The person I worked most closely with was Murray Weiss. He was a Socialist, having come out of a New York Jewish Socialist background. We went out in the middle of the winter to Wierton, Ohio, and Wheeling, West Virginia, to work on the Wierton Steel case. Wierton Steel had refused to bargain collectively and were beating up their workers. They had these hoods who would follow workers around and beat up organizers and who followed us around. They didn't beat us up, but we felt constantly menaced. We'd go back to our hotel, and there would be these hoods following us quite openly. We'd go up in the elevator, and they would be there; we'd be grinning at one another.

POLSBY: This life history is so inconsistent with everything you wrote in *Who Governs?* It just boggles the mind. Did you have a conversion experience?

DAHL: It was gradual. There was great factionalism among people like those at the Labor Relations Board at that time, and foreign policy was polarizing. The Communists were moving through their various stages of united front and popular front and heaven knows what. And the Moscow trials were beginning and the Socialists saw more clearly than many liberals what actually was happening there. Under the influence of people like Murray Weiss, I came to hold a view about the Soviet Union, which pretty much has been my view since then, that maybe it was socialist but it certainly wasn't democratic, and it certainly wasn't the wave of the future, as far as I was concerned. This view brought me constantly into friction with Stalinists.

POLSBY: You got out of the Socialist party?

DAHL: I had come to the conclusion that the nationalization of industry was not a satisfactory solution. This had already crystallized with making me feel I'm not really a Socialist in their sense anymore. When France fell, I realized that the isolationist or semiisolationist position I had shared with the Socialists had depended, in my mind, on the implicit assumption that France and Britain would never fall, and, when it became clear that one of those two had fallen, for me, it was obvious that the United States had to get into the war.

Finding a Vocation

DAHL: I had had this romantic idea that when I finished the Ph.D., after all those years of going to school, I was going to get on a freighter and go around the world. Well, by the time I finished my Ph.D., on June 19th, 1940, if you got on a freighter, you were never going to get around the world. All the time I was here, whenever anybody asked me, I would say I have no intention of going into teaching. I had looked on it with disdain, as a domain for people not concerned with the active world. I was going back to where things were really happening and where I could really make an impact on the world. That was my whole orientation all the time. I was wrong in two very fundamental ways. I was wrong on the extent to which any one person can have that much effect. I was profoundly wrong about myself, in thinking that that was where I fitted.

POLSBY: How did you find that out?

DAHL: We arrived in Washington. I don't remember that I had any connections, but very quickly I got an interview with Paul Appleby at the Department of Agriculture. Paul had a management group of bright young people whom he conceived of sending out into the department to spot trouble and reorganize the department's management procedures. I very quickly got a job with them. I didn't like it at all. I guess I was beginning to get some self-awareness slowly, and one thing I knew is that I was not interested in going around to bureaus and trying to figure out how to make them more efficient. It's a good thing to do, but it wasn't the sort of thing I wanted to do or how I wanted to spend my life. You know, going over to the Bureau of Entomology and Plant Quarantine and learning all about pine rust disease and how to bring about a more effective field agency for controlling the spread of pine rust, or whatever the hell it might be in the western mountains, was not exactly the sort of thing that I had in mind when I was thinking of myself out in the front line there.

I was beginning, slowly, to discover that what I really wanted to do was to be able to play intellectually with ideas, the way we do. Just to have that freedom to play. After Pearl Harbor, the big excitement began to be in the war agencies. So, after six months, I got a job in the Office of Civilian Supply doing economic research. Data about inputs and outputs, such as how much steel would be required to make baby pins for diapers, were virtually unknown, and we were heading towards an allocation system.

POLSBY: Well, here you were erecting a Socialist program under democratic constraints. What could have been more perfect?

DAHL: Absolutely. Learning all about the glories of an administered and demand economy.

POLSBY: But you hated it.

DAHL: That for a while I rather liked. It seemed important and exciting, but then I came to hate it because, again, it was so routine, and there was not enough intellectual play there. I just didn't fit. I wasn't happy doing that kind of thing. And then the army intervened.

I put in an application for the U.S. Navy, thinking I would probably go into Naval Intelligence. I discovered some time later that my application raised a great "to-do" because included in it was a statement on my part that I had been a member of the American Socialist party. At any rate, I was turned down for the navy. Sometime around late 1942, I had this terrible sense of impatience. I wrote to my draft board and said that I did not believe that I was any longer entitled to a deferment on the basis of the work that I was doing. I was then drafted, and, in March, I boarded a train heading for Fort Lewis, Washington, for basic infantry training.

After fighting with the Sixth Army in Alsace and Germany, my division ended up in the Austrian Alps when the war was over. I spent about a week there violently relaxing, and then I got a phone call asking whether I would be willing to go back to the U.S. Control Council, staying in Germany with the occupation, until such time as I got out. Our task was to "de-Nazify" the financial apparatus of Germany. I finally got home in November '45.

When I was over there, I had some time to think about how I would want to use my life, if I had one to use when I came back. In those situations, you think of basic things. I got a flash, like one of those light bulbs coming on in the cartoon. I realized that what I would really like to do is read, talk about things I read, and write. It had become clear to me that what I wanted to do was teach in a university, which I had always rejected up to that point. I came down to New Haven to talk about the possibilities of finding a job somewhere in teaching. They were not terribly encouraging about possibilities. They didn't know of any, but they weren't also discouraging. But it turned out that there was a one-term appointment at Yale teaching American government.

I had this dreadful feeling, which lasted for a long time, that because of the five years I had been away, I was out of touch. There were so many things that I didn't know that I should know. That was true of everybody who came back, and a lot of people who had gone to Washington. That feeling lingered for a long time. What filtered up somehow through the IR wing of the department was, "Here's a guy we can talk to. Why don't we try to hang on to him?" So I was offered an instructorship for the coming year, with a salary of $2,700. I accepted with alacrity.

Politics, Economics, and Welfare

DAHL: Ed Lindblom was in the economics department, teaching labor economics. We discovered that we were both teaching graduate seminars that were rather similar in intention. So we decided that it would make sense to join forces in the seminar. We got together at the beginning of the term and outlined what we wanted to do. We would meet for a couple of hours before the class and work out a rough sketch of the dialogue and the topics. I think it was mutual that we would both participate, we wouldn't lecture. We would make some statements and contribute something.

When we initiated this, we didn't know one another very well, but, in the course of that teaching, we got to know one another very well. By the second time around, we realized that there was a potential book in our seminar. It took us a long time to get the structure of the book clear in our minds. In 1949, we both applied for Guggenheims to write it. We outlined the chapters of the book and agreed on who would take what topics. The one to whom a chapter was assigned would prepare an outline, and then we would sit down for many hours and discuss what the argument was going to be for that chapter. Then we would revise it and go through that process a second time. Then the person who had developed the chapter would write it. Then we would go through the same process again.

It was very, very intense. Somehow our respect for one another and our friendship sustained itself. There were times when I certainly felt irritated with Ed—I don't know if there were times when he felt irritated with me; he certainly should have—and wanted not to have to go through this. We finally got a manuscript that was more or less complete and then went through the process of rewriting it. It would be very difficult for anyone to tell for sure who contributed what. If you look in that book, you find about everything that we both have done, even though both of us have done rather different things. It's all there in one way or another.

It is a difficult book. It is hard to read and hard to grasp. The reviews, on the whole, were favorable. But nobody saw this as a landmark in the integration of political and economic theory, which is what we had aspired to do.

POLSBY: It wasn't then, but became one, retrospectively. Even in social science, it doesn't do to get out too far ahead. It was a sleeper.

A Preface to Democratic Theory

DAHL: I had been teaching a seminar in which I was taking up those topics, one by one. Then the University of Chicago asked me to give the Walgreen Lecture, and I accepted because I wanted to convert the subject of the seminar into the lecture. I wrote the lectures out. I had a draft of the lectures when I went to Chicago, and then I spent a year rewriting the lectures after Chicago.

POLSBY: It would be very comforting to get the word around that it took a couple of years to do, because you can't imagine how daunting it would be for somebody to think you just dashed off these lectures!

Dahl's Favorite Book by Dahl

POLSBY: Do you have a favorite book of yours?
DAHL: I don't think I do.
POLSBY: Of course, there's a sense in which they're all one book.
DAHL: That's right. That's how I see them.
POLSBY: It's like a kind of a soap opera.

DAHL: Absolutely. In fact, I'm a little bit worried sometimes about that: that it's all one big, long book. I'm always astonished when people see these great discontinuities. I think it's quite the other way around.

POLSBY: I'm convinced, as a fox, that it's the hedgehogs who provide the real leadership, and I definitely see your work as hedge-hoglike.

DAHL: It sure is.

POLSBY: So you do have a favorite book, but it's that one book.

DAHL: It's the family. It's like asking which are your favorite children. It's all of them.

Who Governs

POLSBY: In the fall of '55, you came back from the center with a large draft manuscript. We had a week where we read the manuscript and criticized it, and, as we were with all the other materials we had at our disposal, we were utterly brutal with it.

DAHL: It was that year at the center that the notion became much clearer in my mind that what I wanted to do was go back to New Haven and see whether it was possible to study power empirically. One theme was a strong discontent with simpleminded power theories. A second theme was announced in the very opening sentences of *Who Governs?* which is how is it possible, if you have a good deal of inequality in resources, for a democratic order to exist? And a third factor is that the *Preface* was behind me. I spent the year at the Center in pretty abstract stuff and developed a strong desire to get into the real world with a piece of research, so that I would know something about something instead of these abstractions.

POLSBY: Remember how much of a break you gave Floyd Hunter's methodology? We began with a chart on the wall with peoples' names on it, and you gave people cards and attempted to find out who knew whom, in an attempt to chart the sociogram. And one day you looked at the chart and said, "We're getting mush. Let's get rid of it and start learning something." It's an interesting point because it's widely perceived that Floyd Hunter got short shrift.

DAHL: He got more than he deserved.

POLSBY: Did you give a thought at the time to the problem of only doing one city?

DAHL: It was so obvious that a single city was going to tell you a lot about that city, but how much you could generalize was going to be a problem. We had some confidence—perhaps more confidence than we were entitled to—that New Haven was, to some extent, generalizable to other cities. What I may have missed was the extent to which the Lee administration was not generalizable to other cities. I didn't think New Haven was atypical, and it had, of course, the great advantage of being convenient.

POLSBY: The reception of *Who Governs?* has been fundamentally different from the reception of everything else you have written. How do you explain that and respond to it?

DAHL: *Who Governs?* is an extremely well-written book. I think that *Who Governs?* is a very persuasive book. For people who disagree with it, it's a dangerous book because it is so persuasive. It's a fair comment that *Who Governs?* doesn't pay a lot of attention to the relationship between New Haven and the limits that are set by the state and federal structures. It takes for granted that the city of New Haven and the United States are a part of a private enterprise and capitalist economy. Therefore, no mayor is going to socialize the industry or try to drive out the industries, which will remain privately owned. A lot of the criticism of *Who Governs?* is by people who imagine that I should have been directing my attention to that fact that Dick Lee and others were making their decisions in the context of an essentially private enterprise economy. But that's a set of issues that have to do with this whole question of the limits of structures on alternatives. That's not what the book is intended to be about.

I decided early on that I didn't want to spend my time dealing with all the criticisms of any work. One view is that you have a scholarly obligation to continue the discussion because that's a part of the progress in the field. I, for a whole variety of reasons, have not wanted to do that. I just don't want to spend my time answering critics. It may be that I've done less of that than I'm properly obliged to do. But I've always wanted to get on to something else. By the time the particular book is out, I'm off running on something else and absorbed in it, and I don't want to spend my time going back over it.

The Audience

POLSBY: When you sit down to write, do you have an audience in mind?

DAHL: It's a good question, but I don't really have the answer to it. There is a hypothetical audience somewhere out there that I'm writing for. It doesn't quite fit with my image of political scientists as an audience, though they are certainly a part of it. Much of the time I am writing quite independently of who actually reads it. There is some conception of an intelligent and educated, thoughtful person interested in this subject but not necessarily any political scientist who's up on all the political science literature. The image in my mind is somebody who's broader than that—at any rate, not identical with that.

People other than Americans are in this picture. I even have in mind nowadays when I write that there are people who are living in nondemocratic regimes, and I don't want to write in such a way as to give strength to the people controlling these regimes. Therefore, cynicism is not attractive to me. Cynicism is all right among Americans, where you've got a lot of common assumptions, but not to people who may be searching for an alternative way of thinking about the world.

Administration

POLSBY: You were chairman of the department. In fact, *Who Governs?* came out while you were chairman of the department, and that must mean that you were a neglectful chairman.

DAHL: Yes, I was in some ways. I felt, at the time, that it was a terrible burden. The provost put the arm on me and gave me this story that it really wasn't very difficult to do, and he could help out from time to time. It was to be just for one term. I was chairman for five years altogether, and then I was so sick of administrative work I vowed I was never going to take on administrative tasks again.

POLSBY: Why does administrative work annoy you so much?

DAHL: It's a distraction from things that I really like to do. I like to teach, and I'd like to read more than I do. And it distracts me from writing. Mainly what I wanted to do was to help to build up the department into a first class department. There were some appointments that were made while I was chairman that helped to give us the critical mass of well-known scholars.

The Yale Department

POLSBY: How is it that political science emerged at Yale? The first time the ACE [American Council of Education] did their ratings, Yale political science came out number one.

DAHL: Partly through a series of accidents going back to appointments. But Kingman Brewster as provost and John Miller as dean of the graduate school made a very powerful team for the social sciences. There was sympathy with the ideal of strengthening political science and some conceptions of what quality might be there. Several of the appointments or promotions during Jim Fesler's chairman ship had important long-run consequences—Walter Sharp, Herb Kaufman, Bob Lane, me. Later, when opportunities came along to get Karl Deutsch and so on, there was a recognition that the department needed strength.

Some of us in the department had a conception of the kind of department we wanted, or at least the directions in which we wanted to expand, and we had a notion as to what political science was all about. To some extent, we arrived at these through separate trajectories and then converged, and our discussions with one another helped it to emerge. There was a sense among a number of us that the more systematic, empirical side of political science needed to be strengthened. We wanted people who knew how to go about doing that. And some of the other members of the department were persuaded of the desirability of doing that. But I think it was a lot of accident. And there was also a lot of retooling going on. A number of us felt that what we had learned in graduate school was inadequate.

Harold Lasswell didn't become a member of the department until 1953 or '54. That was symptomatic. Then there was this awareness within the department that we have the world's leading political scientist in our midst here, why isn't he in this department? We were receptive to the political behavior ferment that was going on. I was receptive to it. I studied calculus, and I spent the following year studying statistics. I've never been very good at either one, but there was a lot of that going on.

POLSBY: As a hypothesis, it may have been the very weakness of the department that led to the receptivity.

DAHL: Well, it may have been one of the necessary or contributing conditions. I don't think it was sufficient. There had to be that small critical mass of people here who, out of their own origins and their own educational development, felt that this was something that was going to satisfy their understanding of how political science ought to be moving.

Heinz Eulau

Heinz Eulau was born on October 14, 1915, in Offenbach, Germany. He received his A.B. (1937), M.A. (1938), and Ph.D. (1941) degrees from the University of California, Berkeley. After several years of wartime service in government agencies and an editorial position on the New Republic, *in 1947 he took a teaching position at Antioch College in Ohio. In 1958, he moved to the political science department at Stanford University. He served two terms as chairman of that department, 1969–74 and 1981–84. He retired in 1989 and remains very active in research and writing.*

In 1962, along with three colleagues, he authored The Legislative System, *a four-state study of legislative systems and roles, the seminal work in comparative legislative studies. Subsequently, he turned his attention to local legislative bodies, directing a study of city councils in the Bay Area, which led to a number of publications, including* Labyrinths of Democracy: Adaptations, Linkages, Representation and Policies in Urban Politics *(1973). His research interests are far-reaching, extending to both theoretical and methodological questions, on such topics as theories of representation, networks, political elites and elite recruitment, and levels of analysis.*

His professional contributions extend beyond his own research. He was instrumental in the establishment of the Inter-University Consortium for Political and Social Research and served as the first chairman of its executive council (1968–70). He was the first chairman of the Board of Overseers of the National Election Studies (1977–84). He has been a leader in the organization of comparative legislative studies, including the conference that led to the Handbook of Legislative Research *(1985).*

Eulau was president of the American Political Science Association, 1971–72. He has a wealth of experience as an editor and editorial board member, and he edited Political Behavior *from 1980 through 1989. He has been a fellow of the American Academy of Arts and Science since 1972 and of the American Association for the Advancement of Science since 1965.*

Heinz Eulau was interviewed in Los Angeles, California, on January 28, 1988 by Dwaine Marvick, a professor at the University of California, Los Angeles. His research interests extend to a variety of aspects of political institutions and political behavior, with a particular interest in political party activists.

Early Background and Education

EULAU: We lived in Offenbach, a suburb of Frankfort in Germany. It was an industrial town, then sixty thousand. I grew up in an atmosphere of political terrorism, but I never experienced it personally because, you know, I came out of an upper middle class family. My father was a lawyer and, until the coming of the Nazis in 1933, I was rather untouched, actually, by the political environment of the larger scene.

I had a so-called classical education. That meant you studied Latin for nine years six times a week, and Greek for six years every day, French three times a week for seven years. But, somewhere when I was about fifteen years old—this was during the Depression—I became aware that there was such a thing as Socialists and Communists in my hometown. I began reading Marx and very early giving up on Marx. I think, largely, because the dialectic never made very much sense to me. I could never understand why a thesis and antithesis had to be resolved somehow in a synthesis, why they couldn't coexist forever. That kind of Hegelian nonsense, as I have since come to understand it, simply didn't appeal to me. I saw conflicting things coexisting, and that, in turn, probably is what later on made notions like ambivalence so attractive as a psychological concept. You can love and hate at the same time. These contradictory things can be built into reality and can be lived with, without having to be solved by either violent means or politics, you see. I wasn't aware of being Jewish until the Nazis came in. Actually, I didn't take the anti-Semitic component of fascism very seriously prior to 1933. I knew it was there, but in my school, among the two or three in my class who were "Nazis," whose parents were Nazis, the anti-Semitic component never was emphasized, and I always saw fascism really from the left perspective rather than from an anti-Semitic perspective. When I said left, I meant liberal left, Social Democratic left rather than Communist left.

MARVICK: Your whole family emigrated?

EULAU: No. My father, in his wisdom, shipped me out of the country as soon as I had finished gymnasium—high school—in May 1934, and they stayed on in Germany until a month before the outbreak of the war.

I became aware of being of Jewish background, but I never became a religious person nor am I particularly involved in Jewish affairs. I'm just at the margin—a marginal man at the margin of a marginal culture in that regard. And, in part, this may be related to my whole orientation towards political science. I have always felt that, if there was to be or is to be a "science of politics," the practitioner has to bend over backwards not to be overly committed to anything. That creates problems, I realize, but I've always tried, even in days when I was politically very active and even when I played the role of a liberal journalist, I always tried to look at myself from outside of myself, and that makes it very difficult to be committed in the sense in which you would expect a committed person to act. It's extremely difficult to be committed and to be an objective observer of yourself.

I came to this country via the Philippines, where I had to wait for my immigration quota in June 1935, and, you know, I was a European liberal. I came to this country and landed in San Francisco, visited Berkeley, found it a very charming place, and decided to get an A.B. degree there. I was supposed to go on to law school. Then, for some reasons, ended up with a Ph.D.

I majored in International Relations, which was a sort of a interdisciplinary major, largely because it gave you a lot of elbowroom on what you could study, and I didn't work very hard. I tried to balance some C's and D's against A's and B's, depending on whether I liked the course or not. I had no idea of going on. It made no difference what grades. You could get into graduate school or law school with a C average. I mean, a C average was an honorable grade, and, I think, as an undergraduate, I probably graduated with maybe B–, C+ average, and it was because, if I liked a course, I would get an A, and if I didn't like a course, you just didn't go to lecture and did something else. It was a very easy and free-floating life being an undergraduate in Berkeley, and I should have finished in June of '37, but I went to summer school and finished December of '36.

The objective was to go to law school in the fall, and I was going to do some political science because I had nothing else to do, and, in that quarter, suddenly I became a Ph.D. candidate instead of going on to law school. How it actually happened is that I took a seminar with Eric Bellquist, who was a very down, low-key Tennesseean of

Swedish descent, who didn't talk very much and was very old fash-
ioned in his orientations and values. Anyhow, it happened that political science is located in an old brownstone brick building on campus
called South Hall, and there was a john downstairs, two urinals—and
I had been in Bellquist's seminar on comparative politics or comparative government—and I was standing in front of the urinal. He stood
at the next urinal, and he spoke in a very grim voice, and he just said
to me, "Why don't you apply for a teaching assistantship?" And that
gave me encouragement, not going to law school. I took a dim view of
going to law school, in any case, because I had seen how hard the law
students had to work, and that didn't appeal to me. So I applied for a
teaching assistantship, and, in fact, I became Eric Bellquist's first
teaching assistant.

They, of course, had a classical political science curriculum in the
late '30s, with the major fields—American government, comparative
government, public administration, public law, international relations.
There was one professor for each. I offered political theory—which
meant everything from Plato on down to Walter Lippmann or whatever—comparative politics—government it was called—international
relations, international law, which was a field, and Modern European
History from 1815 on down. So we had to prepare in all these fields.
But, then, it was fairly easy to prepare because it was all very super-
ficial. In order to prepare in comparative government for the exam,
which I took—by the way, there was no written exam, I just took
orals—all you had to do, or what I did is, I read from the two volumes of Herman Finer's and Carl Friedrich's, who was then sort of
the new comparative government.

In the seminars, we had to write some very thorough "research
papers." And in Bellquist's seminar, I originally wrote a paper on a
French theorist, Benjamin Constant, who was the first one who properly interpreted the English Constitution, out of which came my doctoral dissertation on early theories of parliamentarism. And in
Bellquist's seminar, I did the article which is the first listed on my
bibliography, "Federalism during the Holy Roman Empire," which is
very learned, with all kinds of literature. But these seminars were not
very helpful for the exam, where you are supposed to master the
field. But you basically mastered the field by reading the textbooks.

I was rather dissatisfied very early. Carl Friedrich and George
Sabine's books were the fresh wind which was blowing, and then, in
1936, Lasswell came to teach a course. And I went to listen. I didn't
understand much of it, but there was something going on here which
was different. In those years too, I did a lot of work—actually I audited courses in psychology with Edward Tolman. I audited some

more of Brunswick. I audited courses in anthropology. So I heard a little bit about culture and personality.

If I had known (that's how provincial Berkeley was) that there was something going on at a place called Chicago, I would have gone to graduate school in Chicago. But I didn't have the vaguest idea. And, in Berkeley, if anybody knew what was going on in Chicago, they certainly wouldn't talk about it, or they would be critical of it, needless to say. But I don't think I raised the issue. Berkeley was an extremely nice place to be. I assume that, as an undergraduate, I thought that becoming an academic meant continuing living on this very pleasant life of reading books, talking to people, not exerting yourself. If I had known what a senior professor has to do in his prime, I'm not sure I would have gone into this business.

The Legislative System

EULAU: Why don't we begin with the project which culminated in *The Legislative System*, which, I think, is generally considered to have been a sort of an epoch-making or guiding or pioneering enterprise. Sometime in the early '50s, the Committee on Political Behavior of the Social Science Research Council had published a report, which actually was written by Oliver Garceau, on political behavior and the political process. It was published, in 1951.

MARVICK: Appeared in the *APSR*.

EULAU: And the people at SSRC, of course, realized that this very intelligent, programatic statement could not stand by itself. Some people, sooner or later, would have to do some research with it, and, apparently, they got a small amount of money to hand out to younger scholars who were willing to see whether they could put some empirical bones on some of the ideas which were floating in the air.

In 1954–55, the SSRC announced a competition for funds for research; and the field of state politics was chosen because that could serve as an arena for comparative research. The American states really had never been used as chambers or laboratories for genuinely comparative research, and then they invited proposals for comparative research, as it was called, on American state politics. I think they had not a very clear idea what they meant by comparative at that point because what actually came in—and I think some twenty or thirty proposals came in—were simply studies by younger scholars in various states submitting a proposal for the study of some phase of politics in one state. And that's exactly the way I came into this project. I had long been interested in urban/rural politics, and I made a proposal for the study of urban/rural differentiation in politics in the state of Ohio. It provided for interviews with state legislators.

I submitted this proposal, and it got, apparently, through the first hurdle, and I was invited, along with about, I think, twenty-five others, to a two-day meeting in June of 1955, where they put us into a fairly large room, maybe as large as your living room here. We were sitting around in a circle; and also present were V.O. Key, who had been the chairman of the committee. Now, David Truman was the chairman of the committee, but V.O. Key, who had been a previous chairman, was there. Pendelton Herring, of course, the president of SSRC, was there, and Avery Leiserson was there, and they asked us each to make a presentation.

And so we all made presentations on the first morning, and it was quite clear we were competing against each other, because there was a fairly limited amount of money—I don't know how much money altogether, it may be a hundred thousand or maybe a hundred and twenty-five thousand, altogether. Then, in that first meeting, there was a fellow sitting across from me, whom I understood. That was John Wahlke. There was an almost immediate symbiotic relationship. That is, he practically took words out of my mouth, and I could have taken words out of his mouth, and so on. He was interested in interest group politics, and he was then living in Tennessee, and he was going to do a study of interest groups in Tennessee. Well, interest groups and urban/rural differentiation sort of meshed together. We talked, and so on. In the afternoon, we again assembled and suddenly Dave Truman said, "Well, there are four people here—Wahlke, Eulau, Buchanan"—that's William Buchanan—"and Leroy Ferguson from Michigan State. I think the four of you should go in the next room with Professor Key and talk some more." And they shoved us off into a room. We were told that if (this was in June) by the fall, after the APSA meetings, we came up with a joint proposal—that's a proposal which would include the original proposals, a compromise among the original proposals of the four of us—they would consider funding us as a group. It wasn't quite clear what we would be doing, whether we would be doing our share of data on topics which interested us which would be collected in four states or whether we would collect only data in our state and then try to, sort of, relate it to data in the other states. It was very unclear what comparative meant at this point. And we didn't know each other.

We spent the summer writing some more working papers and reassembled; for instance, I wrote one on the notion of role system and tried to bring the interests of the others into that. Wahlke was interested in interest groups. Buchanan, who was then living in Mississippi, had proposed a study of legislators' constituents, and Ferguson's proposal was about state parties; and I tried to bring all this into one intellectual framework. Wahlke wrote something on interest groups and so on. The APSA was meeting in Boulder in 1955, and we reassembled after that meeting in Estes Park for about three or four days. With us was Avery Leiserson, sort of as the agent of the SSRC, and, in about three or four days, we worked out a proposal which wasn't longer than four or five single-spaced pages, which we sent to SSRC, and they finally gave us the go ahead.

MARVICK: You still hadn't really devised the instruments or anything.

EULAU: There were no instruments. We spent the academic year '55–'56 meeting three or four times. We met in East Lansing, we met at Antioch College, where I was then; we met at Vanderbilt. We met three times and started to develop questionnaires. I think the whole project initially had maybe SSRC funding of about fifty or sixty thousand dollars, and that was to cover all these meetings and the interviewing and God knows what. That was a lot of money in 1955.

We must have spent that year writing further working papers, developing questionnaires. I think gradually we came to recognize, though we were still mutually suspicious, that we would collect the same data in every state, that is, we would have a uniform interview schedule. Then we got together at Northwestern for four to six weeks to put the whole questionnaire together, which is now a very long interview, and do some pretest interviewing in the state of Illinois. That's why we had to go to a state where we would not be interviewing.

The joint proposal we made to SSRC, in the fall of 1955, called not only for interviews with legislators, but also interviews with lobbyists, with constituents, and with live party politicians. We had committed ourselves to notions of social role—role analysis—and we wanted to interview the significant others. Well, there was no money for this. They said, "Well, sorry, you can't do any of this." If we had done constituency interviews we would have had to assemble teams of students to send them out in the constituencies and do, you know, several hundred interviews.

But that was our proposal. It was rather utopian. Needless to say, subsequently, when the wise guys—you know, after the fact in the '60s—when the wise guys came around they said, you know, they, quote, "failed to interview constituents and lobbyists." I mean, we didn't *fail* to interview them, we *didn't* interview them.

By that time, Buchanan had moved from Mississippi to California, to USC, and Ferguson would ultimately not interview in Michigan, as we had expected, but in New Jersey. So, of course, subsequently, we rationalized all this. You see, it now included every part of the country. We had no such notions originally. It also, then, turns out that New Jersey is a competitive, strong, two-party state; Ohio is somewhere in the middle; and then comes California, which, in the '50s, is a no party system; and Tennessee is sort of a multifactional system and one party. So we, later on, made intellectual, analytic use of this sort of thing, but that was not designed in any way.

The Legislative System, even before it was published, had some influence on the course of research in that field. A lot of people picked up the questionnaire and, you know, it was sort of a flowering of this kind of research, and it became one of the many fads which we have lived through in all these years. But it's interesting what people pick up. I mean, this representation typology. You know, if you want to become famous in this profession all you have to do is have a typology that somehow catches on.

MARVICK: You're talking about trustees and delegates and politicos, of course.

EULAU: But, the other stuff that was a little bit more complicated they didn't pick up.

Bay Area Study of City Councils

EULAU: Then, from the very beginning of the legislative study, people always thought that the so-called behavioral revolution somehow was noninstitutional. It wasn't so at all. I mean, we were very institutionally oriented. Yet it's very difficult, even if you analyze the institution in terms of individuals, to come back to that institutional level, because it's difficult to talk about "The legislature does this," and so on, and yet, one makes public statements of this sort. Our language is macro and the legislature *is* the decision-making body; I mean, it's simultaneous. There is a simultaneous relationship between the individual behavior and the group's behavior.

I was always interested in how the institution behaved because I think that institutions and groups are "real" in the ontological sense, in contrast to methodological individualism, which, of course, denies that groups have any reality at all. It occurred to me that, given an interest in legislatures, city councils would be rather congenial and convenient research sites, small enough to be observed in much more detail. You have more knowledge about the group as a whole and there were many more of them.

The San Francisco Bay area has as many as ninety institutionalized units to deal with statistically. That led to the city council research project. I think the stimulus was to look at legislative political processes in settings on which we could get a more precise handle. Where we could have more confidence—I use the word with some hesitation—in aggregating the individual data, in manipulating the individual data—interview data or observational data—into grouped data. That's how we then moved into the city council project. It was closely related then. I've always been interested in this linkage of units of different size and the so-called level of analysis problem. As I very often told people, I never had any overwhelming interest in state legislatures or in city councils; they are simply real-world research sites in which one could observe what's going on rather than having either some normative conviction about legislatures being the most important institutions in society or having any particular interest in the doings of them.

This is how it came about actually. I was invited to be the legislative research professor in Berkeley in 1961–62. I was supposed to have a seminar (you know, Berkeley in the early '60s was still very antibehavioral), and I thought the best thing I could do would be to start out really as a training project. I thought, well, very simple, we just use the state legislative questionnaire translated into city council terms. And I'll have the students go out to do some interviewing and to learn about city councils, and we can talk about legislative behavior in the seminar.

MARVICK: So this all started in the upper Bay area then?

EULAU: It started in Berkeley. Sid Tarrow was my research assistant, now a specialist in comparative politics at Cornell. He had been at Columbia and had worked with David Truman. At least he knew a little bit about what was going on in political science, in contrast to the students I encountered in that seminar. In a very short period of time, maybe within two, three, four weeks, we worked up a questionnaire. And they went out and started to interview. They interviewed in a number of cities; this in the fall of 1961. Kenny Prewitt and Betty Zisk were at Stanford and had been in my introductory seminar on methodology, so-called, and I got them interested. I said, "Look, this would be an ideal time to start a project on which we all could collect data," and I persuaded them of the importance of small groups, and *The Legislative System* had just come out. And I had to have a project to justify my existence at Stanford. So we went over that Berkeley questionnaire and started to change and improve it and whatnot, and I did another pretest. By now I looked at the Berkeley thing as a first pretest, sort of. We did some more pretesting in cities around Palo Alto and Atherton and Menlo Park and wherever, and collected about a hundred interviews. This is 1962–63, and Kenny Prewitt and Betty Zisk wrote their doctoral dissertations with what later was considered the pretest data.

And at that point, Prewitt and I wrote up a big proposal for the National Science Foundation, which at that point had not funded political science projects. I ran into Henry Riecken, who at that point was running the sociology section. He said, "Try to encourage political scientists to apply," and so we wrote a proposal which was very, very thick. Gabriel Almond, who had come to Stanford that fall in '63 when we worked on this, he said, "Well, if you don't get the money for this proposal, we'll publish the proposal."

The 1954 Summer Seminar at Michigan

EULAU: I have a very vivid memory of the summer of 1954, when I was up there in Ann Arbor for the summer seminar.

MARVICK: Yes, I recall. That was a memorable seminar, because it represented really the first occasion when the Young Turks of the political behavioral movement had been together for a sustained six weeks or so of work.

EULAU: To work and not just talk because, previously, of course, within the Social Science Research Council, a Committee on Political Behavior had been set up, and they had published shortly thereafter a kind of programmatic manifesto.

MARVICK: It appeared in the 1952 *APSR*.

EULAU: But very few of them were really doing research or analysis, especially analysis of data. We had, in the summer of 1954, the first working seminar; the Survey Research Center had conducted its really first full-fledged political survey in 1952, and we were given access to the data and could block out little secondary analysis projects within the data. There were about eight or ten people there. The two I was closest to were Bob Lane, who was then an assistant professor at Yale, and Bob Agger, who, at that point, was an assistant professor, I think, at North Carolina. Our tutor in that enterprise was Warren Miller.

That summer seminar was a rather remarkable thing in a number of respects. For one thing, the very notion that scholars not involved in a research project could share data collected by other people for other purposes. This was unheard of, and, out of that, ultimately, came the idea of the Consortium. That people would deposit their data in an archive, and the data would be shared, so that not only people could do secondary analysis, but possibly replicate—keep the original investigator honest—check up on him. The whole notion of replication became a very live issue.

MARVICK: I hadn't thought of it that way before, Heinz, this notion that people did team research and that they worked together on a project where the data had already been gathered together in sizable amounts.

EULAU: Then you could publish it under your own name. For Bob Lane and me, that experience, quite apart from learning how to handle quantitative data (and we also took a course in statistics that summer) was all new stuff. We published articles within a year; Warren Miller was an extremely good mentor and tutor. He knew the data backward, forwards, and he helped us to develop fairly simple scales. The technology was a very simple one at the time. We only had these counter-sorters standing down there.

So even doing a simple scale analysis was very complex business. You would stand, possibly, in front of a counter-sorter for several hours in order to just sort the cards. And, in between, the cards, of course, would tear, and you would have to replace the whole set— sometimes you could replace from the torn card— but sometimes the cards were so mangled that you had to have the key puncher do it.

MARVICK: I suppose the pleasure we all feel at the computer revolution is poignant partly because we remember the prerevolutionary days.

Development of the ICPSR

EULAU: By 1962, we had the first "founders meeting," and, as I recall this (Warren and I have somewhat different memories), I think that I felt that if we had ten, twelve people in the Consortium, that would be a big success, and he thought, well, fifteen to twenty-five people. We expected it to be a very limited kind of operation, and, in the early years, it operated on a shoestring. Membership was fifteen hundred bucks for the institutions, which were mostly the big research universities.

MARVICK: There must have been thirty representatives, or twenty-seven or twenty-eight, represented at the first meeting?

EULAU: No. The first meeting was very small, as I recall, and that was some time in the springtime of 1962. They didn't dare to bring people to Ann Arbor in the wintertime then, but there were a small number, because we all fitted into one room. But then later, we'd go up to about thirty. And, of course, what made the Consortium take off was basically the computer revolution. By 1964, the big digital computer was put in in Ann Arbor.

MARVICK: I remember Angus Campbell, at the first fall meeting in '62, sitting there, and somebody said that you were going to send these results of each of these surveys, including the 1962 national survey, to all members very shortly, and Angus said he was going to send them by cards through the parcel post, and someone said, "Well, why not put them on magnetic tapes?" and Angus said, "Oh, you can't be sure that they'd go on magnetic tapes. It's too risky."

EULAU: Yes. I became aware of the big digital after I came back from Vienna in '65, and I went to the meeting in Ann Arbor, and they showed us the machine they had down in the basement in the new building, and I came back to Stanford and I told my colleagues, "I have seen the future, and it works." And from then on, you know, the Consortium just simply grew.

Development of the National Election Studies

MARVICK: There is the story about forming the National Election Studies project.

EULAU: That is an incredible story. I really hadn't worked in elections at all since the 1950s. It was not my major concern. But, sometime in the spring of 1976, I got a call from Warren Miller that he was forming a committee which might draw up a proposal to the National Science Foundation that would make it possible to put the National Election Studies, which had been conducted since 1952, or '48 even, on a more permanent basis. Up to that time, in order to conduct these studies every two years, Miller or somebody else had to go out and hustle the money from year to year.

But, in the spring of 1976, apparently there was encouragement. There must have been some policy change in NSF that NSF was willing to put some social science data collection enterprises on a more permanent basis, provided that the operation would not just be a "Michigan operation" but would be fertilized, influenced, supervised by the national scholarly community, and that the national scholarly community should play an important part in the development of the studies. So he called me in the spring of '76. He was very vague. He had been encouraged, I think, by David Leege, who at that time was the program director for political science at NSF, who in turn must have been encouraged by somebody higher up in NSF. So I agreed. We talked a little bit about whom we would want to have on the board.

Warren and I traveled with our wives in Europe during the summer for two weeks in England in July or August 1976, and, the interesting thing is, we never talked about this at all, not once. It was vacation. When we came back in August, we put together a committee; the committee was to write a proposal to the National Science Foundation for permanent funding of the National Election Studies. An important member was Merrill Shanks. Let me point out, we tried to avoid, as much as possible, people who were connected with Michigan. We really tried, and Merrill was the only one who had been a Michigan Ph.D. He was in Berkeley, at that point, as director of the Survey Research Center. Others were David Sears, social psychologist, John Sprague, Ben Page, Jim Davis, sociologist who had been at NORC in Chicago and was now at Harvard, Ed Tufte, who had done a number of things, but was primarily a statistician. There may have been one or two others and I can't remember. How could we make this proposal a proposal of the national research community? The members of the board individually wrote the same standard letter to friends out there in the country asking them for ideas and what should be done about the National Election Studies, and we got a hundred to a hundred and fifty responses, which were worked into the proposal. At that point, the major areas of interest were party identification, the whole problem of the issue orientation, and, was the electorate really getting more sophisticated or not.

Political Behavior

EULAU: By 1980, I thought I was about to retire, and I had an office in the Hoover Institution. But I was asked to take over the editorship of a little magazine called *Political Behavior*, and I said, "Well, sure, why not, if you let me run it," and they have let me run it. Now, the journal differs from other journals. First of all, I make a decision whether to publish something or not. After I've made the decision, and I think the thing should be revised, or there is some problem with it, then I send it to somebody for technical advice. But I'm not just sending out every article to two or three referees. You know, eight out of ten articles are just . . .

MARVICK: Unpublishable.

EULAU: And I can decide that as well as anybody else can. Then, I named an editorial committee. There's an editorial board. I've never used them. It was just dressing. But there is an editorial committee, and it's all colleagues of mine at Stanford. So, if I have something on elections, and I think it needs some checking up on it, I give it to Richard Brody or to John Ferejohn or to somebody there. We can only, fortunately, publish four or five articles in an issue. So, every three months, there is a period of relative intense work. I wait until I have a stack of manuscripts and then they all get taken care of in one day.

MARVICK: So it's not time consuming, but you have a sense of being able to decide things on the basis of merit.

EULAU: I don't know whether it's meritorious, but it's basically on what I like, and it's much more in the style of what editors used to do in the early part of the century. When there's this notion of a complex, anonymous, referee process, it is a result of the politization of the professions. Nelson Polsby told me once he never looked at a manuscript. He read the article when it was in print, in the journal. I don't believe it, but that's what he said.

I think it just happened because now the membership controls the organization. The journal is there for the benefit of the members, and so everybody should have an equal chance, and you cannot trust any one individual. For some reason you can trust a two-to-one majority. And you know damned well that whether an article gets in or not in depends on to whom it is sent. Then, the argument is, we older folk have to help the young people improve their writing and their style and their analysis; and the Association owes it to its members to educate them. I don't think the Association owes anything, you know. On *Political Behavior* I try usually to read a manuscript within a week of its coming in, and, if it's negative, I almost immediately inform them, turn them down. If I sort of like it, I usually stew over it a while, and then I may still turn it down.

Eulau as APSA President

EULAU: How you get nominated to the presidency is a total mystery. There is always a nominating committee, which overlaps from one year to the other. Every president appoints three new members, so there are three old members, three new members, and the year when I got nominated the committee was split (later I found out). David Singer was the chairman of the committee. He was a friend of (Karl) Deutsch, and he held out for me. The committee, I was told, was split three to three (it was Eulau-Morgenthau) and the nominating committee was willing to consider Morgenthau. I got a call at ten o'clock at night. It was David Singer, calling from Colorado, would I accept the nomination? and Herb McClosky was standing there, and I said to him, "Should I accept the nomination?" Totally unexpected and out of the blue sky.

Well, in contrast to Lane and Easton and Deutsch, I did not try to make policy for the APSA. I used that year to get out of as much teaching as possible. I don't think I did any teaching, maybe one seminar that year. I just told them I couldn't do it. But one thing I thought I could do as I went to all the regional and even state meetings was to give speeches. I thought that was a proper function for a president to perform. I visited New England—they met in Providence, Rhode Island. In fact, it was an interesting experience. They had a dinner that night. It was hot, beastly hot, and, of course, there was this very stuffy kind of—you know, people on long tables and a big head table and I, of course, sat in the middle. And, after a while, I started, and I took my coat off, being a good Californian, and everybody else up and down the head table, but not Sam Beer, who always wore a pin-striped suit. You know, he introduced me to give my greetings. I think I didn't have to give a speech, just had to bring fraternal greetings from Washington.

I was at the Midwest, of course, and at the Western, and I was at the Southwestern, and I was at the South Carolina Political Science Association and, oh, very small ones, and the Southern. I was all over the country. In the same year I gave an endless list of lectures here, there, and everywhere. Some of them paid, which was not bad; some of them not so well paid. The Association is like the university. When you get dragged into these things, they look very important at the time, and maybe they are important in some global perspective, but, in a few years, as soon as you're out of it, you miss it a little bit, but after two or three years, it might as well not have happened. At least I discovered I'm not a political person.

Comments on Discipline

EULAU: Political science is clearly not a discipline that operates within a paradigm. That's what I think of the whole attempt to interpret what goes on in political science in terms of Kuhnian paradigm: it just ain't so. There is no such thing as anything that Kuhn had in mind when he talks about physics and chemistry or even economics; it just doesn't exist. We have things going on, ranging from the very hard-nosed methodological stuff to the softest, undisciplined kind of current history stuff. But I never thought like Dahl did, some others did, you know, that suddenly we would become a unified kind of discipline where everybody would march to the QED of the Survey Research Center at the University of Michigan, or to the QED of the Committee on Political Behavior of the Social Science Research Council.

I remember when the Straussians brought out that attack that Herbert Storing edited. There was some discussion whether there should be a reply, and I remember talking about this with Herbert Simon and with Morton Grodzins and they said, "No, just forget it," and the interesting thing is that the very long and critical book review which was done on that book was done by Sheldon Wolin and Jack Schaar in the pages of the *American Political Scientist*. They really took the Straussians on, including defending what the political behavior folk were trying to do, although they themselves were not particularly sympathetic.

I have always felt the expression "revolution" was unfortunate, which some people used, I probably did. The word revolution, as far as I can determine, was first used in connection with the title of that book David Truman edited for the Brookings Institution. That was called *The Impact of the Revolution in the Behavioral Sciences on Political Science.* There was not a behavioral revolution in political science, but, then, he talked about behavioral movement. But the lack of a paradigm, I think, is crucial to an understanding of what was happening in that movement. There was none for the movement itself or for the discipline.

There is sort of a general understanding; I think if it meant anything it was an openness that politics is not unrelated to other phenomena in society, namely, to social structure on the one hand, and to basic psychology. The psychoanalytic thing never made much of an inroad, but social psychology in a generalized sense, certainly did. There were electoral studies and legislative studies, where we talked about attitudes, roles, social roles, and all that. I think that the mood of the '50s, '60s, and into the present, hopefully, is that you draw on whatever seems to be germane. That seems to be the paradigm.

I think the unfinished business of the so-called behavioral revolution is that the social sciences have to have much more long-term planning. I mean, in astrophysics they plan twenty, thirty years ahead. Lasswell used to talk about having these social observatories, which we haven't got, for a long period of time, which is indicative of the basically low status which social science enjoys. We're in the business of keeping the undergraduates off the street. But the foundations lose interest in this in no time, and then they complain that there are no payoffs for the investments. For the little money which they have given, they want enormous payoffs. Take the election studies, which now have a thirty-year time series; the best justification you can now make for the national election studies is that they give the historian more detailed information about what has gone on the last thirty years. So much for the behavioral revolution.

David Easton

David Easton was born on June 24, 1917, in Toronto, Canada, where he lived until he completed his master's degree. Both his B.A.(1939) and his M.A.(1943) were awarded by the University of Toronto. He obtained his doctoral degree from Harvard University in 1947. He joined the faculty of the University of Chicago in 1947 as an assistant professor and remained at Chicago until 1982, being honored with a chair as the Andrew MacLeish Distinguished Service Professor in 1969. In 1971, he also accepted a joint appointment with Queen's University. Upon his retirement from the University of Chicago in 1982, he accepted a position as a Distinguished Professor at the University of California, Irvine. His professional writings have centered on political theory.

His works The Political System, A Framework for Political Analysis, *and* A Systems Analysis of Political Life *defined politics in a systems theoretic framework, a view that was new to political science. His book* Children in the Political System *(with Jack Dennis) was an empirical exploration of the adaptation of children to their political environment.*

He served as a consultant to the Royal Commission on Bilingualism and Biculturalism in Canada. He was elected to the vice presidency of the American Academy of Arts and Sciences. He served as president of the American Political Science Association in 1968–69.

David Easton was interviewed in April and November of 1988 by John Gunnell, who has taught at the State University of New York at Albany since 1972. His research and writing have been in the field of political theory.

Canada and a Broad World View

EASTON: I came from a poor family and was the first to go off to college, to the University of Toronto. The years that I spent as an undergraduate were 1935 to 1939, which means that I started at the pit of the Depression. That has a certain significance for the kind of intellectual atmosphere I found at college. That was during the period when the second coming of Marxism in North America was taking place. The ideological currency of the university, the language that people spoke, was formulated either in Marxist or in anti-Marxist terminology, so it was very difficult for anyone to escape the influence of orthodox Marxism. In my first year at college I was not very much concerned about these matters, but by the time I entered my sophomore year and had been exposed to my future wife's interests in politics, I became much more sensitive to what was going on in society. The politically concerned young people at the time distributed ourselves across a spectrum that ran from reformist socialism to Marxism to a revolutionary socialism that was opposed to Stalinism.

I found myself sympathetically inclined toward the youth movement of the Cooperative Commonwealth Federation party, a small-scale equivalent of the Labour Party in Great Britain, and a great deal of my early political perspectives were shaped by my activities around that organization, particularly its left wing, which was very critical of the more conservative party members and bitterly critical of members of the Communist party—the Stalinists. During those years, I saw myself as preparing myself for an active political life, not for an academic one.

Anybody who went through the '30s and who was exposed to the great debates about the need for vast social transformations could not help but think of specific social problems in terms of the whole social system. You were likely to absorb an orientation that did not encourage you to think about things piecemeal but rather to see individual social problems as bound up with the whole way society operates. So I think there was laid down in my early political socialization a tendency to think in terms of wholes, to try to understand the parts in the context of the whole. I'm not sure it was Marxism or socialism, but really the Depression period, that forced one to reassess the whole of society and therefore laid down a way of looking at and analyzing political problems in such a context.

Upon graduating in 1939, I applied for graduate school. At the time, a great debate in Canada about graduate school was whether to follow tradition and go off to Oxford and Cambridge or be more unconventional and apply to an American graduate school. At the university, a lot of us graduating students were reassessing the advisability of going off to Oxford and Cambridge. Some of us came to the conclusion that we might really get a better and more advanced graduate education in the United States.

So I applied to graduate schools in the United States, got offers from Harvard, Chicago, and Columbia, in addition to others, and had to make up my mind where I wanted to go. Harvard had greater prestige, but I decided to accept the Chicago offer for two reasons: it had more money, and I was most impressed by the Chicago program. So I accepted Chicago's offer.

But the war broke out in 1939 in Canada just as I was about to go off to Chicago. In marking time until it was possible to find out what the Canadian government policy would be with regard to study outside the country, I decided to get my master's degree in Canada. Before doing so, however, I took time off to work in government service and then in business, actively maintaining my political interests all the while. At the same time, I returned to academic life part-time for a couple of years to get my master's degree in what we would now call political economy. I finished this degree at the University of Toronto in 1943.

By then, Canada had decided to allow students whom it did not require to participate actively in the armed forces to continue their education in preparation for the post-war period. Of course, since it was impossible to go to Britain during wartime for graduate studies, that meant the United States, where I still wanted to go in any event. I reapplied to Chicago and Harvard, and this time Harvard offered me more money than Chicago. Again on the basis of financial need— by that time Sylvia and I had married—I went to Harvard, even though it seemed to me I might have gotten a better education in political science at the University of Chicago.

When I first came to Harvard and went to introduce myself to the chair of the department, Ben Wright, he greeted me by saying, "Oh, so you're the David Easton, are you, from Canada? You're the only chap I can remember who ever turned down a fellowship from Harvard." Those were the days when that sort of thing just wasn't done. So, in a way, I got some reverse kind of recognition before I even came to Harvard for having done that, quite innocently.

Graduate Studies at Harvard

GUNNELL: If you could, give me your first impressions on arriving at Harvard—intellectual, physical, whatever they might be.

EASTON: The offerings were very sparse. My first general impression of the program, which was reinforced the longer I remained at Harvard, was that I had probably made a mistake in selecting

Harvard over Chicago, from the point of view of the intellectual content and the kind of training I hoped to get. So it was with a little sense of disappointment and of opportunity lost that I continued the program. Part of this may have been because of the shortage of instructors during the wartime and a certain diminished interest by the instructors, many of whom were commuting between Washington and Cambridge. William Yandell Elliott, for example, impressed on us how heavily engaged he was in government service during that period and, as he told it, was clearly the dominant figure in Washington during the period, even though it soon became clear he played only a minor role.

I did not know what was happening at Chicago except through the criticism that was offered by Carl J. Friedrich, in part, but in larger measure by Elliott. From them, unknown to me at the time, I got a very distorted view of the "Chicago school." Gosnell, Merriam, Lasswell, Frederick L. Schuman—if they were mentioned at all in the Harvard curriculum or classroom, were treated largely in a hypercritical if not a somewhat arrogant fashion as people in whom we really ought not to be interested. Despite their frequently disparaging comments—or perhaps even because of them—my appetite was whetted to know more, an appetite I was never able to satisfy in the classroom at Harvard. It was that concern for rigorous empirical inquiry that I intuitively missed during the whole of my stay there. It is difficult today to appreciate fully how inimical the whole atmosphere in the Department of Government was, at least among many of the senior professors, to scientific method for the study of politics and society.

I quickly discovered that it mattered little what you studied at Harvard; in the end it all turned out to be theory, a standard joke among us graduate students. So it was really a misnomer at that time to say that you concentrated in anything else, because almost every instructor had pretensions to being a theorist. This was probably the single greatest virtue of the curriculum at the time. You could not graduate from the program without being sensitive to the importance of theory in political research.

This direction was reinforced for me by my slight exposure to Talcott Parsons. It happened that, for many years, Friedrich's wife was the secretary to Parsons. So, if for no other reason, I was quickly alerted to his existence and to the way sociology was being transformed into the new theoretical sociology in his hands. I got a little flavor of that discussion, which revived my interest in sociology. I also got an incidental exposure to Max Weber through my friend Ozzie Simmons, whom Parsons selected as an assistant to help edit his, Parsons's, translation of Weber's work.

These are the little pathways that develop within a university community and make it so exciting; one follows down these paths without the faintest idea of the import they may have at a later stage. It's clear now that what was being laid down for me was an interest in a view of society or parts of society as a system of behavior. I didn't realize that at the time, and I did not become very self-conscious about it until I left Harvard, went to Chicago, and began my initial work on *The Political System*. So even though at the beginning I felt I'd made a mistake in going to Harvard and was disappointed in the formal nature of the education, the informal aspects helped to prepare me for bringing in, more systematically and more self-consciously, my concern for a different kind of theoretical approach to political problems.

I should remind you that I went into graduate work in political science not because I wanted to become a scholar. I had no very sharp awareness of what I wanted to do, except that I was very much concerned about solving social problems. I became focused in political science because I thought I wanted to become a practical politician of some sort and that political science would be a good preparation for that. It was only after I got to graduate school that my vocational interest began to shift.

I was in graduate school to try to get some answers to social problems, but what I found was a series of discrete inquiries into rather narrow aspects of what were said to be problems of government and politics. Very gradually, what was built up in my mind was a sense of the disaggregated quality of my instruction. When I moved from one class into another, I really wouldn't know what made these classes part of the training of a political scientist—no sense of any central intellectual focus or real coherence. I was not getting any sense of the whole. By the time I left Harvard, I just didn't know what political science was all about. Writing *The Political System* was a way of forcing myself to face up to the issue intellectually.

The Spirit of Chicago

EASTON: I began looking for a job about the middle of the academic year 1946–47. I did get a number of offers. One from the University of Texas, one from Redlands University in California, where I was cautioned that I would have to give up wine, smoking, and be careful about sex! I was invited to remain on at Harvard after I got my degree and, in fact, even accepted a faculty appointment, if somewhat reluctantly, as a hedge. I then had an inquiry from the University of Chicago, which came about, as I understand it, not because I had applied for a job there but through the recommendation of Herman Finer. He had been visiting at Harvard for a couple of years, and I had done a few minor research jobs for him and had been his class assistant for a short while. After he went to Chicago, he recommended me for an opening there, not in the department, but in a general education program being opened up, in the graduate Division of the Social Sciences, that would involve a joint appointment in political science.

When I went down there to be interviewed for the job, Sylvia was invited to come with me. We got off the IC train at 55th Street, and, as we walked toward the university, we saw the dirt, the bars, the rubby-dubs sleeping on the streets, the dilapidated condition of the buildings. Sylvia reacted more sensitively to all this than I did. And before we even got to the university, she protested, "This is not the place where I would like to go," and I said, "Well, dear, if we get a chance, let's go for five years at any rate, and we'll be able to do what we want to do afterwards." I stayed there for over thirty-five years and, for at least the last thirty of those years, Sylvia was very discontented with the environment, if not with the university itself. And I always argued, in jest, that she had failed to hear the "thirty" that preceded the "five" when I muttered "thirty-five years."

GUNNELL: Let's turn to your introduction to the faculty at the University of Chicago.

EASTON: It quickly became apparent to me that I'd stepped into about as different an intellectual world, compared to Harvard, as one could find. My discussions about these differences evoked the imagery of Harvard as a broad, slow, meandering stream with considerable force, not through the power of its currents, but only through its breadth and the distance that it covered, whereas Chicago seemed like the Tiber River—violent rapids, churning, exciting, adventurous, and bubbling over with ideas. I felt suddenly as though I had come alive intellectually. It took no effort at all to plunge into this maelstrom. In fact, it would have taken an effort to prevent oneself from being dragged along. Undoubtedly, the first five or ten years at the University of Chicago represent one of the most exciting intellectual periods in my life. It was just one great intellectual high. I was exposed to a whole new range, not only just of ideas, but of fundamental assumptions that I was able to contrast with those I had absorbed unconsciously from the Harvard intellectual atmosphere. The exciting thing about Chicago was that there was a multiplicity of differing, if not clashing, assumptions, and these were constantly being raised for questioning. And a tremendous emphasis was placed not only on the substance of the ideas but on the procedures and means that were used to attain these ideas, or, in common parlance, upon methods.

So methodology and philosophy of science became problematic and inviting subjects for discussion. And this, it gradually dawned on me, was indeed the key that I had been looking for. I learned in the first five to ten years at a tremendous and thrilling pace, almost self-consciously trying to make up for what I had failed to discover at Harvard, perhaps to unlearn much of what I had seemed to learn there.

At Chicago there were two contrasting tendencies: those who immersed themselves in data collection and were "hyperfactualists" and those who were theoretically oriented. One of the things I came away from Harvard with was a reinforcement of the importance of theory in all areas of endeavor. This helped me to overcome a strong, factual, empirical tendency at Chicago and, if I may be presumptuous enough to say so, helped to reshape the Chicago Department of Political Science itself, moving it in a more theoretical direction.

When I first came there, Charles Merriam—"the Chief," as he was called—had just retired, but he remained a dominant figure around the department. I inherited his chair—his room and his physical chair, that is. Within a few years he deteriorated badly and died. Nevertheless, I had the opportunity to talk about his experiences and gained many insights about the development of the profession. At Chicago, the whole atmosphere and rhetoric was one of interdisciplinary research, the sense that all the social sciences were indeed one. Symbolic of this was the story of the construction of the Social Science Building itself. Merriam was instrumental in getting funding for the building. At the time when the cornerstone was laid, Merriam had to be out of town. When he came back, he looked at the cornerstone with the name of the building engraved on it and hit the roof. The source of his fury can be seen to this day. If you look carefully at the cornerstone you will see the words, engraved in stone, "social science," but to the right of these words you will note that the letter "s" had been ground out. The cornerstone, when it was initially laid down, had the words "social sciences," a concept that was anathema to Merriam, who believed that there should be only a single body of social science knowledge, not an aggregate of different social sciences. In that interdisciplinary spirit a program had been organized to develop a common course for all entering students in the graduate Division of Social Sciences called Scope and Method of the Social Sciences. The philosophy behind it was that what unites the social sciences clearly cannot be their subject matter. Indeed, what joins all the social sciences—if not all the sciences—are the methods they use. My best judgment is that this team-taught course was a disaster for the students but a tremendous learning experience for the participating faculty. We met regularly, in long sessions, to work out the curriculum for the course. We engaged in great debates about the nature of the subject matter and methods and the differences among the various social sciences. In this one course we were being called to undo three hundred years of increasing specialization of knowledge. This was clearly too heavy a burden to put on the shoulders of a dozen very junior faculty who themselves were recent products of that three hundred years of development. Although it was too heavy a burden, it was one we each enjoyed sharing because it opened up our minds to some of the major epistemological and ontological problems in the social sciences and reinforced the interdisciplinary ambience of the university as a whole.

This period offered the opportunity for a tremendous proliferation of friendships and, through friendships, intellectual contacts. Part of this was made possible by the great period of expansion in higher education in the 1950s. There were a lot of people of my own age group at the university at the time, and this opened the door to the development of a wide network of generational friends without having to go through the less easy exchanges that often characterize relations among persons separated by large generation gaps. Within this wide interdisciplinary network, I was no longer comfortable thinking of myself as a political scientist. I began to feel more strongly than ever like a social scientist who just happened to be interested in political problems.

"The Decline of Modern Political Theory"

EASTON: The second article I ever published was "The Decline of Modern Political Theory." What was really bothering me was that here I'd come into graduate school at Harvard wanting to understand how politics worked. I wanted to do something to be able to change society, to bring about a better society and to use politics as the instrument for that change. And yet, when I graduated, I felt I didn't know very much more about politics than a reasonably well-trained journalist. And having concentrated in political theory, thinking that it would give me the fundamental understanding I was looking for, I failed to find it. I was searching for a kind of theory that I had not been taught, which seemed to diverge considerably from political theory—the history of ideas largely—as it was taught. I wanted theory that was explanatory rather than only historical.

I came to graduate school somewhat starry-eyed, thinking I was going to discover something that would help me to change the world. I looked back in history and I looked at the great political theorists, and they had very significant things to say. They were worldly oriented. But the political theory I was studying at the time was largely commentary on what others had written. The creation of new visions of the world was not integral to the project. Comparing political theory as I saw my seniors teaching and doing it with what the great political theorists had done, I felt the business had declined, if not indeed died. I now understand that in some way I needed to get this disappointment out of my system. My 1951 article on the decline of modern political theory was cathartic for me. So I got out of my system the feeling that there had been a decline associated with the severe reduction in attention to moral issues, the imaginative quality that had traditionally been built into political theory. Saying that freed my mind to turn to other functions of political theory. I was then able to select out the empirically oriented area and say, well, now, here's an area that had also always been part of political science but had never been extricated for that kind of special attention that would permit it either to rise or decline. Out of this began my long quest for a more solid theoretical grounding for empirical political science.

GUNNELL: Whether correctly or incorrectly, many people have understood your 1951 article to be the first shot fired in the behavioral revolution.

Systems Analysis

EASTON: When the scope and method of the social sciences course collapsed, I was invited to join the Department of Political Science full time. It was clear after I was there for a while that the senior members of the department didn't think I was doing the kind of traditional political theory that I ought to be doing. Some of the senior members of the department were a little worried about me because they couldn't quite figure out what I was doing. Initially I am not sure I understood fully myself. It later became clear to me that I was desperately groping for something, trying to assess what I had and had not learned, reading voraciously, and worrying about my own discontent. Out of all this came the draft manuscript for *The Political System*. I was very uneasy about my manuscript. I gave it to Leonard White, the chairman, who would occasionally ask me how I was getting on with whatever I was doing. He didn't pretend to be a political theorist, but after reading it he became so excited about it that he got hold of the field representative of Knopf, whom he knew very well, and Knopf decided to publish the book. From that moment on my position in the department was secure. Strangely enough, however, within the department there was not much sympathy for the position that I was staking out for behavioral science. So, in a way, at the very moment when I seemed to be finding my intellectual way, I felt rather isolated among my most immediate colleagues. Initially, I found my support group largely in the other social sciences.

Gradually, however, in the recruitment of newer people to the Department, the Department itself was being influenced by what was happening in the rest of the country in political science. By that time, public opinion research—the leading edge of the behavioral movement—was taking root.

GUNNELL: This is an interesting point, because the perception of many people is that at this time the department in Chicago was very much at the forefront of the empirical movement in political science.

EASTON: I think the profession as a whole was moving further at the same time. I think it was Heinz Eulau, in trying to account for the popularity of *The Political System*, who said the reason was that it was the autobiography of a generation, that I was really expressing the dissatisfaction of a whole generation with what political science had become. I was not very self-conscious about what I was doing and where it was going, however, or that I was representing anybody. I just felt that I was expressing my feelings with regard to my own education in political science in the face of my personal desire to develop a more reliable type of political science and to find an empirically based theory of politics. I had great doubts as to whether anybody would really be interested in what I had to say or the remedies I would prescribe.

The book did not have a very dramatic impact at the time. Initially, it seemed to be accepted as just another book. I was doubly grateful therefore that some did seem to recognize it as representing something new that was developing in political science. Perhaps those who understood the broader message in the book were therefore encouraged to look to me as they began to express an interest in these newer developments, and, in this way, I became somewhat representative of a a generation. The other side of the coin is that I also became the primary target of those who resisted these behavioral changes and took much of the flak that was aimed at the major transformation that was getting under way in the discipline.

In 1952, while I was working full speed on the manuscript for the book, a group of us at the university organized what we called a committee on behavioral science. That was a group who converged because we were all interested in what at that time were newer developments that did not have a name but were beginning to emerge with regard to the notion of system and cybernetics. This group gave me an opportunity to do dry runs of ideas I was developing on the implications of systems thinking for political science. Those who went off in a direction called "general systems theory" were trying to formulate a general theory of systems that was applicable at every level of human knowledge, from the subatomic level to the galactic level, including human societies. I never was interested or attracted to this. In thinking about the use of systems analysis and applying it to politics, I had to introduce many modifications that left a formal systems way of thinking about phenomena rather far behind. Otherwise, it seemed to me, it would have been trying to fit the data of politics into something of procrustean theoretical bed. So I found myself less able to derive benefit from those thinking in general systems theoretical terms and more able to modify, adapt, restructure, systems thinking itself, to make it more useful for the understanding of the particular kind of system that political behavior and institutions represent. Unfortunately, some of those who have been critical of my use of systems analysis in political science have mistakenly assumed that what I was talking about was exactly what the general systems theorists were concerned with. It seems to me that they have misused criticisms that might be applicable to general systems theory and automatically, arbitrarily, and mechanically applied it to political systems analysis.

Nevertheless, for better or for worse, the fact that there was a group of us at the University of Chicago who had this close intellectual association for a considerable period of time provided a forum for the development of my own ideas, however idiosyncratic from a general systems point of view they might have been. It also represented my major interest in the interdisciplinary character of our understanding of human behavior and the necessity to pursue that in a vigorous way, which I have continued to do. And it made for intellectual friendships and connections that have endured over the years.

On Systems Analysis and Schools of Thought

EASTON: In the 1960s, I was working very intensively, virtually seven days a week, on what later became *The Framework for Political Analysis* and *A Systems Analysis of Political Life*. I had to make a very explicit decision as to whether I ought to respond to my critics, who were numerous from all directions, or whether to keep my nose to the grindstone and get my own positive work done. When *The Political System* was published and the reviews came out, I found people who, it seemed to me, had read my book very poorly, making outrageously erroneous statements. I asked Leonard White, "Do you think I ought to respond to these critics? Look what this one says, look what that one says." In his calming and patrician way, he said, "David, if you spend your time answering your critics, you won't have very much time left to do anything else, so why bother? Nature will take care of it." And, to this day, my initial combative spirit is restrained by what Leonard White, forty years or fifty years ago, counseled me. And I think he was essentially correct.

Schools of thinking are very constraining. They become prisons in which students become trapped, from which it is very difficult for them to extricate themselves at a later time. One develops acolytes and a movement rather than a process of inquiry for the maturation of understanding that is at the heart of the intellectual enterprise. So I typically opened my class in political theory at Chicago by saying something of the following sort: "You must feel that anything I have to say is untrue until you have some basis, independent of what I have to say, for demonstrating to yourself its validity. And if you feel that you've not got the time or the expertise at this moment in your life to be able to make such an inquiry, then you must be very agnostic about what I have to say." So I constantly discouraged students from considering that systems analysis was indeed a truth around which a movement could develop in the European sense.

It may seem peculiar that *A Framework for Political Analysis* and *A Systems Analysis of Political Life* were published in the same year— 1965. From 1953 to 1965, I was working on the theoretical development of a systems analytic approach. I had a contract with Wiley to publish this book. I didn't want people tampering with my work; I thought I knew what I wanted to say. I didn't feel I needed to go through the hassle of having outside readers chipping away at this piece and chipping away at that piece. The editor, Bill Gum, sensed this and volunteered to bypass the normal routines and not send it to an outside reader if I didn't want to. So I developed the manuscript almost to the point of completion without benefit of readers. But it was very long. Others, especially Jim Murray of Prentice-Hall, were constantly pressing me to write a text or a monograph for them. One day after a pleasant dinner with Jim when, once again, he raised the question of doing a book for him, Sylvia casually came up with the thought: "Well, Dave, you know, that manuscript is growing too long. Why don't you chop off the first part of it and give it to Prentice-Hall, and the second part, which is not quite complete in any event, you can give to Wiley." That comment gave birth to the two books in place of one, to the improvement of each.

Behavioralism and Empirical Research

EASTON: So far as I was able to influence the department at Chicago along these lines, behavioralism meant not only the attempt to apply quantitative research where possible, but also to bring in the interest and substantive findings from other disciplines such as economics, anthropology, sociology, and psychology. From my point of view, of course, it also meant the development of empirically oriented theory.

Behavioralism was not a clearly defined movement for those who were thought to be behavioralists. It was more clearly definable by those who were opposed to it, because they were describing it in terms of the things within the newer trends that they found objectionable. So some would define behavioralism as an attempt to apply the methods of natural sciences to human behavior. Others would define it as an excessive emphasis upon quantification. Others as individualistic reductionism.

From the inside, the practitioners were of different minds as to what it was that constituted behavioralism. In retrospect, Dahl's article on the nature of behavioralism and mine were attempts to define for our behaviorally inclined colleagues what indeed was taking place. And few of us were in agreement. For example, those who were particularly interested in quantification and the use of survey research were very critical of the work I was doing, which was very theoretical. They saw me as a person who was articulating a defense for them, but not as a practitioner. And, although they accepted the importance of empirical theory, for them theory meant a much lower level of generalization than I was seeking. So those who criticized me as a behavioralist incarnate were driving me into the arms of the behavioralists, yet the behavioralists didn't have their arms wide open. I was getting it from both sides. That offered me a degree of independence from which I could say, in a sense, that I need not identify fully with the position of either side. I tried to define the terms of the dispute to show the behavioralists that there was an important theoretical component that they were missing and, at the same time, to show the anti-behavioralists that to be a behavioralist did not necessarily exclude an understanding of the importance of values or moral discourse. But insofar as I defended the development of moral positions, I was talking past my behavioralist colleagues, and insofar as I was talking about the importance of measurement and of rigorous empirical research, I was talking past the critics of behavioralism.

So I found that, despite perceptions to the contrary, I had no real support group among the behavioralists or among the critics of behavioralism. And it has always been thus, for me—a rather lonely path in political science. This may be one of the reasons why most of my sustenance has come from close intellectual ties with scholars in many other disciplines—in the natural sciences, the other social sciences, and the humanities as well. And the atmosphere at Chicago facilitated and sustained connections such as these and encouraged strong multidisciplinary habits that remain with me to this day.

Those of us who were interested in changing the character of political science were beginning to recognize the need for moving away from a traditional approach to political phenomena and toward the introduction of newer techniques of empirical research as part of our interest in more reliable understanding. When we'd see each other at national and international congresses, we would weep in our beer over the slow rate of change that was taking place. In the late 1950s, to speed things along and obtain a medium for the expression of our developing point of view, we seriously thought of organizing a new journal to take the place of the traditionally oriented *APSR*—and this was a period when new journals were not being organized with the relative ease that we see today. We began to doubt whether we should or could any longer tolerate what appeared like systematic exclusion from the program at the annual meetings of APSA. We felt ignored and neglected—if not openly rejected—yet we were confident of our behavioral message. At one time some of us even seriously wondered whether the only solution would be to break away from the APSA and set up a professional association of our own.

As part of this, we saw that one of the problems was how to provide for the training of students and of unskilled faculty in the methodology necessary to hasten the transformation of the discipline toward more rigorous empirical research. At that time, if you looked around the departments of political science in the country, there were very few persons who had the skills necessary even for their own work, let alone for training upcoming students in quantitative research. It occurred to me, and perhaps to a number of others at the same time, that we ought to have some kind of central training facility.

Let me just give you an illustration of what impressed these needs on us. In 1957, I submitted my manuscript "An Approach to the Analysis of Political Systems" to the *APSR*. Harvey Mansfield, Sr., the editor at the time, promptly returned it to me saying that, for my own good, it shouldn't be published yet, implying that it required a great deal more thinking, which looked like a none-too-friendly brush-off to me, to say the least. I turned around and submitted it to *World Politics*, a journal that had already acquired a reputation for being sympathetic to newer currents in the disciplines. They immediately accepted it, and, to my surprise, even paid me what seemed like a handsome honorarium for it, unheard of in the social sciences, even in those days. That article has been published, to my knowledge, in close to a hundred different anthologies since then, something of a record, I believe, for that journal.

When I began talking about this rejection with my colleagues in the profession, to my amazement (and innocence) I found that others interested in behavioral research were having the same sort of difficulty. Some of us began to compare notes and discovered, to our dismay, a systematic pattern of difficulty in breaking into the few established journals in the discipline. Out of frustration, anger, and probably wounded ego, this even led some of us to think of founding an alternative journal. We even came to the point of considering who the editor of such a journal might be and how we might get it funded. And we came very close to embarking on a course of action that could have led to a basic split in the Association. If it had not been for the, at the time, secret sympathy and concern on the part of Evron Kirkpatrick for the transformation of the discipline itself, we might well have hived off to attempt to set up our own association. If not our own association, at least certainly our own journal. Kirkpatrick kept us in check, however, by privately cooperating with us and even encouraging the necessary changes in the APSA as an institution. In fact, he played a critical role in bringing about a change in the editorship of the *APSR* itself.

The behavioral transformation inspired and was further aided, of course, by the organization of the ICPSR [Inter-University Consortium for Political and Social Research], in the founding of which I was closely involved. In a sense, the Consortium was a real bootstrap operation, and for the hole that it filled at the time it deserves the highest praise. It gave us the opportunity to accelerate the whole shift toward more rigorous standards of empirical research. Yet, strangely enough, after the next generation of teachers—formally trained for the first time in quantitative techniques—were in place, the very strength of the Consortium contributed ultimately to a certain weakness. A kind of theoretical narrowness emerged from the way it carried out its early overwhelming commitment to survey research as a major tool for behavioral work in political science. For many years this almost single-minded approach led to a very serious handicap for the theoretical enrichment of the whole behavioral movement—narrowed it and produced a much more arid approach to political research than might have occurred if the Consortium had been more a product of the currents in the various behavioral components of the profession as a whole rather than largely of the perspectives of those around the Survey Research Center. This may have contributed to retarding the theoretical growth of the discipline. As I saw this developing early on, I felt increasingly uncomfortable with its narrow perspectives on research, and finally voluntarily dropped off the governing council. I did not want to hamper the good job it was doing in retraining the discipline by raising other contentious issues that might have weakened the very forces that were helping to bring about necessary changes.

There is another influence on the evolution of the behavioral approach that can be easily overlooked. I think a detailed study of the development of the discipline would demonstrate that McCarthyism had something of an impact. In the ranks of those numerous academics who'd had any association with left-wing or liberal causes there was a great deal of legitimate fear of disastrous political harassment. Political science was at that time just starting up in the behavioral movement. The emphasis upon the basic character of research, upon pure science and the need to deal with fundamentals rather than with policy issues, served political scientists well at a moment when liberal positions on policy issues might expose and reveal them, or invite unfavorable attention to them. So the movement toward a pure science that took its agenda for research from the internal dynamics of the discipline rather than from urgent social problems external to it had the incidental benefit of providing a relatively safe haven, even if it was never explicitly thought of in this way. The turn to basic research was, of course, largely dictated by the nature of the behavioral revolution, which was stressing the importance for the direction of research to be set by the theoretical needs of the discipline rather than by policy matters. By one of those accidents of history the existing political situation and the direction in which political science was moving, methodologically and theoretically, converged.

To return to the 1957 article: one of the reasons why I published it was that I was under a nagging pressure from my critics, both those who were opposed to the development of behavioralism as such, and even those who were more friendly toward me, to indicate what I really had in mind about behavioral theory. Some of the anti-behavioralists did manage to get under my skin. I can recall one of them remarking at a public meeting: "Well, you can see where behavioralism leads, a dead end. Easton publishes the book in 1953 and hasn't done a thing since." As it turned out, the 1957 article laid out a pretty good statement, in very condensed form, of a plan of research for the next ten or fifteen years.

My direct experience with the implications of a behavioral commitment to research was not confined to opening up this new kind of theory, general theory. I felt the need to flavor and share the experience of that growing number of scholars who were engaged in empirical research, if only to find out what there was there that I might be missing. I felt the need for hands-on experience. This interest ultimately led to *Children in the Political System*, one of the earliest studies in political socialization. Another reason I was pleased to move into the area of large-scale empirical research was because theoretical work is very draining intellectually. So it was a welcome and exciting change of pace. Of course, the major and driving motivation for the research was the hope of sharpening and elaborating some of my theoretical ideas about the input of political support.

Post-Behavioralism

EASTON: I was president of the Association in 1968–69. It began with a phone call from Gwendolyn Carter, who was then on the council of the APSA. She phoned to inform me that the council had voted to nominate me for the presidency, and she wanted to inquire whether I'd be interested in accepting the nomination. I was at that time very hard at work on a number of things and genuinely felt that the presidency would seriously interrupt my work at a time when there were others who could do the job as well if not better. So I told her that I would want to think somewhat further about it before I made a decision but that, initially, I was fairly negative. I did not consult my colleagues in my department at Chicago because I could guess in advance what their recommendation would be. Upon further consideration and back-and-forth debate with Sylvia—and not without some misgivings—I felt, ultimately, that I should accept. In the first place, above all else, it was an honor from my colleagues in the discipline. Second, given my identification with empirical theory and behavioralism, it would have to be viewed as symbolic of transformations that had taken place in the profession. Third, since the country was now mired in the Vietnam war, at the height of the countercultural revolution, and since the University of Chicago had experienced its own sit-ins and student militancy, it was apparent that these issues would also be peaking in the professional associations, in all areas of knowledge. I thought the presidency would give me an opportunity to participate more effectively in what was going on in the country. This appealed strongly to my activist nature, which had been suppressed all those years.

The post-behavioral position that I sought to define during my presidency was not simply a product of a sudden concern for moral issues that 1969 somehow brought to life. It was part of the way I had always looked at society. What ultimately became my presidential address "The New Revolution in Political Science" reflected the application of points of view that were well established in my mind, in my make-up, in my outlook on life, and my basic social philosophy. Most of my professional life had been devoted to trying to develop a theoretical point of view for studying political behavior and institutions. It had not appeared necessary or appropriate to bring in the discussion of issues that would have reflected my social values. But, given what was happening in the world, in the country, in the Association itself, I felt it was now important and appropriate to change direction and allow social issues to set at least part of the agenda for research. Hence, moral judgments, in the selection of such issues, marched self-consciously toward the front of the research process.

Behavioralism was under attack not only because of its presumed intention to exclude values but also because of the now presumed inadequacy of the methods of science to deal with important social issues. The latter attack on behavioral science, it seemed to me, had some reason to it. It raised the question of the extent to which we needed to part company with the extreme positivist conception of the methods for acquiring knowledge. In other words, was it time to reconsider just what we might mean by the scientific method itself? Here I sought to broaden our conception of scientific method and to take into account changing ideas that post-positivists were already discussing. I had always interpreted science not as a product, but as a process. The process begins with the very source of the idea that is considered to be important and that generates a problem for inquiry. This posed the question as to whether the process of discovery ought to or could be excluded from the scientific process. It represents where all science begins, so why exclude what is an essential part of the practice of science?

Science involves good thinking, and in certain areas only does good thinking ultimately lead over time to refinement into measurable phenomena. What is historically interesting about the 1950s and '60s is that primarily one part of the scientific process—that relating to measurement—was lifted out for special attention. When we discovered that there are certain phenomena that can be refined sufficiently so that they can be converted into measurable units, that great discovery helped to trigger "the behavioral revolution." And we began then to refine and measure many trivial problems that really didn't need measurement and weren't worth the time and effort that was spent on them, except that they helped us to sharpen and refine our measurement tools. An important part of the discipline fell prisoner to that one component of science and seemed to feel that this was the be-all and end-all of science.

Long before I became president, it was apparent to me that there had been such a commitment of resources and energies to that one end of the process, that the other parts of the process had been neglected, if not totally forgotten, and that they merited some special attention as well. That part of the process is "the process of discovery," as Popper had instructed us. It involves using one's imagination to discover the problems worth investigating. In that process of discovery one uses kinds of methods very different from those used in the process of refinement and confirmation or justification.

So it came about that I said, "Well, we've gone beyond the behavioral stage now. We are now entering a new stage—post-behavioralism." I very self-consciously introduced that term to describe this whole cluster of other things that I thought we had begun to do and should be doing. Post-behavioralism involved the selection of issues by moral as well as theoretical criteria, the acceptance of a new understanding of science, and the notion that qualitatively confirmed ideas, if they are the best we have, need not lie beyond the pale of scientific discourse.

Committed behavioralists accused me of having abandoned behavioralism. Then the anti-behavioralists, in seeing the shift in emphasis that had taken place, cried: "Aha! Easton has abandoned behavioralism." I felt I was not in any way diminishing the significance of the behavioral revolution. To my mind, post-behavioralism was not an abandonment of the behavioral revolution. It was a way we could continue and build on it, opening it up in new directions. Unlike the behavioral period, when we were concerned with increasing the rigor of political research and refining our tools of analysis, we needed now to be more concerned with substantive issues. Political science itself needed to pay more attention to the applications of its knowledge to the solution of social problems. And having devoted an exaggerated amount of attention to the place of the tools of research in the whole scientific process, we now needed to draw back and identify and articulate the importance of other aspects of that process. So once again I found myself trying to define a middle ground, which seems to be my recurring fate!

What happened when it became clear that behavioral science was not the millennium, that political science did not stop developing just because it had discovered adequate methods for doing empirical research? It seriously affected the composition of departments, the institutional face of the discipline, and, of course, slowly eroded behavioralism's earlier position of intellectual leadership. Reflecting the fragmentation of the broader discipline itself, the departments—as well as individual scholars and graduating students—no longer had as clear a sense of alternative directions that was once a major source of strength. And thus, again mirroring the discipline, there was no longer a dominant intellectual tendency or group to give a new and firm sense of direction or coherence to the profession. By the 1980s, there were few new and exciting intellectual impulses arising that appealed to the profession as a whole. Nor was any such compelling impulse coming from any one or another department around the country, or around the world for that matter.

Not that there has been a dearth of new tendencies in recent years, but none of them has caught the imagination of the discipline as a whole and swept it along with the sense of a common and compelling purpose. This is not to be taken as a counsel of despair about the discipline. We ought not to fall into the trap of mistaking deep changes for chaos or failure. What may look like *volte-faces*, disintegration, disorganization, blurring of focus, competing and irreconcilable perspectives, are undoubtedly just the normal signs of critical changes that are clearly in process of birth. What we are undoubtedly witnessing is the grand reassessment that all knowledge is undergoing in the world today, awaiting, perhaps, some new synthesis too far off the horizon to detect at this moment. And, if the discipline is to be faithful to its recent heritage, it should be one of the first to have its periscope up, peering over that horizon for a glimpse of new intellectual worlds to conquer.

Austin Ranney

Austin Ranney was born on September 23, 1920, in Cortland, New York. He received the B.S. from Northwestern University in 1941, the M.A. from the University of Oregon in 1943, and the Ph.D. from Yale University in 1948. He taught at the University of Illinois from 1947 to 1963 and at the University of Wisconsin-Madison from 1963 to 1976. In 1976, he moved to the American Enterprise Institute for Public Policy Research in Washington, D.C., where he served as a visiting scholar until 1986. Since 1986 he has been on the faculty of the University of California, Berkeley.

Throughout his career, Ranney has pursued an interest in American political parties: their organization, their nominating processes, and their impact on policy. He has also actively participated in the continuing debate over proposals to reform the parties. His first major publication was The Doctrine of Responsible Party Government, *(1954), a critical assessment of the party reform movement sparked by recommendations of an APSA committee. He returned to the topic of reform in his 1975 book* Curing the Mischiefs of Faction: Party Reform in America.

His interest in proposals to change the presidential nominating process, reflected in several of his publications, was also demonstrated by active participation in several Democratic party commissions on the delegate selection process. In Pathways to Parliament, *(1965), he challenged conventional wisdom about the process by which British political parties nominate candidates for Parliament. His tenure at the American Enterprise Institute led to his participation in a number of books on the nomination and election process in the United States and Britain. He has made major contributions to the*

American Political Science Association, including program chairman-
ship in 1956–57, a term as editor of the American Political Science
Review *from 1965 to 1971, and the presidency of the Association in*
1974–75. He was also very active in the Social Science Research
Council from 1964 to 1972.

Austin Ranney was interviewed October 24, 1978, by Nelson Polsby, a
colleague at the University of California, Berkeley. He shares Ranney's interests in the issue of American political party reform and in
elections.

Early Interest and Training in Political Science

POLSBY: Where did the notion of becoming a political scientist
and going to graduate school come from?

RANNEY: I've compared notes with some other people and it's
surprising how many of us backed into political science.

POLSBY: Of course, political science didn't really exist as much of
a discipline in those days, did it? There were courses in schools, but it
certainly didn't have any visibility beyond a college catalogue.

RANNEY: No. It had very little visibility. I well remember even
after I had my Ph.D. in the early mid-1950s, about the great difficulty I had in explaining to people . . . political scientist, well, what's
that! I remember *Time* magazine referring to V.O. Key as "Harvard
Political Historian." Sometimes people would just laugh and say, "Political science? There's no science in politics." I went to Northwestern
fully expecting to go to law school—become a lawyer. The more I did
the debating and the more I was in school, the more I disliked this
adversarial stuff; it was just intellectually very unsatisfying to me.
Also, the more of these professors I was encountering, the more I
thought they were the finest people and lived the finest lives that I'd
seen, and I'd like to be like that, too. So what I really wanted to be
was a college professor, not a political scientist or an economist or a
professor of speech but a college professor.

In my senior year, I had pretty well decided I was going to be a
college professor. I wasn't quite sure, a college professor of what, I
really hadn't thought about that much. Meantime, all of these expectations that I was going to go to law school continued, and I figured,
well, maybe I'd be a professor of law. So I applied to law schools, and
I was admitted several places but was given a pretty good scholarship
at Stanford.

I was all set to go, literally. That summer, I had graduated from
Northwestern and I was back in Corona and this high school teacher,

James D. Moore, who had such an influence in getting me interested in things when I was in high school, was over and said, "Have you decided what you want to be?" "Yeah, I want to be a college professor." "Well, that is very interesting. What do you want to be a professor of?" And I said, "Well, I don't know, maybe a professor of speech, maybe political science, maybe law, I don't know." "So, what are you going to do this fall?" "I'm going to go to the Stanford Law School." "Do you want to be a lawyer?" "Oh no, I'm quite sure I don't want to be a lawyer." "Well," he said, "It's crazy as hell that you should be going to law school . . . it's just a waste of a year of your life." And he said "You should be going to some kind of graduate school." So I thought, geez, that's right. This is in July when I'm supposed to be someplace in September, presumably at the Stanford Law School. July of 1941.

So, I called up the dean of the speech school, a man by the name of James McBurney back at Northwestern. I said, "I have decided that I want to do graduate work in speech, but I need a teaching assistantship to help pay the freight. Are there any of those available?" And he said, "Well, I'm delighted to hear you want to do graduate work in speech, but this is awfully late in the game. Let me see what I can do." So a couple of days later he called back and said, "Yes, there is a teaching assistantship that's open at the University of Oregon." "University of Oregon?" I said, "Gee whiz, that isn't much of a school, is it?" He said, "It's a good school."

I withdrew from my Stanford scholarship, accepted the TA's job at Oregon. Well, when I got to Oregon, I discovered that they didn't offer graduate work in speech. I had to get a master's degree in something because that was part of my deal with Northwestern, so I figured, what the hell, I'll take it in political science.

My year at Oregon was also very formative. I taught four sections of Introduction to Public Speaking. I am not going to waste our valuable time talking about what a dull, barren, boring, and horrible exercise it is teaching Introduction to Public Speaking.

POLSBY: With whom did you study political science?

RANNEY: There was a very important guy there in my life, who, also, incidentally, was a very important guy in Warren Miller's life. Warren was an undergraduate at Oregon about four years after I was there for my master's degree. The same guy, Fred Cahill, had a terrific impact on both of us. Fred Cahill was a freshly minted Yale Ph.D. This was his first teaching position, he later went to be Dean at North Carolina State after having been several years at Oregon. His own field was judicial behavior. He was one of the first modern students of judicial behavior; [he] did that book on the politics of the

federal courts. It was one of the first of that new kind of study of the
judiciary. Fred was a very, very good teacher, and he was very interested in recruiting students.

Early on, he decided that I was bright. I began to have coffee
with him after class and increasingly expressed my gripes about how
"God awful" it was teaching these public speaking courses. He said,
"Well, that's really ridiculous. You don't want to be a professor of
speech." So, I thought, I'll do it in political science. Then I applied
for fellowships at three schools. I hadn't the remotest notion of who
was good in political science or who wasn't. One of them was Harvard, and one of them was Yale, and one of them was Princeton; and
I got offered fellowships at all three. I took the one at Yale; I never
thought of taking the others because Fred, who was really my mentor
in this, had gotten his degree at Yale, and he said it was clearly the
best. So that's how I decided to go into political science, and that's
how I decided to go to Yale.

Research Interests and Colleagues

RANNEY: The Schattschneider story really begins with Sigmund
Neumann, who taught off and on at Yale quite a bit during his career.
Well, Sig taught at Wesleyan but was a guest professor at Yale. Sig
was, all his life, very concerned with his students—he wanted to
know them. He'd take them out for coffee; he'd take them out to
dinner. It didn't matter if he was a visitor, I found Sig exciting, stimulating, interested in lots of things. He was very warm and personally
supportive, just everything that you want a teacher to be. So, after
he'd gone back to Wesleyan after that year at Yale, he said, "You must
come over and see me." I did, and he said, "You might like to meet
the others in the department," and so there was a lunch. You know,
when you come to think of it, for a punk graduate student from another school, it was a very nice thing for him to do. The other persons
at the lunch were the other members of the Wesleyan department,
which I would still argue was person for person the best department
ever assembled because the other people there, in addition to Sig,
were Schatt and Victor Jones and Steve Bailey. Well, of course, I fell
for Schatt like a ton of bricks. I can't begin to say what a tremendous
human being he was—the stories about him as a story teller, and his
kind of warm way; millions of such stories.

He really was an enthusiast, and these political parties, it was just
so fascinating; they were so important and so few people understood
it, and it was so terrifically desirable that they were going to be the
salvation of democracy and, God, if people would only see that—in-
terspersed with lots of great stories about politicians that he'd known

or that he'd read about. I tell you, it was cool, clear, spring water to a man who'd felt like he'd come out of a desert because there really was just nothing of much interest going on at New Haven.

POLSBY: As the Yale department strengthened and grew and flourished in the postwar era, they never really got around to talking politics; they were trying to build a science.

RANNEY: Yes, that's right! Well, Schatt was not trying to build a science. Schatt was trying to think past the surface and get at the things that were really going on. I started going regularly over to Wesleyan. I would go over as often as once a week, and they were always hospitable, always had lunch with me, and I remember when I was getting ready for my prelims they even—can you imagine this?— they even took a couple of hours and we sat around drinking a cup of coffee while they shot questions at me. I claim I am Wesleyan's first Ph.D.

Schatt really got me excited about this political party stuff—about how terrifically important they were and how important it was that we made them really strong and really centralized and really stand for something. That's really the only way you can make a democracy work. Then he said, just in the course of the conversation where he's sparking off hundreds of ideas, we'd really forgotten that one of the greatest traditions in American political science, in fact in all of American academia, was this great tradition of writing about political parties. Some of the greatest men that we've ever had, like Woodrow Wilson and Frank J. Goodnow, the first president of the Association, they'd written and it was terrific stuff. Nobody read it anymore and it was just a tragedy. He said, "Somebody ought to go back and take a look at those guys and see what they had to say and see how relevant it is—just recover that tradition."

Well, he said that at the time when I was thinking about what would I like to do a doctoral dissertation on. I didn't have any ideas; in fact, I was kind of in despair. I said, "Gee, Schatt, why wouldn't that make a good thesis?" and he said, "That would make a marvelous thesis! Do it, do it!" So it was his idea, not my idea. I got it from this conversation with him, and I got to reading these guys. The actual writing of the thesis was done at Illinois during the year of '47 and '48. In that process, Willmoore Kendall played an important role.

POLSBY: Before we leave New Haven, I think you ought to talk a little bit more about Schatt and how he fit into your career.

RANNEY: As I actually got to writing and thinking, I got more and more skeptical about the applicability, the reality, of the Schattschneider prescription, and I also, undoubtedly under Kendall's influence, got to be more Kendall's kind of majoritarian where consensus and majority forbearance and minority acquiescence and all of those things were important. Then I went back to re-read, this time very carefully, Herring's *The Politics of Democracy* and Agar, *The Price of Union*—that whole body of material. That seemed to make more and more sense to me. I remember that was the year I first decided that the direct primary wasn't a very good thing, which was something that Schatt had known all along but which all "right thinking" people thought was a great thing.

So, although I wrote the thesis that Schatt wanted me to write, covered the issues he wanted me to cover, in fact, I first started making any kind of public reputation by attacking Schatt. I mean, the first thing that got any kind of notice was that commentary that appeared in the *Review* in which I attacked the parties committee report of which Schatt himself had been the chairman. So, in some sense, you might say this was really the disciple turning on the master and making his reputation as some kind of heretic.

POLSBY: Did he ever talk to you about it directly?

RANNEY: He wrote me a long commentary. I sent him a copy, an inscribed copy of the book when I'd published it, and he, of course, had read the thesis. Basically, his view was: Well, I think you underestimate the possibility of changing people's minds on this, and you overestimate the importance of institutions in making it possible. But, it is a reasonable, well-reasoned thing, and you certainly deal with the important issues. And I'm just delighted that you've done it.

POLSBY: Talking only now about the thesis?

RANNEY: Talking only about the thesis, but, fundamentally, he felt the same way about the book.

POLSBY: All right, but, now, did he talk to you about *The Dissent*?

RANNEY: He said that it was a committee report and that, in order not to have any kind of minority report, he was willing to give in on some issues that seemed important to him. He said that Fritz Morstein Marx had actually written the report. Schatt had this phrase in *Party Government* that democracy has to take place between the parties and can't take place within them. The main thing is that the parties should be cohesive and responsible and not that they ought to have a lot of internal democracy. Well, the parties committee's report was trying to have it both ways; wanted completely internally participatory parties and implied that they ought to kind of argue themselves into agreeing on everything. Schatt knew that was nonsense. What he had in mind, really, was the British parties, where there is no nonsense about intraparty democracy. The leader says, "This is it," and the troops fall into line. That's what Schatt wanted. So he was in some ways rather defensive to me about the report.

POLSBY: He's now widely cited as the godfather of participatory democracy.

RANNEY: That would hand him a great laugh if he knew that. Sometime in the very early 50s, Willmoore Kendall approached me and asked had I felt that he and I had worked well together doing my thesis? Of course, I told him I thought it was absolutely crucial what he had done. So then he said, "Well, I have been looking over this parties literature. I think it's a very important subject and doing your thesis got me interested in it. It seems to dovetail with a lot of things that I'm interested in." "What I am proposing to you," said Kendall, "is that you and I, together, do a textbook. Now, we'll make some money on it, and it'll help both of our reputations, which could both use a little improvement. We'll talk about what we want to say, and then you write the first draft. Then I will rewrite it and edit it. You don't have to accept everything that I do but we'll find an agreement. Your name will appear as the senior author. It will be clear because of appearing out of alphabetic order that you are the senior author. We'll divide the royalties, two-thirds for you, one-third for me. What do you think?" Well, that sounded terrific to me because I had this genius here to ensure the book's quality. That's the way *Democracy and the American Party System* was written.

I honestly think it is the highest-quality project I've ever been associated with, and I would say that, although I did the research and I did the first draft, there is no question that if that book has real quality, and I believe it does, Kendall is responsible for more than a third of that. It's a very pro-Herring book, with much quotation of Herring and much reliance on Herring's analysis and defense of existing party system. Still, our book is a very Schattschneiderish book in the sense of its selection of issues. I think it, if I may say so, it is a more systematic defense of the existing party system than Pen's book, which is a book just chock full of rich insights, but not very systematically put together. I also think our book states the case for responsible party government better, more completely, more systematically than Schatt ever did.

POLSBY: Did you know V.O. Key?

RANNEY: I knew him quite well. I was never a student of V.O.'s. I had never met him. In the early 1950s I got interested in measuring degrees of party competition, which finally wound up in that *APSR* article Kendall and I published on "The American Party Systems." And I very timidly wrote to V.O. saying that I had this little idea, and did he think that there was enough merit in it that would be worth working out, since he was playing with something like that himself, as the state parties book later showed.

Well, back almost by return mail came a five-page single-spaced letter pecked out—his typing became famous. You hadn't lived unless you had a letter from V.O., and he typed all his own letters with typical typographical errors on a typewriter that must have been made around 1890.

I was much encouraged by his reply, and he had carefully read what I had said, thought about it, had a number of excellent suggestions, and I had rarely had treatment like that from any senior scholar, let alone someone I didn't know. V.O. was always very generous to me, and I think he was a great human being as well as a great scholar.

After that—really one of the nicest things that ever happened to me—V.O. became one of my champions. He wrote a nice, long letter about *Democracy and the American Party System*; he liked it a lot, and he talked about some things that the parties book was going to influence in his future work and to some degree it did—the subsequent editions of *Politics, Parties and Pressure Groups*. And when I first started deaning, V.O., when he was getting ready to take his leave to go to Ann Arbor, called me up and asked would I like to come to Harvard to be his replacement that year? Still later, he was very interested in the work that I was doing when I went to England. And I kept up some correspondence with him while I was in England. The year that I got back, 1962–63, was the year that he got sick, and he went to the hospital.

POLSBY: Had you already concluded that you wanted to go to England on your SSRC grant?

RANNEY: Yes. To be honest about it, I had decided I would, in order of importance: (a) like to spend a year living in England, and (b) do something academically respectable, as an excuse for being there.

POLSBY: Tell me a little bit about how you chose your project: how you narrowed it down, how you decided what to do, and how you went about it.

RANNEY: One of the things I remembered most from my graduate school days was hearing Cecil Dreiber talk about British parties and one day remark in a seminar that one of the great unknown areas of British politics was how the parties select their candidates and how important that was and how nobody'd ever seriously studied it. What little there was was in A. Lawrence Lowell's book published in the 1880s. Nobody had done anything since, and it took an American to look into that question. I thought, yes, that's kind of interesting. Then I forgot about it. Then I got into the responsible party government stuff in a big way, and it became more and more evident that, explicitly or implicitly, these people had the British model in mind whether they knew it or not. Pretty clearly, candidate selection was important.

I got the idea from bits and pieces in textbooks and other places that in both the main British parties there was an absolute central veto power over locally selected candidates. If the candidates strayed the slightest bit from the party line, then boom, down came the national veto. Then, when I read Leon Epstein's stuff about what had happened to the Conservative rebels over the Suez venture, it suddenly occurred to me that the axe was descending not from the national headquarters but from the local associations, and I wondered: just what is the situation?

When I first got there, with one notable exception, almost everybody said, "Well, there really isn't much to study there. You know, everybody knows about it. There is an absolute veto power in the national offices and just not much to study." The one person who said it was a good subject was David Butler. Now, David himself had for several years thought he was going to write a book on British local party organization. It was clear to him that by far the most important part of that book would be about candidate selection. He had done a lot of interviewing and had a lot of notes. He had finally decided he was never going to write that book. So, he, with incredible generosity, simply turned all of his notes over to me. He went out of his way to give me little letters of introduction or personal introductions to all sorts of local party leaders in both parties. Of course, as I got to talking to people, I found that when you got away from the academics and started talking to the central and local politicians they had no sense at all that there was any absolute central veto power. In fact, the picture that came out was that the central offices intervened only rarely and hesitantly. The notion, for example, that the central office of either party could place a candidate in any local constituency they wanted to not only was wrong, but, in fact, if they were even seen to be trying to push a particular candidate in most cases it would hurt him.

I spent almost the entire year gathering data. I got a great many biographical facts out of those *Times'* "Guides to the House of Commons." For the first time in my life, I tried fairly elaborate quantitative analysis. First of all, I put the facts about the candidates on "key sort" cards and tried to get analysis by hand. I soon discovered that that was an enormous waste of energy, very inefficient. So then, for the first time in my life, I had my facts put on regular IBM cards. I did a great deal of interviewing, I attended a number of selection conferences and even screening committee conferences. I got to know (Hugh) Gaitskell during this period. Gaitskell was doing his annual tour of the East Midlands region, and I tagged along and was privileged to be present at a couple of very small dinners—only five or six people with Gaitskell.

I was at the 1960 Democratic convention and was close to the Minnesota delegation, and one day I was standing around outside the Minnesota delegation suite with David Butler, talking to Art Naftalin. Art was just about to go in to their big secret caucus about what they were going to do about their three-way split. Just before they went in, Art turned to David and said, "David, you might find this very interesting. Would you like to come in and hear us do this?" David said, "I certainly would!" So I started to walk in, too, and Art said, "No, no! David can come in because he's a foreigner. Sorry, Austin." David, as a foreigner, had much better access than I did. The reason that I mentioned it is because I became convinced that when I did my research on British candidate selection, I had access that no Englishman could get. So I saw it both ways. Even though *Pathways to Parliament* did not shake the academic world, I enjoyed writing that book. I was more pleased with it and, in many ways, consider it a more original contribution to knowledge than anything else I've done.

Political Activity

RANNEY: When Hubert Humphrey made his try in 1960 for the presidency, when that movement got going fairly well into 1959, Max Kampelman called Jack Peltason and me and said would we like to be in the campaign, and we certainly would. We were both strong Humphrey people. We went up to Wisconsin at our own expense and punched doorbells and organized meetings, were his advance men for a couple of weeks before the Wisconsin primary.

Then I remember 1968 only too well. Early on in the campaign, Wisconsin being one of the early primaries, there was an effort to try to set up an organization for Johnson and Humphrey, and Les Aspin asked me if I would head up a Wisconsin Professors-for-Johnson-Humphrey. I really didn't want to do it, but I learned a lot. The McGovern-Fraser Commission was the first national Democratic commission that I served on. And most of what I know about McGovern-Fraser I know from having read Byron Shafer's dissertation. I've learned from it that all sorts of things were going on of which I was not aware at all. For example, all the stuff that was going on at the staff level—I had only the dimmest notion of that. You know, I was only dimly aware that there was an executive committee of the commission and that it was making a lot of critical decisions. I just wasn't very clued in.

POLSBY: And then there's that famous moment at the commission meeting which Teddy White memorialized. Austin Ranney opens the Pandora's box of quotas.

RANNEY: As it turns out, I now know from reading Byron's thesis that he was giving me a little more historical credit than I deserved. Everything he says is correct, but, had I not done it, somebody else would have done it. But on the other hand, you know, I greatly regret it. I can recapture my reasoning very clearly. I thought that something ought to be done for blacks, that blacks were very important Democratic voters. They really were discriminated against in a lot of places and something ought to be done to make sure that blacks were adequately represented, and I was perfectly willing to have some kind of a quota for them. And that was what I was arguing for. Then David Mixer said we should also have a quota for young people. I guess it was Ann Wexler who said, "That's right. And we ought to have a quota for women." Then I said, "Hey, wait a minute." I didn't think that was the same thing at all, that blacks really had been discriminated against because they were blacks, and I'd never seen any evidence in my party work that women had ever been discriminated against because they were women or young people because they were young people. Nevertheless, it was clear that it was a losing argument. By the time it was clear that you're going to have quotas for youth and women as well as blacks, then I was against the whole idea of quotas—I mean, better nothing special for blacks if you were going to throw in the whole quota system.

POLSBY: Your reward for this was to be put on the Winograd Commission. How do you get put on these things?

RANNEY: Well, how did I get put on the McGovern-Fraser Commission? I hadn't the remotest idea until I read Byron's explanation.

Now, the Winograd Commission originally was a very different deal. It was originally set up primarily because of Mark Siegel and Bob Strauss, who were very concerned about the proliferation of primaries. And so the commission was set up to look into what was causing the proliferation. It was the Commission on Presidential Primaries. It was intended to be primarily a committee of scholars, hence Jeane Kirkpatrick and Tom Mann and I were put on it. The original charge that we got from Strauss was to answer about six or seven questions about the primaries and their effect, and we then designed a big study, and Strauss agreed to fund it.

And then, at the '76 convention, because this was the only commission in being, the convention suddenly converted us into a brand new kind of commission that was to deal with party rules, and it became a very different kind of an affair. And our whole object from the beginning was to try to roll back some of the damage we felt the McGovern-Fraser Commission had done. We, for example, wanted to get a rule to set aside 10 percent of the delegates for *ex officio* slots for governors and senators and state chairs.

POLSBY: Austin, do you think the fact that you've been politically active from time to time has helped your scholarship, has fed it in any way, or, vice versa, has your scholarship helped your activism?

RANNEY: One always has mixed motives for being active in politics. Why, for example, would a guy like me accept an appointment to the McGovern-Fraser Commission, which I knew would take up a lot of time? Well, a lot of motives—one, flattery. The national chairman calls you up and says your party needs you. That's one thing. Secondly, it's a national kind of an operation instead of a local one. That's exciting. Thirdly, there's the feeling of being on the inside; instead of writing about it back in your ivory tower from the outside, you see it from the inside, and that's exciting. And then I think there was some feeling that maybe I would see some things and some relationships that would get me closer to the way things really were than I could get by looking at it from the outside.

Certainly you do know from your own life of participation in university politics and decision making that what appears in the written record and what the student newspaper says about why universities' decisions are made the way they are has relatively little relationship to what you know really went on. Now, if that is the case in university politics, maybe it's the same in national politics as well. Even that experience alerted me to some questions, some academic type questions that seemed to be increasingly critical. I got a deep sense out of my McGovern-Fraser experience that the really central question is the question of who ought to be thought of as a party member, who are the Democrats that we ought to open up participation to, whose views ought we to reflect? I'd thought about the problem before, but I don't think I'd ever quite seen its centrality.

POLSBY: Well, why is it central?

RANNEY: Well, you go back to Schattschneider. If you define the party as a collection of partisans, then the whole necessity of being participatory and open becomes very different. I think many of my colleagues who have never been directly active in politics tend to overplay the importance of ideology and the battle of liberals versus conservatives. For example, it's important to know that the Lyndon Johnsons and the Eugene McCarthys were very good friends and spent a lot of time together and that one of the reasons that McCarthy turned such venom and bitterness on Johnson in '68 was that he thought that he was going to be tapped for the vice presidential nomination in '64 and felt personally as well as politically betrayed in a way in which I think you and I might have felt betrayed if we had been in Gene McCarthy's shoes and had been in each others' houses many times. To see this all as Johnson's rejection of McCarthy because of his ideology or McCarthy's attacking of Johnson solely because he opposed the war and wanted to get the war stopped is an oversimplification.

The more difficult question, I regret to say, is this: Did I, as a political scientist, bring anything to my participation that made me a more effective contributor? I would answer: Only in a very minor way. The only things that I ever did on the commission that I thought were any kind of contribution beyond what any reasonably intelligent person would make was that I knew a little bit more about the way they did things in other systems. I could say they tried that in Britain with all of the following consequences.

APSA Activities and Comments

POLSBY: Why did you take the job as editor of the *APSR*?

RANNEY: When I first became a political scientist in the late 1940s and began to be conscious of the Association, I didn't have any very strong views as to whether it was especially good or especially bad. But then, as I got more and more into it, heard my fellow graduate students talk and then my fellow assistant professors when I went out to Illinois, I was very well aware that there was a great deal of discontent that it had been Fred Ogg's private preserve for some twenty-three years. A lot of people said that it had become an extremely fuddy-duddy journal, nothing interesting in it, not attuned to the new developments in political science, and, of course, this was the time when the behavioral revolution (or whatever it should be called) was going on. One of the real great elements of the establishment that we thought ought to be reformed was the *Review* as it was being administered by Fred Ogg. A group of prominent people in the Association, of whom I know Pen Herring was one, and I'm pretty sure Harold Lasswell was another, engineered the removal of Ogg.

So they finally got him out, and Taylor Cole became the first editor of the *Review* other than Ogg for the better part of a quarter-century. And I can well remember when Taylor Cole's first issue came out. Just about everybody I identified with said it was just a tremendous improvement. Gosh, all of a sudden really scholarly pieces were being published, and there was evidence, and there was analysis, and there was good editing. So that was my first vivid memory of the Review. I generally thought that it was a very good journal under Taylor Cole, and then there was the Hugh Elsbree interim editorship, and, of course, Harvey Mansfield, Sr., took it over in the mid-1950s. Harvey had it about ten years.

A fair amount of what I did as editor was to try to avoid some of the errors that I thought—and I think my whole generation thought—that Harvey had made. I think I felt that the quality of what Harvey put out was good. I thought Harvey did a very good editing job. He carefully read, I guess, all the manuscripts himself, and, at least in my experience, had excellent suggestions about how to make them stronger.

POLSBY: He had a screening system, I think.

RANNEY: Yes, I later learned about this. He had a couple of young people in the Ohio State department. And also, of course, the other big rap against Harvey was that the magazine kept getting later and later and later, so that the March issue would in fact appear in April or May or June.

I put right at the top of my agenda getting quick decisions to people and getting the journal out in the month on the cover. And I came pretty close actually to living up to those promises. What I found was that, of course, the unanticipated consequence of quick decisions was the backlog, because if you make quick decisions, then you accept more articles than in fact you can run in the next issue and then the next two issues and then the next three issues. I generally took the position that, as editor, it really was not appropriate for me to put my personal stamp on it, to publish only stuff that I personally thought was good political science and weed out stuff that I personally didn't think was good political science. It seemed to me that my job was not to solicit manuscripts but to take those submitted to me and refer them to people who I thought were eminent authorities in the field and would give me candid reviews.

POLSBY: Was it the case, as some people have said, that you gave a slight boost to things that you regarded as new, young tender shoots in the field, such as the formal theorists?

RANNEY: Yes, it is true. I felt that, having said everything I've just said and sticking to that, that I was still entitled to give a little push to exciting new ventures, and I thought at the time that formal theory was the most exciting. In retrospect I've kind of come to think that maybe that was a mistake.

POLSBY: Why?

RANNEY: Well, because I don't think it's ever really paid off. It's been going long enough now that if it really were going to yield major new insights and give us major new explanatory power, we'd know about it by now. I think that formal theory didn't pay off. The relatively small number of people who have had enough math that they could evaluate those things almost never gave an adverse review of any manuscript. If one believed in conspiracy theories, one might guess that some of these guys got together in a hotel room and said,

"Let's agree everybody will rave about everybody else's manuscript, and that way we'll all get published." You almost never got an adverse review. At the very most they would say this particular equation is a little bit wrong and ought to be written in thus and such a way, but this is a pioneering breakthrough, sensational, great piece that you ought to publish.

POLSBY: The traditional theorists also complained, didn't they, that they weren't getting their fair share?

RANNEY: Yes, but I don't accept that as a fair criticism. The knock on me that I unduly favored formal theory is correct. The classical theorists' criticism, however, is not correct, because they themselves were at fault. It was hard to get any consensus among the readers. When I would send out a manuscript in classical theory for review, I would send it—particularly the first couple of years—to people in some general reputational way known to me as eminent students of political theory. And back would come the most wildly varying evaluations. Thus, critic A would say, "Outstanding, magnificent, changes our whole understanding of Machiavelli, a true breakthrough." Critic B, equally eminent, would say, "Absolutely ridiculous, obviously a semester paper by some first-year graduate student that deserves a C, and it's an insult that it would even be reviewed by the professional journal." Both comments about the same piece! Whereas in some other fields, of which I suppose the most outstanding case is the voting behavior field, my experience was that I got high consensus on the manuscripts, and, unlike the formal theorists, it wasn't all positive.

Did I ever tell you the great story about Easton and the bright young man? I received a big, thick manuscript on how we ought to think about comparative government all in a big systems framework. So I sent it off to Dave as one of the critics. Back immediately comes a report from Dave saying this manuscript obviously won't do. It isn't quite up to a professional level. It's written by a person who obviously shows considerable promise, and, when he learns some discipline and completes his graduate training, he will show real promise. Then in closing he added a little note to me: "Dear Austin, I know this breaks your policy of anonymity—but could you tell me who this young person is, because I think he has great promise, and we might be interested in hiring him at Chicago."

So I laughed and didn't reply. Then a couple of months later I saw Dave at the Midwest meetings in Chicago, and he drew me aside and said, "Say, you never answered my letter. I mean, I really want to know. That was a young graduate student, obviously very uninformed, but obviously very bright, and I think that if we had him in Chicago, we could really make something of him. Now, tell me who it is." So I said, "All right, Dave. I'm going to break my rule. I'll tell you who it was. It was David Apter," who was at that time, of course, his colleague at Chicago.

POLSBY: Now, when you became president of the Association.

RANNEY: I was president in '74–'75.

POLSBY: Did anything happen that year? Was it a quiet year?

RANNEY: I think I ought to say that professionally it's the nicest thing that's ever happened to me. There's no point in trying to be coy about it. When I decided that I really wanted to be a professor and not a dean or a college president, then to be president of the Association seemed to me to be the highest honor to which I could aspire, and I wanted it, and I was enormously pleased when I got nominated. I worked very hard in my campaign for the election.

And, you know, even though my margin over Peter Bachrach was pretty modest, nevertheless, I was delighted to be elected. The fact is, though, that my year as president was, in some respects, a pretty tough one, although in other respects it was kind of fun. The reason that it was tough was that I became president at the year in which we had the uncontested election, the time when the ad hoc Committee endorsed Jim Burns, and ad hoc put on no campaign, and as a result five members of the caucus were elected.

So all the time that I was president, as you well remember, I faced a council that was nearly evenly divided between caucus people and ad hoc people, by far the largest number of caucus people that had ever been on the council, and it was a year in which a major decision was to be made, the decision to pick the new editor to succeed you. I was very clear in my mind that it wasn't going to be any caucus type. It was also clear that any candidate I would favor, there would be a lot of caucus opposition to, and so I knew right at the beginning that it was going to take a great deal of politicking.

I really felt from the beginning that it was my constitutional prerogative to recommend a name. The council could certainly vote it down, and, given the nature of the Council, I thought they might. But it was my prerogative to name one person, the person that I thought would be best, but I thought it was extremely useful to have the committee's advice.

Warren
E. Miller

*Warren E. Miller was born on March 26, 1924, in Hawarden, Iowa.
He received the B.S. and the M.S. degrees from the University of
Oregon in 1948 and 1950 and the Ph.D. from Syracuse University in
1954. After two years of teaching at the University of California,
Berkeley, he moved to the University of Michigan, where he taught
from 1956 to 1980. In 1980, he moved to Arizona State University.*

*Warren Miller has had a major impact on the field of voting be-
havior as a researcher, writer, and administrator. He organized the
biennial surveys of voters in presidential and congressional elections
that have been carried out at the University of Michigan since the
1950s. Working with a number of colleagues, he has analyzed the
findings from these surveys in a number of books including* The Voter
Decides *(1954),* The American Voter *(1960),* Elections and the Political Order *(1966), and* Leadership and Change *(1976), and in innu-
merable articles and conference papers.*

*He was instrumental in transforming the structure of voting sur-
veys into a new organization, the National Election Surveys, which
gives the national scholarly community control over the content of the
surveys. He has served as principal investigator of the NES since its
founding in 1977. His scholarly interests have also included issues related to legislative representation, party elites, and the nominating
process, which produced* Parties in Transition: A Longitudinal Study
of Party Elites and Party Supporters *(1986) and* Without Consent:
Mass-Elite Linkages in Presidential Politics *(1988). One of his major
contributions to the academic community has been his role in establishing and helping to direct the Inter-University Consortium for*

Political and Social Research (ICPSR), which collects and disseminates social science data to scholars at participating universities.

He has been president of the American Political Science Association (1979–80) and of the Social Science History Association (1979–80). He has also been active in many other organizations, including the European Consortium for Political Research and the International Political Science Association, and he has served on editorial boards of a number of leading journals.

Warren Miller was interviewed in Scottsdale, Arizona, on February 11, 1988 by Heinz Eulau, who recently retired after three decades of teaching at Stanford University. Eulau's research interests are wide ranging and include comparative legislative studies, political elites, and theory and methodology. He worked closely with Miller in the development of the ICPSR and the National Election Studies.

Early Interest in Political Science, and College Experience

MILLER: I grew up in South Dakota in a small town. Forerunners of the future were there in my interest in current events. I did a lot of work in debate, extemporaneous speaking, oratory; forensics was the big extracurricular activity other than sports and music. I was interested in public affairs but decided when I was, I think, a sophomore in high school, that I was going to be a metallurgical engineer. To me metallurgy meant melting metals. I was so committed that I took extra courses in advanced algebra by correspondence so that I could be sure to be off with a head start at the South Dakota School of Mining and Technology, which is where I started college.

I found that I didn't like it as much as I thought I was going to, and the School of Mines had hired a new personnel man who must have specialized in testing. I took aptitude tests, a whole slug of them, and they were all perfectly consistent, that I might make a good social studies teacher or a YMCA director or a journalist. The only occupations or professions for which I was clearly negatively endowed had to do with engineering.

Whatever those tests were worth, they had me absolutely properly pegged. The Second World War came along, and the army sent me to the University of Oregon in the Pre-Meteorology Program. I discovered Oregon had a very good journalism school and so all of my extracurricular activities were journalism. Subsequently I went overseas and spent three years in the Azores.

After the war, I went back to Oregon and enrolled in journalism. I contracted for my room off-campus and discovered that I was living in a small rooming house where the other occupants of the second floor were Fred Cahill and his father. Fred was a brand new Ph.D. from Yale in political theory, and, at some point, he thought I was worth a little proselytizing, so he persuaded me that I ought to switch majors, and my senior year I gave up the editorship of the yearbook and switched to political science. And then, of course, sat down and took my master's there. And it was clear I was interested in political science, interested in politics.

There was a long time when I wanted to be a theorist, and Fred was a theorist, and I eventually got the clue that Fred didn't think I was going to be a great theorist. So I scratched that. Bert Wengert was the chair, and he was firmly committed to the notion of interdisciplinary work, and so the senior seminar that he ran for the political science majors was very interdisciplinary. And so I read Robert Morrison MacIver, *The Web of Government,* and got to know all about Ruth Benedict and *The Chrysanthemum and the Sword* and Ralph Linton and *The Study of Man.* A heavy dose of applied anthropology and found it all absolutely fascinating, although I'd never had a course in sociology. I did a master's thesis on roll call analysis. I had run across a book by Herman Carey Beyle called *Attitude Cluster Block Analysis.* Beyle had done a study of the Minnesota legislature in 1927. So I set about trying to figure out how to do something, maybe like Beyle.

Ultimately I learned that there were not only things like central tendency and dispersions around central tendencies, but there were tests of significance like chi square and there were analytic techniques like analysis of variance. And so my master's thesis turned out to be the development of a very crude mode of analysis of roll call behavior, but it did involve screening with chi square analyses for significant clustering of votes. It was the beginning of learning about statistics.

I applied to Syracuse in 1949–50 for Ph.D. work, and they offered me a $1,400 a year teaching assistantship. Syracuse had Floyd Allport, who was offering at that time, I thought, a curriculum in political psychology named as such, and one of the political science departmental members there was Herman Carey Beyle, who had twenty years earlier done this attitude-cluster block analysis. When we came up to the dissertation in 1954, there was nobody around to even chair the committee. I had a hard time finding somebody who would take responsibility for me. I was very much self-oriented, self-directed. Consequently, I became interested in the difference between inner-directed and other-directed and discovered that, apart from such anecdotal experience of having been one or the other, there was nothing that really made that very credible as the basis for research. The one thing that was unique was Syracuse would permit me to take a Ph.D. with this sort of very eclectic collection of research experiences, and it meant then that the transition to the University of Michigan was very easy, because I just assumed that everybody was aware of attitudes and perceptions and values.

University of Michigan and the Center for Political Studies

MILLER: The Survey Research Center had always been organized in terms of major programmatic groups. So you had the Organizational Behavior Program, the Economic Behavior Program, and the Public Affairs Program, originally—that's when I came to SRC—which we transformed into the Political Behavior Program. And there was an Organizational Change Program, and, if you go back to Ann Arbor today, you will still see within SRC the baronies are organized around sets of barons who have their research programs. And we'd had our research program very much organized around the election studies, very, very heavily American, but with an increasing interest in non-American activities.

The Center for Political Studies was the haven for those who didn't want to have to cope with the department. Intellectually, we were a department unto ourselves. ISR Center for Political Studies doesn't offer a degree, doesn't offer a course. All of our disciplinary pedagogical commitment had to be through the department, and it was there without reservation. There was no tension with Sam Eldersveld at all on intellectual matters. But when it came to where are you going to live day by day, where are you going to do your research, Sam would never take advantage of, or never be seduced by, the center.

Those of us in the center, the institute, had no question about our identity. We were political scientists. We were without exception committed to teaching. I always taught the equivalent of a half-time load at Michigan, and there was no intellectual tension between us and the department. There was real organizational tension. One was that graduate students got a real sense that if you want to be tabbed as something other than an area specialist, if you wanted to be a political scientist, you better have your credentials established by being a research assistant in the institute, not a TA in the department.

We had started to do work outside the United States. Sam Barnes had been very interested in Italian studies, Phil Converse had been very interested in French studies. Ken Organski came to Michigan and was very much interested in, of course, international relations. And interestingly, this was shortly after the Camelot scandal, so-called, in which it turned out that social science activities being carried out were suspect in terms of their American political purposes.

Nevertheless Kalman Silvert, who was a program officer at the Ford Foundation, had been aware of our work, particularly *The American Voter.* Under Kal, the Ford Foundation had embarked on a very aggressive program of trying to train Latin American political scientists to be empirical political scientists. And they had organized a graduate program. A lot of their activity was focused on Brazil. They had a program at Bello Horizonte and a program in Rio, and they were trying to develop a program in Buenos Aires. Very interested in promoting a program of indigenous development in Chile. Kal was persuaded that what he ought to do is really invest enough in us to get us to export our technology, our methodology, data analytic techniques, and so forth, to Latin America. He came up with a proposal that Ford Foundation grant essentially a million dollars to launch a series of comparative studies in South America. One of our early "complementary" studies was to be a study of political socialization directed by Ken Langston. The Center for Political Studies would administer the study. Phil, Kent Jennings (who was the socialization expert), and I would consult.

NSF granted the money, but they would never transmit any money. We discovered that Nixon and the State Department intervened very explicitly and said, "No. No American participation." But Kal in the meantime and the Ford Foundation had indeed invested their money, and we spent a lot of time exploring first in Santiago and then Buenos Aires and then in Rio the possibility of developing close collaborative research relationships. The point of this tale at this juncture is it was that Ford funding which made it fiscally possible for the center to be established. If you're working on a base of a million dollars and it is twenty years ago, even a small percentage of indirect cost meant a large number of dollars with which one could talk about a staff that would be independent of the Survey Research Center. As with the Center for Research on the Utilization of Scientific Knowledge—which also spun off from the Survey Research Center—having been the program of organizational change, so the Political Behavior Program of the Survey Research Center became the Center for Political Studies.

In part, it was a matter of the center being populated by political scientists, and our research agendas were just simply very different from that of the other centers. We were self-contained within the Center for Political Studies. That became very, very helpful later on to the center and to the department, because of what we could offer faculty, with pretty minimal support from the center. They had offices, they had dependable colleagues, they were in a setting in which their research could be administered, so it was a very reasonable location for them for their professional research activities. We could not only offer summer salaries, but buy off part of their teaching time. Again, the objective within the center was that senior staff members, who are tenured within the Institute, attempt to support themselves. However, we are faced with the fact that the external world hasn't kept apace with the developing appetite and demand for political science, and it's hard to fund political science research, particularly outside of NSF. The Ford grant was almost the last major grant that was received from a private foundation. How do I understand the Center for Political Studies? It's there to facilitate scholarship, the doing of good research. It's not there to make money and accumulate reserves, and in order to be viable there has to be income. Income has to at least equal the outgo. And if you don't have any income, you can't support those things that need supporting. My sense is the external world doesn't have much appreciation for the Center for Political Studies and its contribution, because it has never been anything other than a local organization. And yet, in listing the things I've tried to do and am proud of having done, I think of organizing the Center for Political Studies and making possible this whole series of studies of representation.

Collaboration with Stokes and Converse

MILLER: In some ways, my one true claim to fame was that I saved Phil Converse from a career as a specialist in English literature. He was an English lit. major and had taken his master's degree in English literature at Iowa and had come to Michigan intending to do his Ph.D. in English. He and Jean were Students for Stevenson fans, and it must have been in the spring of '53 I gave a talk to the Students for Stevenson—based on the '52 study. It could not have been elegant methodologically, but they were just totally unfamiliar with this way of thinking about politics. And they came up after the talk, and we talked at great length, and I invited them over to our apartment. My interest at that point was in persuading Phil to become a science writer, because we were all depressed with the fact that most of us doing social science were not good writers.

I loaned him a whole slug of books and gave him a bibliography of stuff that he ought to read which was almost entirely, of course, in those days sociology, social psychology. There was virtually nothing in political science. They then took off for France, for his junior Fulbright, continuing long laid plans, with an interest in French literature and language. And I took off for Berkeley. Phil came back from his Fulbright and enrolled in the social psych. program. He took his master's in sociology and went into the social psych. doctoral program, and Phil was just clearly head and shoulders the star of the graduate program. And Phil was hired by Angus Campbell while I was still in Berkeley. Don, in the meantime, had come to Michigan to study math.

EULAU: Don Stokes. Where did he come from?

MILLER: He came from Yale, A.B.D. to do a pre-doc. in mathematics, and he came without any attachment to SRC, but simply because of Michigan's luster as a center for powerful methodology in the social sciences. Technically, he wasn't on the staff, but we got him an office in the old hospital where we were housed. And so the three of us started working together as soon as I returned in '56.

Studying Elections and Developing Party Identification as a Concept

MILLER: In the early 1950s, I thought it was quite unclear whether the empirical study of mass political behavior was going to be in the province of the social psychologists—the sociologists a la Janowitz, Lazarsfeld, and Lipset who didn't even think of being a political scientist—or whether it was going to be in political science, where you had Key. But it was very unclear what the disciplinary orientation of the empirical study of mass politics was going to be. The SSRC committee submitted a proposal to the Carnegie Foundation for funding of the '52 election study and the funding was given to the SSRC. The Survey Research Center was really the committee's "chosen instrument." I helped Sam Eldersveld design an Ann Arbor study in 1951, which was the first time that party identification was ever asked, at least by the Michigan group.

EULAU: I dug up that the question had been asked in 1944 in an unpublished dissertation by *Sheldon Korchin.*

MILLER: So much of the progress, if you will, between *The Voter Decides*, published in '54, and *The American Voter,* published in '60, had already occurred, unbeknownst to all humankind except *Sheldon Korchin* and his committee and his dissertation, where just all sorts of evolution from the Erie County studies had taken place in their thinking. I think it proper at some point to recognize that *The American Voter* was in some sense really a product of the intellectual climate, at least as we experienced it.

EULAU: I think in the social sciences one cannot identify really a discovery in the same sense as in the physical sciences.

MILLER: The trail is much, much more complex, less well documented. I think the biggest change that I would take credit for is the notion that people had predispositions which we called orientations, and so the language of *The Voter Decides* is issue orientation, candidate orientation, party orientation. And in the ensuing couple of years I had come to the conclusion that party identification really was not coordinate with issue orientation, candidate orientation. Those were both short-term evaluations. And it did seem indeed that party identification really was a basic enduring commitment and was the way in which people identified themselves and really was the extension of ego to an external object. And so some of our early discussions with Don and Phil were around that theme of rethinking the causal structure of decision making. Rather than having three coordinate causes, we started to think in terms of causal chains, and that got us into the infinite regresses of working back to all of the causal origins. All of a sudden you could see a funnel, if you started looking at the small end. So the innovations really came in our interpretation of data and data analysis, rather than in the specification of the data.

Political Institutions and the Representation Study

EULAU: Tell me about the representation study.

MILLER: Let me get into that by drawing attention to what was not a very self-conscious feature of life when I first came to the Survey Research Center and yet was a very deliberate feature. Although at the time I don't think I would have recognized the meaning of a research agenda, nevertheless I had accumulated, in my graduate student years—and it was literally just a couple of years at Syracuse—a whole host of things I wanted to do. I think this was manifest in the very first thing that I ever published—"The Index of Political Predisposition Revisited" with Janowitz, which was entirely the relationship between social structure and political choice.

I was interested in social structure. I was very much interested in social psychology, but I was also interested in political institutions. And, at one level, that has been the continuing, ultimate point of interest for me as a political scientist—trying to understand what difference political institutions make. In the narrow sense I would say, sure, I'm interested in the vote, but I'm really interested in the institutions having to do with the vote.

It seems to me that political science is distinct from sociology because of our interest in political institutions rather than social institutions. In any event, I've had a persistent interest in the impact of political institutions on individual behavior, have always wanted to be able to say something about the way in which institutions actually work. Somehow, out of this interest in democratic theory, the study of political institutions, their impact on individual behavior, came the notion of doing a study of representation. It was an inspiration basically born out of sampling theory. Of saying that when you talk about representation and the connection between the representative and the represented, you can think of it as just a whole host of bilateral relationships, each voter with his or her representative. And particularly given the American penchant for single-member districts, you can say, "Hey, look. What we have in a national sample of the electorate is a national sample of one end of twenty-five hundred bilateral connections between a citizen and a representative, and we really would have a sample of representative-represented relationships if we could only collect data from the other end, namely the representative."

The first draft of our "forthcoming" manuscript on representation, which never came forth, still had the individual dyad as the unit of analysis. V.O. Key was visiting with us in Ann Arbor, and we showed him our early analysis. The tables we were showing were the bivariate tables showing the intersection of individual voters and individual congressmen. And he would say in effect, "Well, where is Willie Brown's district in this table?" and we would say, "Well, here's Willie Brown in the third row from the left, very liberal Democrat, but his district is scattered all throughout the row because all we have is a sample of his constituents." And V.O. just boggled at the notion that we would represent a congressman with a whole series of points in a table being his constituents, rather than his constituency. And V.O. thought very much in terms of constituency, not a sample of constituents.

We became convinced that, if we couldn't explain to V.O., who was very sympathetic, what we were doing and what the significance was, it was probably hopeless. Moreover, we were smart enough to realize that, by turning from individual data to grouped data, our correlations would start to look bigger and significant and relevant. So we immediately redid everything with the constituency or subsets of a constituency as one end of the dyad. We then became convinced that what we really had to do was go back to '56, because whatever the congressional district sentiments as of '58 were, to some extent they were a consequence of what had intervened politically. And so we wanted to have both a backward looking and a forward looking model that would have '56 as the first point for the mass data, '58 as the second, and '60 as the third.

EULAU: It's an enormously complex data set. And you published one very famous article in the *APSR*, out of this. But the book never came out. I assume either it was because of the intellectual complexity or because of certain other events.

MILLER: It was the other events. In part, the book never appeared because we were too ambitious. The straw that broke the back really was the notion that we had to get a temporal theme into it. So we would not only have to do a lot of rewriting, but would have to extend the analytic work, both forward and backward. If we had been content to do a more modest volume that would have been knowingly static, I think it would have been finished.

But, basically, what happened was—and remember the timing—the data were collected in '58. Now, *The American Voter* was well under way. It came out in '60. We got the Stern Family Fund grant to organize the consortium in '61. That interrupted also my plans at that time to go to Nuffield and work with David Butler on the British election study. We had made sort of an institutional commitment to get involved there. Once I started organizing the consortium, then it was up to somebody else, namely Don Stokes, to pick up the Nuffield obligation, and he spent about a year and a half in England then, over the next couple of years. We simply were overcommitted, and, consequently, years went by and the study became more and more antiquated, and our sense of what really ought to be done became more sophisticated. Ultimately, it just fell of its own weight and all the competing demands.

The Development of the ICPSR

EULAU: Tell me a little bit about that institution you are alleged to have built, namely the Inter-university Consortium for Political— and now also—Social Research, which takes us back to around 1960: the evolution of the idea, your role in it, the role of other people.

MILLER: I think it's probably less the institution I built and more the one I invented. The building rested on such scholars as yourself, who provided the demand for the supply that we then invented. The idea for the Consortium really came fairly directly out of the experiences with the SSRC summer seminars in 1954 and 1958. And it became clear out of those experiences how important it was to have access to the data, to the evolving machinery of data analysis, and to be provided with the kind of training that was still absolutely nonexistent for political scientists (although I suspect there was more in sociology and social psychology than we were aware of).

In any event, it became pretty clear that the resources that we were developing in the election studies simply weren't going to be very heavily used unless somehow the access to those resources was given institutional support. This was an era in which we'd started to become accustomed to individual research grants. This was well before the NSF came into being as a source of research support for us.

Very few if any universities had internal research funds. There still is no norm of equipping social science departments for research in the same way that you equip chemistry departments and physics departments.

I had developed the idea of the Consortium and the basic notion of a need for institutional support for individual research out of the summer seminar experiences. But there also had been a very important document that is almost never referred to these days, and it was a report by Stein Rokkan to the Ford Foundation, I think. They had been commissioned to look into the possibility of archiving data for what was then uniformly described as "secondary analysis." Their focus was very much on comparative research.

We had a copy of that report, and I read it. By combining the notion of archiving and making accessible through card-sort equipment the data for research and the idea of providing training of the sort that we were in an embryonic way starting to provide in the SRC summer seminars, you might really be able to do an "Operation Bootstrap" and transform—at least for the study of American politics—the way in which political scientists did research. But you would need to get a staff dedicated to the archival and training activities.

So it seemed to me that it was quite possible, if one could come up with the right organizational format and the right scheme of governance, that one might inveigle some small subset of the research universities into a commitment to provide support for this new creation. I think it was actually Angus Campbell who came up with the idea of calling it a consortium. I talked the idea over with Angus at some length, and I think the first time it really started to take form beyond our personal discussions was in '58 where a meeting of the SSRC Political Behavior Committee, in Ann Arbor, for quite other purposes, seemed to be an appropriate place to test with V.O. Key and Bob Dahl and so forth, the question whether something like this might not be a good idea. And my recollection is that it was treated as something that might really be very helpful and got a lot of verbal support from them. Consequently, I wrote up a memorandum to the SRC Executive Committee, basically doing as we would always do, requesting formal permission to submit a proposal and started trying to find funding for the initial organizational costs. I had very little success in the period from '58 through '62. It was a period in which I couldn't find the seed money that would be necessary to hire just a minimal core of staff and try to get the thing off the ground. I think it was in November 1961, all of a sudden I received word that an almost forgotten proposal submitted to the Stern Family Fund requesting seed money to start the Consortium had been acted upon favorably and they granted SRC and me as the principal actor.

The initial thought was that, gee, we'd be lucky if would could get a half a dozen, maybe ten such universities. In fact, the first meeting had twenty-four. We ultimately held an organizing meeting, I think, in June of '62. Evron Kirkpatrick came to that meeting and, as executive director of the Political Science Association, gave it his imprimatur. And I think that was very important as a legitimating act. We started shipping out decks of cards, and the card image, which is probably unknown to a large fraction of the current research community, is still the metric by which the volume of Consortium data transmission is gauged. We set up very early on the summer training program which initially wasn't very different from the training program the Survey Research Center had offered, but federal fellowships provided a lot of support for subsidizing participation in the program.

The major schools always had a couple of people there, because this was before any school other than Michigan—and Michigan just by accident of being where we were—had anything like a graduate program in research methods. And so for a fair period for the major universities, the summer program stood in lieu of their trying to hire a staff member to teach what would then be a very small handful of people interested in the new empirical methods. But there was very strong participation from the leading universities.

EULAU: When did the computer come in?

MILLER: I think the first computer that we got was in '64 or '65. This was a period in which I was more current with the new technology than I have been since, but a period of great frustration because they were constantly changing the software. Using the Consortium's need to handle large quantities of data as the rationale, I persuaded Angus that the Survey Research Center ought to underwrite the initial investment in the computer, arguing that I was sure the volume of activity would mean that fairly rapidly you could amortize that investment. And Angus, very much as an article of faith, said, "All right, fine." He provided the support. It was just one of many instances in which Angus supported the Consortium.

The National Election Studies

EULAU: Do you want to discuss just how the election studies evolved after the Social Science Research Council basically lost interest in the studies?

MILLER: In hindsight now, one can look back on certainly the '50s, but to some extent the '60s, as really the golden days for the support of modern social science. I think it was almost single-handedly the Ford Foundation that did so much to legitimate empirical social science. Today it is perfectly clear that there wouldn't be any election studies were it not for the National Science Foundation. None of the private foundations who have the resources to support a million or two million dollar a year venture are supporting basic research in social sciences of any sort, and certainly not in political science and certainly not in order to extend a continuing series of studies that is already well established. So raising money to support these studies really became an excruciating job. By and large my life in the '60s was writing research proposals. In the period of the '50s and '60s I would occasionally characterize myself as "the Willy Loman of political science," from *Death of a Salesman*. I was on the road selling empirical political science and had developed a lot of good friends around the country and a lot of them were quite aware of what could be done with survey research.

In '74, we finally had pieced together a study, and it was the third election year in a row that NSF had been called upon. And between then and 1976, activities that I would identify, as far as I know, almost entirely with Dave Leege, who was then program officer for the Political Science Program in NSF, developed support within the foundation for transforming the election studies from a Michigan private enterprise operation, if you will, into a national communal effort to create the first national research resource for political science, for the social sciences in general.

As a precursor to the creation of the National Election Studies, NSF accepted a proposal for the '76 study, which included a provision that that study be shaped with the intensive consultation of an outside group. That was followed very immediately by my submitting a proposal on behalf of the Center for Political Studies to the National Science Foundation for the creation of the National Election Studies. There were guidelines set up to define the role of a board of overseers that was to link the election studies to the national community of users.

In setting this up it seemed to me that we were creating a very different kind of organization than had ever existed before, because it really was to create a board of overseers that was supposed to operate in a quite unique fashion. There was a lot of attention placed on transforming the studies from Michigan property into national property and limiting the Michigan control. Seeing a unique organizational form—namely the board of overseers—and seeing the set of political problems basically having to do with creating and maintaining national confidence in the organization, I made a strong argument that *you* had to be the chair of the board of overseers. It seemed to me it needed somebody who was vastly experienced in the conduct of research, somebody who had broad experience in the national politics of social science. Now I must say, as you are probably aware, there was a lot of opposition because you had not exactly developed a reputation as a gentle mediator of affairs in the past. Well, obviously my judgment was correct, and I thought you played just an absolutely invaluable role in creating norms for collegial behavior among the nine folk who then got to be named as the board of overseers. We were both well aware that we were creating a new institution that we hoped would have a long life and that one had somehow to balance deep intellectual understanding of what we were doing, provide leadership for a national research community, and at the same time avoid not only the reality but the appearance of serving special interests. And given the rapid proliferation of intellectual concerns that really turned to the National Election Studies for the data for their research activities, the problem of avoiding a log rolling, negotiating collection of special interests and really having a set of people who put aside both personal and representational roles in order to craft the best intellectual vehicle possible for the widest possible range of promising research is not an easy thing to do. But I think through cajoling and admonishing and setting examples, that did indeed get accomplished. And the board has functioned, really from the very beginning, as collegial set of people trying to do their best to promote good research.

From the beginning we've had a very small staff, but a highly expert staff, that has been able to accomplish a mountain of work with very little person power engaged. Although there never has been anything in the proposal specifying where the data collection was actually done, clearly one of the reasons for locating this in Michigan was the fact that the Survey Research Center and its facilities manifest in the sampling section, the field section, the coding section, the data processing section, had all the technical support needed to transform our ideas and the interview schedules that we would construct into a national data collection.

EULAU: How did your board go about soliciting information from the national community?

MILLER: We started the enterprise with a fairly long agenda of topics that needed to be addressed such as limitations that had been felt in the Michigan studies over time, one of which, for example, concerned the fact that we had measured party identification in a single question. There had been a growing barrage of criticism, great dissatisfaction with continuing to rely on this one measure without seeing whether there were other alternative ways of better reflecting the same concept. And so the second item on the agenda was a conference on party identification, which ultimately was held at Florida State. The first conference, however, to respond to the agenda was a conference on congressional elections research which we held in Rochester in 1977. We sent out memos outlining our research interests and inviting people to respond with memoranda of interest. And for each of these conferences we had, as I recall, responses from something on the order of fifty or sixty people. The interested board members, although ultimately with a review from the whole board, then went through these letters of memoranda of interest and selected people who were then invited to attend a conference. One of the really innovative features was a lot of people who were invited to conferences that we had never had direct contact with before.

So the Florida State conference was a conference on party identification, and ultimately out of that came a whole host of ideas that only showed up a full two years later in the 1980 studies. Dick Fenno was one of the early members of the board, who was deliberately brought onto the board because our past pattern had been to do off-year congressional election studies. Dick was *the* person who would provide the best entré to the community of scholars wanting to continue and improve the election studies for the study of congressional elections. He was clearly the major figure in designing the stimulus letter for the Rochester conference. And following the conference, we chose a committee, really, of nonboard members to participate in the detailed design of the '78 study. The sense that here was a study that was going to be focused from the very beginning, in terms of design, on congressional election behavior, meant there was a tremendous head of enthusiasm to participate in that study. The committee that we appointed was then divided into two subcommittees, one of which was charged with the responsibility for helping the staff and the interested board members in designing the interview instrument. The other was to specify the collection of contextual data, where the campaigns and the candidates of each of the one hundred and eight districts provided the context for the individual voter or potential voter's electoral decision. And so to collect contextual data and to design an interview schedule that would resolve some of the perplexing questions about voting in congressional elections were the two major objectives of these two subcommittees.

Designing the study has really been very much a collegial mix of the principal investigator and the Ann Arbor staff, the board members who choose to participate, and the outside scholars who have been invited to participate. In some ways one can indeed say, we now have demonstrated you can design some pretty good research by committee. The NES has worked. Each of the studies has, I think, become a really marvelous vehicle for research because the participants are all active members of the invisible colleges. They know each other's work. They're coming out of a common body of theories. They may not at all agree on the theories, but they are aware of or familiar with the full range of work that has been done. And it is really not difficult at all to come together with consensus on the definition of the problems that now need study.

I have been disappointed in the lack of exploitation of the juxtaposition of panel and successive cross section in '80. There are a lot of methodological explorations that could be done with NES data, and I could imagine the Consortium becoming a center for development of methodological explorations. There is too much ad hoc, doing this thing that's interesting or that thing that's faddish, and I would like to see the fruits of the National Election Studies provide the foundation for more continuity for a given line of inquiry. I'm disappointed that the vision that I got from Dan Katz and others in the summer of '50, that the future of social science is programmatic research, turned out not to be a very widely shared vision.

The Question of a Social Science Foundation

MILLER: Evron Kirkpatrick, as executive director of APSA, had developed the Congressional Fellowship Program and had very good contacts on the Hill. In one of his acts of outreach, he mobilized an assault on NSF and he asked all of the members of the House and Senate, who by now thought well of the Association, to start petitioning the foundation as to why no political science. There was a brief period in which he apparently immobilized the National Science Foundation. The director and the associate directors and everybody else were all being queried, and he turned the Hill, or his fragment of contacts on the Hill, loose on the foundation, saying, in effect, political science simply has to be included in. The foundation very shortly therefore went to Congress and got a minor change in the legislation which put political science in as an accredited discipline.

It didn't do much for total resources, but it did mean that a couple of years later you wouldn't have to go to sociology, you could go to political science. Well, that was the beginning of Kirk's interest in really trying to develop resources for political science. He was a supporter of the Consortium from the beginning. He decided that the thing to do was to create a social science foundation and really not as an aftermath or sequel, but continuation of his development of strong contacts on the Hill. I think he had things absolutely greased for congressional authorization for a national-social science foundation. Then some of our great leaders like Bob Dahl came down and testified against the creation of a social science foundation.

EULAU: You were in favor.

MILLER: Oh, I was strongly in favor. I said then as I would say now, look, social science has no credibility among the natural and physical sciences. And I don't know how we're ever going to achieve credibility there, but, as long as we are there at their beneficence, social science is never going to have the magnitude of support that it absolutely has to have to mount the scope of research, the complexity of research, that's needed to do what we think we can do. But then about a decade later, there was another move to create a separate social science foundation, this time out of the National Academy and the National Research Council. The conservative voices always argued tha‧ it was much better to hide behind the physicists and the chemists and take our share but don't make ourselves vulnerable to direct attack by Congress.

APPENDIX

Transcripts of the following interviews are available on loan from the Pi Sigma Alpha Oral History Collection in the M. I. King Library of the University of Kentucky.

Gabriel Almond	1978		Harvey Mansfield	1982
Vincent Browne			Robert Martin	1985
James M. Burns	1988		Warren Miller	1988
Gwendolyn Carter			Louise Overacker	1980
Taylor Cole	1980		Clara Penniman	1989
Robert Dahl	1980		Howard Penniman	1989
Manning Dauer	1980		Don Price	1980
Karl Deutsch	1989		Herman Pritchett	1980
David Easton	1988		Austin Ranney	1978
Leon Epstein	1989		Emmett Redford	1980
Heinz Eulau	1988		William Riker	1979
James Fesler	1979		David Truman	1979
Ernest Griffith	1984		John Turner	1989
Alexander Heard	1989		Vernon Van Dyke	1987
Pendelton Herring	1978		John Wahlke	1988
Charles Hyneman	1979		Belle Zeller	1985
Marian Irish	1988			

INDEX